Th

OXFORD BROOKES UNIVERSITY
LIBRARY   HARCOURT HILL

This book is to be returned on or before the last date stamped below.
A fine will levied on overdue books.
Books may be renewed by telephoning Oxford 488222
and quoting your borrower number.
You may not renew books that are reserved by another borrower.

31/3/14

WITHDRAWN

The .... onsible for
the te .... mprehensive
introd .... ing support
for bu

Illu .... on where to
find a .... ecifications,
softw

Ke

- C post–16
- T .... echnologies
- A
- P
- S
- T
- P
- S

Writt .... English and
intern .... designed to
suppo .... hools.

Roger Crawford is Senior Lecturer in Education specializing in Information and Communication Technology (ICT) and Computing, at the School of Education and Professional Development, University of Huddersfield, UK.

OXFORD BROOKES
UNIVERSITY
LIBRARY

D1412839

00 963795 03

The ICT Teacher's Handbook

Teaching, learning and managing ICT in the secondary school

2nd edition

Roger Crawford

with chapters from John Higgins and
Dave Luke, and contributions from
Emma Little, Daniel Midgley and
Rebecca West

 Routledge
Taylor & Francis Group

LONDON AND NEW YORK

First edition published 1997
This second edition published 2013
by Routledge
2 Park Square, Milton Park, Abingdon, Oxon OX14 4RN

Simultaneously published in the USA and Canada
by Routledge
711 Third Avenue, New York, NY 10017

Routledge is an imprint of the Taylor & Francis Group, an informa business

© 2013 Roger Crawford

The right of Roger Crawford to be identified as author of this work has
been asserted by him in accordance with sections 77 and 78 of the
Copyright, Designs and Patents Act 1988.

All rights reserved. No part of this book may be reprinted or reproduced
or utilised in any form or by any electronic, mechanical, or other means,
now known or hereafter invented, including photocopying and recording,
or in any information storage or retrieval system, without permission in
writing from the publishers.

Trademark notice: Product or corporate names may be trademarks or
registered trademarks, and are used only for identification and explanation
without intent to infringe.

British Library Cataloguing in Publication Data
A catalogue record for this book is available from the British Library

Library of Congress Cataloging in Publication Data
Crawford, Roger. The ICT teachers handbook: teaching, learning and
managing in the secondary school / Roger Crawford.—2nd ed.
p. cm.
1. Information technology—Study and teaching (Secondary)—Great
Britain. 2. Computer science—Study and teaching (Secondary)—
Great Britain. 3. Educational technology—Great Britain.
I. Title. T58.5.C72 2012
004.071′241—dc23
2012030388

ISBN: 978-0-415-69694-4 (hbk)
ISBN: 978-0-415-69695-1 (pbk)
ISBN: 978-0-203-14133-5 (ebk)

Typeset in Bembo
by Book Now Ltd, London

ACC. NO. 96379503 FUND SECS
LOC. ET   CATEGORY   PRICE £22.99
03 MAY 2013
CLASS No. 373 · 1334 CRA
OXFORD BROOKES
UNIVERSITY LIBRARY

MIX
Paper from
responsible sources
FSC   FSC® C013056
www.fsc.org

Printed and bound in Great Britain by
TJ International Ltd, Padstow, Cornwall

Contents

Figures

Tables

Notes on contributors

Collectively, the contributors to this text book have considerable experience of ICT-related education in English secondary schools.

Roger Crawford has a keen interest in teaching Information and Communication Technology (ICT), Computing and Mathematics. He is a Senior Lecturer in Education specializing in ICT and Computer Science at the School of Education and Professional Development, the University of Huddersfield. He has considerable experience as a teacher of ICT, Computing and Mathematics in multicultural, urban secondary schools in the UK, New Zealand and Australia. He has experience as: a Chief Examiner for GCSE ICT and for ICT Functional Skills; an OFSTED inspector for secondary schools, post 16 and teacher training; an Ofqal subject expert; a researcher; author and consultant. His work is predominantly practitioner- orientated, and he has published: textbooks and other resources for teaching and learning; articles in practitioner publications and refereed academic journals; a book on the management of ICT in secondary schools; and GCSE specifications and teacher support materials. He is an experienced and well-qualified teacher and ICT practitioner (Fellow: CIEA and HEA; Member: BCS and ITTE; Chartered IT Professional (CITP), EdD, MSc Computing, MSc Education, C.Eng., PGCE, BSc Mathematics), and worked for several years as a systems analyst/computer programmer in commercial companies in London and New Zealand before employment as a teacher and lecturer.

John Higgins has been a passionate devotee of ICT for over 20 years, teaching and managing ICT curriculum and resources within a number of secondary schools. Vastly experienced, both in UK and international arenas, John has not only taught a multiplicity of examination syllabuses but has examined candidates for UK and international examination boards, including in his current position, Principal Examiner and Senior Moderator for a major examination body. Widely travelled, having taught in Spain, Jordan and Kuwait, John brings to this textbook an understanding of how ICT can support twenty-first-century learning and how to limit the effects of ICT in distracting from the main purpose of schools, namely, advancing the learning of students. John is currently HoD of ICT and member of the Senior Leadership Team at Outwood Grange Academy, Wakefield.

Emma Little is an ICT Teacher at a West Yorkshire secondary school. After completing her degree in Business Information Systems at Sheffield Hallam University, she worked in Sheffield and London as a Market Analyst, Consultant and Account Manager for various IT Software Houses for several years before deciding to move into teaching. She successfully completed the PGCE ICT at the University of Huddersfield.

Dave Luke is a School Improvement Consultant. He was Head of ICT for 21 years in a comprehensive school and became involved in developing and delivering ICT courses to pupils, staff and parents. He has worked as a full-time INSET/CPD trainer since 2002 and has delivered many well-received training days and consultancies for Kirklees Local Authority on all aspects of Subject Leader Development, ICT, E-safety and Learning and Teaching. He has contributed to the Yorkshire and Humberside ICT consultants networks, leading sessions on E-learning, sequencing instructions and APP and has spoken at conferences and given occasional lectures at the University of Huddersfield. He is a trained Ofsted inspector and has advised SLT and ICT departments on Ofsted inspections.

Daniel Midgley is a teacher of ICT in Hull, East Yorkshire. His specialist areas of ICT are image engineering, 3D design and video production. He studied Multimedia Technology at Leeds Metropolitan University and completed the PGCE ICT at the University of Huddersfield. Daniel's foci in education are the use of Web 2.0 and social media to help develop assessment and collaboration skills. Prior to teaching, Daniel had a career in retail management at a leading UK supermarket chain.

Rebecca West is a teacher of ICT and Creative Media in South Yorkshire. She studied for an MSc in Computing and Management at the University of Leeds and then completed her PGCE ICT at the University of Huddersfield. Rebecca has a keen interest in mobile communications, animation and programming which she likes to share with her students. Before teaching, Rebecca had 15 very successful years working in telecommunication organizations, including BT and O2.

Preface

This book will be of particular interest to ICT and Computing teachers in English secondary schools, including prospective trainees, trainee teachers, teachers, curriculum leaders, Heads of ICT departments, ICT directors and senior managers.

There are helpful hints for those applying for teacher training and for NQTs and those wishing to develop their teaching careers. This book will help teachers, senior managers and governors who are concerned that the ICT and Computing curriculum should be relevant and meet statutory requirements; that learning should be effective and engaging; that teaching should make appropriate use of ICTs to improve learning; and that the organization and management of ICT should be effective and efficient.

The book begins by describing the characteristics of schools where pupils have high levels of ICT capability. It looks at issues of current interest such as the place of Computing in the ICT curriculum, and safeguarding and inclusion when using ICTs. There is consideration of how assessment, and hardware and software resources can be organized and managed effectively, including sections on security, and health and safety. Various models of the ICT curriculum are identified, and their impact on the school curriculum, and resource provision considered. The applications of ICT in school administration and management are reviewed. An organizational structure for managing ICT is suggested, and there is practical advice on writing a whole school policy for ICT. There are concise summaries of the new GCSE, IGCSE, Functional Skills, Cambridge National, BTEC First and DiDA ICT specifications. Classroom teachers of subjects other than ICT may also find the book helpful in placing what they do in a whole school context. The use of technical jargon has been avoided wherever possible.

The views expressed in this book are those of the authors. Where possible, these are supported by reference to research evidence, statistics and professional consensus. However, much of what is written is based on our shared experiences.

Abbreviations

AfL	Assessment for Learning
AO	Awarding Organization
AoL	Assessment of Learning
APP	Assessing Pupils' Progress
AQA	Assessment and Qualifications Alliance
ARG	Assessment Reform Group
AST	Advanced Skills Teachers
AT	Attainment Target
AUP	Acceptable Use Policy
BCS	British Computer Society
BETT	British Educational Training and Technology
BIS	Department for Business, Innovation and Skills
BTEC	Business and Technology Education Council
CAS	Computing at School Working Group
CEDP	Career Entry and Development Profile
CEOPS	Child Exploitation and Online Protection Centre
CiDA	Certificate in Digital Application
CIE	Cambridge International Examinations
CIEA	Chartered Institute of Educational Assessors
CPD	Continuing Professional Development
CRB	Criminal Records Bureau
CSS	Cascading Style Sheets
DDE	Direct Data Entry
DfE	Department for Education
DiDA	Diploma in Digital Applications
DPA	Data Protection Act
DTP	Desktop Publishing
EAL	English as an Additional Language
FSA	Financial Services Authority
FTE	Full-Time Equivalence
G&T	Gifted and Talented
GPS	Global Positioning System
GTP	Graduate Teacher Programme
HEA	Higher Education Academy
HoD	Head of Department

HSE   Health and Safety Executive
HTML   hypertext mark-up language
ICT   Information and Communication Technology
I/GCSE   International/General Certificate of Education
INSET   In Service Education and Training
IPD   Initial Professional Development
ISCTIP   Independent Schools Council Teacher Induction Panel
ITT   Initial Teacher Training
ITTE   Association for Information Technology in Teacher Education
IWB   Interactive Whiteboard
KS   Key Stage
MIS   Management Information System
NC   National Curriculum
NCSL   National College for School Leadership
NQT   Newly Qualified Teacher
NS   National Strategy
OCR   Oxford, Cambridge and RSA Examinations
OEM   Original Equipment Manufacturers
OFSTED   Office for Standards in Education
PGCE   Postgraduate Certificate in Education
PoS   Programmes of Study
QCA   Qualifications and Curriculum Authority
QCDA   Qualifications and Curriculum Development Agency
QTS   Qualified Teacher Status
RAID   Redundant Array of Independent Disks
RCD   Residual Current Device
SCITT   School Centred Initial Teacher Training
SCORM   Sharable Content Object Reference Model
SEN   Special Educational Needs
SLT   Senior Leadership Team
TA   The Teaching Agency
TES   *Times Educational Supplement*
TF   Teach First
TTA   Teacher Training Agency
UCAS   Universities and Colleges Admissions Service
VLE   Virtual Learning Environment
WJEC   Welsh Joint Education Committee

Chapter 1

ICT capability

Introduction

This chapter describes features of ICT and considers what is meant by ICT capability. The characteristics of secondary schools where pupils have high levels of ICT capability are noted and some related issues are discussed.

What is ICT?

Information communication technology (ICT) is a powerful tool as it significantly extends people's abilities, and as a learning tool, it is particularly effective. Pupils encounter different facets and levels of knowledge using ICT. Learning experiences can involve learning about a topic, and learning how to use the ICT tools required. For example, suppose a pupil is using ICT in English to produce a magazine. The pupil would learn the skills and knowledge associated with an understanding of English, such as spelling, grammar, or punctuation, and also how to write for a particular audience. At this level, the ICT skills learnt would be those that were required to operate the software used, such as page layout, using different text fonts and sizes, importing pictures, and publishing the finished product. In addition, learning also takes place at a much deeper level. In common with all technologies, ICT embodies the accumulated understandings of its makers. ICT hardware and software are the products of extensive human thought; these are physical and intellectual, and highly organized and structured. Pupils learning how to use ICT actively interact with them and learn dynamically.

Activity

Describe three learning experiences when pupils use ICT when learning about a topic in your subject. List what they learn about ICT and what they learn about your subject.

ICT is an interesting teacher as it can make learning easier and more attractive, for example, a resource for learning about animals could include written information about their habitat, and show pictures of it. There could be sound recordings, and video showing the animal running, accompanied by animated diagrams of the operation of their skeletal structure and muscles. This could be done using multimedia software. Multimedia is a means of constructing flexible and attractive teaching and learning resources, integrating text, pictures, animation, video and sound.

ICT is a patient and responsive teacher. Software does not tire of waiting for a response and can give pupils immediate feedback. Pupils are rewarded as they make incremental progress. This can be particularly helpful where pupils have learning difficulties. Rewards can be structured so that pupils are motivated to learn. Many computer games are attractive to pupils for similar reasons. Concerns arise when this leads to addictive behaviour and dependence. However, care should be taken not to confuse such negative characteristics with the length of time spent at the computer. In common with other activities, it is not the duration of the experience that is important but its quality.

Activity

Play a computer game. Note the features of the game that might engage the player and help them make progress with the game. How could these or similar features help pupils learn?

ICT is pupil-centred. Unlike traditional didactic teaching, strategies for teaching ICT will emphasize pupil-centred, resource-based learning. This helps ICT teachers with the particularly exaggerated problems they have planning and controlling focus, continuity, progression, differentiation, breadth and depth of learning. However, where ICT resources are relatively immobile, pupils must move to use them and they may need to use them at any time. These features of ICT teaching and learning contrast sharply with traditional teacher-centred, didactic approaches based on inflexible timetables and strict rules controlling pupils' movement about the school.

ICT supports open, independent and flexible learning. Pupils can access the same learning resources at home and at school using the school's Virtual Learning Environment (VLE) and can access a wide range of educational resources on the Web. Students of all ages could have open access to independent learning materials for distance learning in all subjects at all levels. Many pupils already 'attend' online schools and in the future, this might reduce the need for pupils to attend school. Pupils might be expected to provide their own computer in school in the same way that they now have other equipment. This could be a smartphone, tablet or other small, portable device used for personal entertainment as well as education. Schools will need to ensure that the availability of ICT resources in the home or elsewhere is adequate for all pupils.

Activity

Compare an online school and an English secondary school. Describe the advantages and disadvantages to pupils, teachers, parents and the community.

ICT is everywhere. In addition to their experiences of ICT in school, pupils come into contact with a variety of access points to larger ICT networks and systems, for example, supermarket checkouts, the National Lottery, SatNav, libraries, and cashpoints. Swipe cards and biometrics are used for registration, payment and access control in schools and elsewhere. As adults, pupils will directly or indirectly access large ICT systems, for example, online banking, and the Driver Vehicle Licensing Centre (DVLC). Many will work with automated control systems for warehousing and manufacturing. ICT systems are used for road traffic management. Electronic tagging is used to monitor of criminals. An understanding of what these ICT systems can and cannot do, and an awareness of their responsibilities and rights, will help pupils become more effective citizens. Schools need to know what rights pupils have in relation to their record-keeping systems, and what demands will be made of them. New ICT systems and technology will be introduced and schools will need to respond quickly and appropriately.

ICT promotes sharing and collaboration. Pupils and schools can join social networks and extend current collaborations with the community, commerce, industry, colleges and universities. This collaboration can be local or international in scope. For example, pupils might improve their learning of languages by collaborating with native speakers of Spanish who are in Spain using Skype. Social networks can be used to extend pupils' learning but there are dangers and schools need to ensure that pupils are aware of these and act responsibly.

ICT promotes diversity. There are opportunities to learn about world cultures, other religions and political systems. For some people, this is interesting, but to others it is a threat and may lead to conflict. Freedom of access to the Web is denied in some countries as governments and others seek to control information. However, censorship can also be beneficial, for example, children should not have easy access to pornography. Even so, complete control of information is rarely entirely beneficial for all. Unfortunately, it is often difficult for those who control information to resist the temptation to control it for their own benefit. The widespread distribution of information does not guarantee that it is true and comprehensive. Schools are not neutral agents and they have their own values. Careful thought is needed about the impact on the ethos of the school.

ICT is blind to gender, race, age and disability. It is not unknown for people to adopt alternative persona when communicating using ICT networks as personal characteristics communicated using ICT are largely under the control of the originator. This may well extend what disadvantaged pupils can do but there are dangers that all pupils must be aware of, for example, when online friendships move offline. To help prevent this, pupils' access to ICT and social networks should be carefully supervised and constantly monitored.

ICT affects employment. More and more people are using ICT at work and teleworking is becoming widespread as more people are working from home. Increasingly, employers hire employees in a global labour market and pupils leaving school in the UK will have to compete for jobs in this international market. They need good ICT skills to enter the market. These trends tend to increase wages for skilled work but push down wages for unskilled work. The future well-being of our pupils and our country depends on raising skill levels throughout the community. Therefore, schools must ensure pupils leave school with good ICT skills.

ICT is a valuable resource. Schools use the same hardware as many commercial companies, and teach pupils using industry standard software. Schools are often more technologically advanced than some small businesses. This helps schools sell training services to local companies, earning income that can be re-invested in education. Unfortunately, this also makes schools' ICT resources more attractive to thieves.

ICT is unpredictable. It is very difficult to predict how it will develop. This uncertainty makes planning difficult. Many of the above developments could radically affect how ICT is organized and used in schools, and its impact on them. There is still a lack of consensus regarding when, how, where and by whom ICT and Computing should be taught in secondary schools, and the extent to which ICT should be integrated with the whole curriculum. A flexible whole school policy for the development of ICT is essential.

What is ICT capability?

What is meant by ICT capability changes over time and different groups approach ICT capability from different perspectives (Crawford, 1998; Kennewell *et al.*, 2003); these perspectives are 'strongly influenced by their biographies and prior experience of computer use' (Somekh, 1996, p. 119). Understanding what is meant by ICT capability has evolved, and tends to reflect current beliefs and technology. Some trends are evident in schools (Crawford, 2011):

- There is more emphasis on ICT skills to support teaching and learning than on the need to develop those needed for employment.
- There is more emphasis on the transferable ICT skills needed by users. Specific technical skills become obsolete more quickly and have narrower application.
- Approaches to teaching and learning are constructivist. This affects the ways in which the curriculum is elaborated and the construction of training materials. For example, instead of writing detailed worksheets that instruct pupils in the technical operation of specific software, teachers encourage learners to develop strategies that enable them to select and use appropriate ICT resources, whether or not they are initially familiar with their use.
- There is a tendency to be technologically conservative. Pupils are more likely to learn about the technologies currently available, rather than unusual, state-of-the-art or potential future technologies.
- Technological determinism, that is, the idea that the development of technology is independent of social influences, is more prevalent than understandings of the relationship between technology and society in terms of social shaping that is interactive and cyclical.

ICT capability is defined in the National Curriculum for England (QCA, 2007b) where it is described as the ability to do the following:

- Use a range of ICT tools in a purposeful way to tackle questions, solve problems and create ideas and solutions of value.
- Explore and use new ICT tools as they become available.
- Apply ICT learning in a range of contexts and in other areas of learning, work and life.

Similarly, pupils could be considered to have high levels of ICT capability (Crawford, 2011) if they are able to do the following:

- Use ICT to support their learning in all subjects.
- Use common ICT tools.
- Take responsibility for their own learning, developing strategies to help them learn how to use unfamiliar ICT tools, and work collaboratively.
- Use current ICT hardware and software and understand its potential and limitations.
- Understand that using ICT affects social processes.

These descriptions are not dissimilar and taken together are the definition of ICT capability used in this book.

The characteristics of schools where pupils have high ICT capability

Schools where pupils have higher levels of ICT capability have these features in common (Crawford, 2011):

- ICT is taught as a discrete subject throughout the school, and pupils are entered for external assessment, for example, I/GCSE ICT, at the end of Key Stage 4.
- There are well-planned programmes of study for discrete ICT studies and ICT is also used throughout the curriculum although this may not be planned in detail.
- ICT teachers are aware of the differences between teaching ICT and other subjects, and set realistic, open-ended tasks in authentic contexts that require pupils to use real ICT tools or realistic simulations.
- There is leadership of the development of ICT in the school by senior management; the HoD ICT is enthusiastic and approachable; and there are opportunities for all teachers to be involved in decision-making.
- There is a management committee that includes senior managers, the HoD ICT and ICT teachers; and a user group with representatives from other subject departments.
- ICT is taught by specialist teachers.
- Teachers of other subjects have to use ICT for aspects of school administration and are encouraged to use ICT in the classroom.
- Schools are proud of their investment in ICT resources.
- There is an adequate quantity of modern ICT resources.
- Funding for ICT is well planned.

Some issues to consider are:

- Is teacher intervention critical in developing pupils' ICT capability? ICT teachers tend to encourage independent learning but significant teacher intervention may be needed in each lesson to ensure that all pupils make adequate progress, especially for lower ability pupils in mixed ability classes. The appropriate balance between teacher intervention and independent learning needs careful consideration.
- Pupils' experiences of ICT are thought to be enhanced by rich contexts in other subjects of the curriculum, whereas pupils' experiences of ICT in discrete ICT lessons are sometimes thought to be decontextualized and sterile. However, if the other subject has problems with contextualization, then these may also affect the contextualization of ICT. Even where ICT is well used to support teaching and learning in another subject, its use may not go beyond this because teachers do not relate their subjects to real-world activities. For example, in Mathematics, the use of software that manipulates the graphs of straight lines ($y = mx + c$) may help pupils understand the impact of varying the values of m and c but it does not help them understand why they need to know this. Pupils develop both their Mathematics and their ICT skills but these are decontextualized. However, in discrete ICT lessons, teachers intentionally and overtly model real-world activities. They use the ICT software used in commerce and industry, and set real problems and model realistic contexts.

- Where ICT is taught through another subject, there is often a good balance between the ICT subject content and the other subject, however, where there is a lack of balance, it is the ICT that is neglected.
- Pupils who attend schools that teach ICT as a discrete subject make more use of ICT at home, especially girls (Crawford, 2011). Girls outperform boys at GCSE but 'an alarming low and declining proportion of girls choose ICT or Computing at Advance level' (Ofsted, 2009b, para. 41). Teaching ICT as a discrete subject may help counter the tendency of girls to neglect these subjects.
- The greater emphasis on ICT skills to support teaching and learning than on the need to develop those needed for employment may lead to the neglect of specific ICT skills that are in demand in the ICT industry, i.e. computer programming.

Summary

What is ICT?

- ICT is a powerful tool.
- ICT is an interesting teacher.
- ICT is a patient and responsive teacher.
- ICT is pupil-centred.
- ICT supports open, independent and flexible learning.
- ICT is everywhere.
- ICT promotes sharing and collaboration.
- ICT promotes diversity.
- ICT is blind to gender, race, age and disability.
- ICT affects employment.
- ICT is a valuable resource.
- ICT is unpredictable.

What is ICT capability?

What is meant by ICT capability has evolved, and tends to reflect current beliefs and technology. Some trends evident in schools are:

- There is more emphasis on ICT skills to support teaching and learning.
- There is more emphasis on the transferable ICT skills needed by users.
- There is a tendency to be technologically conservative.
- Technological determinism is more prevalent than understandings of the relationship between technology and society in terms of social shaping that is interactive and cyclical.

Pupils could be considered to have high levels of ICT capability if they are able to do the following:

- Use ICT to support their learning in all subjects.
- Use common ICT tools.
- Take responsibility for their own learning, developing strategies to help them learn how to use unfamiliar ICT tools, and work collaboratively.

- Use current ICT hardware and software and understand its potential and limitations.
- Understand that using ICT affects social processes.

The characteristics of schools where pupils have high ICT capability

Schools where pupils have higher levels of ICT capability have these features in common:

- ICT is taught as a discrete subject and used throughout the curriculum.
- ICT teachers set realistic, open-ended tasks in authentic contexts that require pupils to use real ICT tools.
- There is leadership by senior management; and all teachers are involved. A management committee includes senior managers, the HoD ICT and ICT teachers; and a user group includes other subject departments.
- ICT is taught by specialist teachers.
- Teachers of other subjects have to use ICT for aspects of school administration and are encouraged to use ICT in the classroom.
- Schools are proud of their investment in ICT resources and there are adequate modern ICT resources.
- Funding for ICT is well planned.

Some issues are:

- Is teacher intervention critical in developing pupils ICT capability?
- Pupils' experiences of ICT are thought to be enhanced by the rich contexts in other subjects of the curriculum, however, pupils' experiences of ICT in discrete ICT lessons are thought to be decontextualized and sterile. This viewpoint is problematic.
- Where ICT is taught through another subject, there is often a good balance between the ICT subject content and the other subject, however, where there is a lack of balance, it is the ICT that is neglected.
- Pupils who attend schools that teach ICT as a discrete subject make more use of ICT at home, especially girls.
- The greater emphasis on ICT skills to support teaching and learning than on the need to develop those needed for employment may lead to the neglect of specific ICT skills that are in demand in the ICT industry, i.e. computer programming.

Further reading

Crawford, R. A. (2011) *ICT Capability in English Schools*, Saarbrucken: Lambert Academic Publishing.

Kennewell, S., Parkinson, J. and Tanner, H. (2003) *Learning to Teach ICT in the Secondary School*, London: Routledge Falmer.

Moore, C. D. (2005) 'How should the KS3 ICT National Curriculum be taught so that it delivers capability at KS4?' Available at: http://www.teacherresearch.net/tr_ma_4480_cdmoore.pdf (accessed 18 July 2011).

Chapter 2

The ICT curriculum

Introduction

On the 20th January 2011, the Secretary of State for Education announced a review of the National Curriculum (NC) in England for both primary and secondary schools. It is intended that the revised NC will set out only the essential knowledge that all children should acquire, and give schools and teachers more freedom to decide how to teach this most effectively and to design a wider school curriculum that best meets the needs of their pupils. It will set out a minimum national entitlement organized around subject disciplines.

The key principles of the new NC are (DfE, 2011d, p. 6):

- The new NC will be developed in line with the principles of freedom, responsibility and fairness in order to raise standards for all children.
- Schools should be given greater freedom over the curriculum. The NC should set out only the essential knowledge that all children should acquire, and leave schools to design a wider school curriculum that best meets the needs of their pupils and to decide how to teach this most effectively.
- The content of our NC should compare favourably with curricula in the highest performing jurisdictions, reflecting the best collective wisdom we have about how children learn and what they should know.
- The NC should embody rigour and high standards and create coherence in what is taught in schools, ensuring that all children have the opportunity to acquire a core of knowledge in the key subject disciplines.
- The NC should provide young people with the knowledge they need to move confidently and successfully through their education, taking into account the needs of different groups, including the most able and pupils with special educational needs and disabilities.
- It is important to distinguish between the NC and the wider school curriculum. There are a number of components of a broad and balanced school curriculum that should be developed on the basis of local or school-level decision-making, rather than prescribed national Programmes of Study. To facilitate this, the NC should not absorb the overwhelming majority of teaching time in schools.
- The NC will continue to be a statutory requirement for maintained schools but will also retain its importance as a national benchmark of excellence for all schools, providing parents with an understanding of what their child should be expected to know at every stage of their school career.

ICT will remain a compulsory subject at all Key Stages at least until September 2014, pending the outcome of the current review of the NC in England. However, the existing ICT Programmes of Study and associated Attainment Targets (QCA, 2007a, 2007b) have been disapplied at all four Key Stages, along with the statutory assessment arrangements at Key Stage 3, from September 2012 (DfE, 2012a). The intention is that schools and teachers will have more freedom to teach ICT and Computing in ways that are creative, innovative and inspirational.

This chapter considers the appropriateness of the previous NC (QCA, 2007a, 2007b) and the National Strategy, looks at some of the arguments for change, considers the likely effects of disapplication, and the impact of no longer requiring teacher assessment of pupils' ICT capability at the end of KS3.

Activity

Below are some extracts from a speech by Michael Gove, Secretary of State for Education, in a speech at the BETT (British Educational Training and Technology) show on 11 January 2012:

> Almost every field of employment now depends on technology . . . But there is one notable exception . . . Education has barely changed . . . The fundamental model of school education is still a teacher talking to a group of pupils . . . A Victorian schoolteacher could enter a twenty-first-century classroom and feel completely at home. Whiteboards may have eliminated chalk dust, chairs may have migrated from rows to groups, but a teacher still stands in front of the class, talking, testing and questioning.
>
> [. . .]
>
> But that model won't be the same in twenty years' time. It may well be extinct in ten . . . It's clear that technology is going to bring profound changes to how and what we teach. But it's equally clear that we have not yet managed to make the most of it.

Discuss:

- Do you agree?
- How do you think education will be organized in 20 years?

The National Curriculum (NC) and the National Strategy (NS)

The NC is mandatory for maintained schools. The curriculum requirements for academies and free schools differ in that they are required only to provide a broad and balanced curriculum that includes English, Mathematics and Science; that makes provision for Religious Education; and that meets their pupils' needs, aspirations and interests.

The organization of education in England and Wales is age-related. Pupils begin compulsory education at the age of 5 and may leave school at the age of 16 although this will increase to 18. School years are identified as Year 1 through to Year 13, and are grouped into five Key Stages. There is an expectation that pupils will achieve within a range of

Table 2.1 The association between age, year, Key Stage and expected attainment

Age	Year	Key Stage	Expected range of NC levels attained
5–7	1–2	1	1–3
7–11	3–6	2	2–5
11–14	7–9	3	4–8
14–16	10–11	4	Not applicable
16–19	12–13	5	Not applicable

levels of attainment during a particular Key Stage. The relationship between age, school year, Key Stage and the expected range of levels of attainment is shown in Table 2.1.

The NC was first published in 2007, and at Key Stage 3 (KS3) pupils study English, Mathematics, Science, Physical Education, ICT, Art, Citizenship, Design and Technology, Geography, History, a modern foreign language and Music. At Key Stage 4 (KS4), this requirement is reduced to English, Mathematics, Science, Physical Education, ICT, and Design and Technology.

The subject content of each NC subject is described in the NC Programmes of Study (PoS). The previously mandatory ICT NC is described in the separate PoS for KS3 (QCA, 2007a) and KS4 (QCA, 2007b).

The Key Concepts that underpin the study of ICT are described as:

- capability;
- communication and collaboration;
- exploring ideas and manipulating information;
- impact of technology;
- critical evaluation.

The Key Processes are described as:

- finding information;
- developing ideas;
- communicating information;
- evaluating.

There are explanatory notes and a range and content section that outlines the breadth of the subject to be taught.

During and at the end of KS3, pupils are expected to achieve and are assessed in relation to levels of attainment and these are described in the Attainment Targets (ATs) in the NC Programmes of Study (PoS). For example, in the ICT NC PoS for KS3 (QCA, 2007a), there is one AT which consists of level descriptions of what pupils are expected to achieve if they attain each of levels 4–8 (the highest). Above level 8, pupils are said to have achieved 'exceptional performance'. There are no level descriptions for KS4 and it is assumed that pupils will be assessed by being entered for external assessment, for example, I/GCSEs.

The NC ICT PoS seem somewhat vague in places. There is little mention of specific hardware or software. For example, in the KS3 PoS, element 2.1.a. states that pupils should be able to: 'consider systematically the information needed to solve a problem, complete a task or answer a question, and explore how it will be used', and similarly, element 2.2.c indicates that pupils should be able to: 'test predictions and discover patterns and relationships, exploring, evaluating and developing models by changing their rules and values'. While these should be interpreted in the context of the ICT curriculum, in other contexts they could be taught without the use of ICT, and so provide little direct guidance for ICT teachers on what ICT skills should be taught. Despite a well-organized structure the ICT NC does not have the detail found in, for example, the Mathematics NC PoS, and progression throughout KS3 and KS4 is not always as clear. This is not expecially helpful to teachers planning detailed schemes of work.

Perhaps as a result of this vagueness and lack of detail, the ICT National Strategy was introduced. Initially this applied to KS3, then later KS4. Detailed resources for teaching and learning were published for KS3 and these were extensive and detailed and included:

- a framework and teaching objectives for years 7–11;
- a scheme of work for ICT;
- sample teaching units, including lesson plans and resources;
- advice on how to organize the delivery of ICT in the school curriculum, including the recommendation that pupils should study ICT for approximately 1 hour each week;
- advice on how ICT should be planned and taught; assessment and target setting; and the management of ICT in secondary schools;
- the ICT coordinator's and ICT subject leader's responsibilities;
- advice on inclusion and differentiation.

The ICT NS scheme of work was organized into units and each unit was accompanied by detailed lesson plans and all the resources needed to teach the lessons, including presentations, data files and pupil worksheets to be completed. All the resources were available electronically and could be completed electronically. The outline scheme of work for the KS3 NS was:

Unit 7.1 – Using ICT
Unit 7.2 – Using data and information sources
Unit 7.3 – Making a leaflet
Unit 7.4 – Introduction to modelling and presenting numeric data
Unit 7.5 – Data handling
Unit 7.6 – Control and monitoring
Unit 8.1 – Public information systems
Unit 8.2 – Publishing on the web
Unit 8.3 – Information: reliability, validity and bias
Unit 8.4 – Models and presenting numeric data
Unit 8.5 – An ICT system: integrating applications to find solutions
Unit 9.1 – Developing ideas and making things happen
Unit 9.2 – Finding things out
Unit 9.3 – Developing ideas and making things happen

Each unit covered several lessons. For example, Unit 8.2: Publishing on the web, included lesson plans and resources for:

Lesson 1.   Introducing the unit and a text mark-up language, HTML
Lesson 2.   Comparing methods of producing web pages
Lesson 3.   Planning the website structure
Lesson 4.   Introducing web page creating, structure and appearance
Lesson 5.   Designing and creating a front page for a section
Lesson 6.   Designing web pages
Lesson 7.   Creating more web pages
Lesson 8.   Completing and evaluating the project

The highly specific detail in the ICT NS for planning and the provision of usable resources were much more helpful than the ICT NC. Teachers could work through the lesson plans and use the resources off-the-shelf. There was sufficient detail for those teachers who did not already have in-depth subject knowledge so that they could teach themselves. However, many teachers found that the subject content or lesson plans were not at an appropriate level for their pupils. For example, the introduction of HTML in Unit 8.2, Lesson 1, soon after the start of Year 8, and Cascading Style Sheets (CSS) in Lesson 4 of the same unit, was thought by some teachers to be too difficult and the progression was too rapid. Nevertheless, the NS materials were very useful, provided detailed and comprehensive guidance and support, and could be adapted to suit a wide range of pupils, and consequently, many topics are still taught and the resources still used in schools. When planning a curriculum for ICT for KS3, the NS lesson plans and resources remain a good starting point.

Activity

Refer to the National Strategy framework (National Strategy, 2008), teaching units and resources. Choose a unit and work through all the lesson plans, doing all the exercises.

For example, you could work through Unit 8.5 – An ICT System: integrating applications to find solutions:

Lesson 1.   Introduction to the unit: Feasibility study for a system
Lesson 2.   Modelling the finances
Lesson 3.   Developing the financial model
Lesson 4.   Using control systems to automate a process
Lesson 5.   Programming and testing the solution
Lesson 6.   Extending the control system
Lesson 7.   Marketing the product
Lesson 8.   Developing a marketing package
Lesson 9.   Producing the project report and analysis of the result

Consider whether the subject content is at the right level for your pupils.

The ICT curriculum at KS4 and KS5

The ICT curriculum at KS4 and KS5 is dominated by external qualifications available from Awarding Organizations (AOs). The specifications for these state what subject content should be taught in much more detail than the KS4 ICT NC, and are the only guidance for KS5. Most of these qualifications at KS4 contribute to the standing of schools in the school league tables. At KS4, these qualifications include: GCSE and IGCSE (International/General Certificate of Education); and OCR (Oxford, Cambridge and RSA Examinations) Cambridge Nationals (for more detail, see Appendix 1).

GCSE specifications exert a major influence on teaching in KS4. All GCSE specifications conform to the mandatory code of practice (Ofqual, 2011a) and are based on the GCSE subject criteria (Ofqual, 2011b). Consequently, they all have similar aims, objectives and subject content. However, the ways in which they conduct assessment may differ.

GCSE specifications in ICT must aim to enable learners to do the following:

- Become independent and discerning users of ICT, able to make informed decisions about its use and aware of its implications for individuals, organizations and society.
- Acquire and apply creative and technical skills, knowledge and understanding of ICT in a range of contexts.
- Develop ICT-based solutions to solve problems.
- Develop their understanding of current and emerging technologies and their social and commercial impact.
- Develop their understanding of the legal, social, economic, ethical and environmental issues raised by ICT.
- Recognize potential risks when using ICT, and develop safe, secure and responsible practice.
- Develop the skills to work collaboratively.
- Evaluate ICT-based solutions.

(Ofqual, 2011b, p. 3)

These aims are accompanied by a statement of the subject content which states that all GCSE ICT specifications must require learners to demonstrate knowledge and understanding of the following:

- current and emerging technologies and their impact on individuals, organizations and society;
- a range of ICT tools and techniques and the ways they are used in different contexts to develop ideas and solve problems;
- legal, social, economic, ethical and environmental implications of the use of ICT for individuals, organizations and society;
- issues of risk, safety, security and responsible use of ICT;
- collaborative working.

(ibid.)

They also state that all GCSE ICT specifications must require learners to demonstrate the ability to do the following:

- Think creatively, logically and critically.
- Select, use and integrate ICT tools and techniques to meet needs.

- Find, select and evaluate information for its relevance, value, accuracy and plausibility.
- Manipulate and process data and other information, sequence instructions, model situations and explore ideas.
- Communicate data and information in a form fit for purpose and audience;
- Adopt safe, secure and responsible practice when using ICT.
- Develop appropriate and effective ICT-based solutions in a range of contexts.
- Evaluate their own and others' use of ICT.

(ibid., pp. 3–4)

IGCSE and Cambridge Nationals, BTEC and CiDA are also regulated by Ofqual and have very similar subject content to GCSE; however, they are assessed in different ways. You should read the relevant specification before teaching and this will give considerably more detail about the subject content and how it is assessed.

Curriculum models

The various curriculum-related documents, such as the NC, NS and I/GCSE specifications tend to specify the subject content but do not always clarify other aspects of the delivery of ICT in schools. An exception is the NS where the three-part lesson plan (starter, main activity, plenary) is implicitly recommended. Even so, how ICT is to be delivered is not usually stated. Similarly, I/GCSE specifications do not always contain a definitive list of the software and hardware that are needed to ensure that pupils' experiences of ICT in schools are sufficient to help them prepare for assessment. An advisory list is provided in Chapter 4 of this text book.

While schools must cover the statutory ICT NC PoS, the ways in which they organize the delivery of the ICT curriculum is not mandatory. As a result, schools can choose to organize the delivery of the ICT curriculum in a variety of different ways. In practice, three basic models have emerged. These are referred to as:

- discrete ICT
- cross-curricular ICT
- hybrid ICT.

Discrete ICT

Discrete ICT refers to ICT being taught as a separate subject. Time is allocated on the timetable for ICT in the same way that it is allocated for Mathematics, English, Science, and the other subjects. It is assumed that pupils will be taught ICT and be assessed in ICT in the timetabled subject of ICT.

If ICT is to be taught as a discrete subject, the following conditions should apply:

- There should be enough specialist ICT teachers to allow all pupils to be taught by an ICT specialist. If not, it is likely that non-specialists will teach ICT in KS3.
- There should be sufficient time available on the timetable.
- There should be sufficient well-equipped ICT rooms.

If this approach causes resource problems, the school could spread its existing resources more thinly. This may meet statutory requirements, but lead to a relatively insubstantial experience of ICT for all pupils. This is particularly unsatisfactory for those pupils who might benefit from more in-depth study. One solution is to offer all pupils a basic course (that covers the NC ICT PoS) and, in addition, provide opportunities for more in-depth study. For example, all pupils could follow a course leading to an ICT Functional Skills qualification at the end of KS4 with a supplementary option available leading to the more substantial IGCSE ICT for those pupils who choose to study ICT in greater depth.

It has been suggested that teaching ICT as a discrete subject is unlikely to provide sufficiently rich contexts in which pupils can consolidate their ICT skills. This is not necessarily so. ICT skills are almost inevitably taught in context. These contexts may be satisfactory whether pupils experience them in ICT or some other subject (Crawford, 2011). For example, when pupils are taught to use desk top publishing (DTP) software, they may develop their ICT skills by producing a school newspaper. That the task is done in an ICT lesson rather than an English lesson, or vice versa, need not influence the quality of their learning experiences.

Cross-curricular ICT

In the cross-curricular approach, ICT is taught and used only in other subjects. There is no time allocated on the timetable specifically for ICT. It is assumed that the teaching, use and assessment of ICT will take place in these other subjects.

The cross-curricular model can be organized in a variety of ways. For example, a few subjects, such as English, Mathematics, Science, Geography, and Design and Technology, may be given the responsibility to collectively cover the ICT NC in their schemes of work. This arrangement can help ensure coherence, continuity and progression in the ICT curriculum, and simplify the associated planning and assessment.

If ICT is taught across the curriculum, the teachers of other subjects who will deliver the ICT curriculum must have sufficient ICT skills, knowledge and understanding, and must be able to plan lessons with ICT objectives as well as learning objectives in their own subject. Teachers of the other subjects given responsibility for delivering ICT may find that the extra work is too great a burden in addition to teaching their own subject, and they may be more interested in teaching their subject and not very interested in teaching ICT. In contrast, teachers of subjects that do not have a responsibility to deliver the ICT NC may feel excluded.

Another possibility is for classroom teachers in other subjects and ICT specialists to team teach. The ICT specialist identifies a coherent programme of opportunities to study ICT derived from the whole curriculum. The ICT specialist then teaches and assesses ICT skills while other teachers concentrate on teaching their subjects. This approach can be successful but it is relatively expensive. It is not unusual to find that too little ICT support is provided and that its availability is limited. There is also an assumption that detailed forward planning of the ICT curriculum is possible across a range of subjects and this may not be so.

It may prove difficult to ensure that pupils are thoroughly prepared for external assessment in ICT. Although cross-curricular ICT can deliver the NC, it is unlikely that pupils will be adequately prepared for I/GCSE ICT or other assessments. For I/GCSE ICT, pupils will need to be prepared for controlled assessment and examinations. However, as there is no timetabled time for ICT, this must happen within the time allocation for other subjects, and revision for ICT assessments may be neglected.

The teaching and assessment of ICT across the curriculum may lead to overly complex organization and administration. There is concern that:

- Pupils may not be taught ICT effectively by non-specialist teachers.
- Too little specialist ICT support will be available.
- Assessment of pupils' ICT skills may be of a variable standard.
- ICT hardware may be spread thinly throughout the school so that whole class teaching of ICT skills is not possible.
- Pupils may not be effectively prepared for I/GCSE ICT or similar external assessments.

Consequently, the cross-curricular approach is rarely entirely successful. In extreme cases, it may lead to the effective disintegration of the ICT curriculum.

Hybrid ICT

In the hybrid approach, pupils are taught and assessed by ICT specialists in ICT subject classes, and use ICT across the curriculum wherever possible. This approach attempts to combine the advantages of both discrete ICT and cross-curricular ICT, and is the most common in schools.

Time needs to be allocated to teaching ICT skills as well as to practising and consolidating them. Pupils should be taught ICT skills as well as using ICT to enhance learning in other subjects. ICT skills should be developed, practised and consolidated in a variety of contexts. This can be achieved through a combination of ICT subject teaching in conjunction with well-planned opportunities to use ICT across the curriculum. In addition, pupils should have the opportunity to study ICT in greater depth.

For example, a discrete course in ICT, taught by an ICT specialist teacher, could prepare all pupils for assessment for Functional Skills in ICT and for using ICT in other subjects. Typically, such a course would occupy 5 per cent of timetabled time. Pupils are prepared for external assessment by the ICT specialist who teaches them. Pupils' use of ICT across the curriculum still needs to be planned and recorded; however, teachers of other subjects will not need to teach and assess ICT skills as this will be done in discrete ICT. These teachers can give due priority to their own subjects, making use of ICT when appropriate. Having acquired adequate ICT skills in discrete ICT, pupils have the opportunity to make use of them in the variety of rich contexts provided by other subjects, and will need a minimum of support when they do so. As the teaching of pupils' ICT skills is done in discrete ICT by a specialist ICT teacher, adequate coverage of the NC ICT can be ensured. Administrative and organizational difficulties are reduced, and the coordination of assessment is simplified. Extending this approach, so that pupils who choose to do so can undertake further study leading to a more substantial I/GCSE ICT will require extra timetabled time.

In summary, the delivery of the ICT curriculum is most effective when there is some timetabled teaching of ICT combined with well-supported and organized opportunities to apply ICT skills in other subjects. When ICT is only taught as a discrete subject, coverage of the ICT curriculum is more rigorous; but there may be insufficient opportunities to apply the ICT skills acquired in other subjects. The cross-curricular delivery of ICT works only when teachers of other subjects are also confident in ICT and structures are in place to effectively coordinate delivery.

Many judgements have been made by practitioners over a long period of time to support this viewpoint. For example, Ofsted used inspection evidence from 240 secondary schools as a basis for similar comments (Ofsted, 1995) and a more recent analysis of Ofsted subject inspection reports notes that '[a] lack of cross-curricular organisation is frequently mentioned as an "Area for Improvement"' and that 'Most "Inadequate" or "Satisfactory" schools have cross-curricular cited as an area for improvement' (Bradley, 2009). Even so, pupils should 'be given opportunities to apply and develop their ICT capability through the use of ICT tools to support their learning in all subjects' and in KS3 and KS4 'there are statutory requirements to use ICT in all statutory subjects except PE' (DfE, 2012b).

The ICT and Computing curriculum

There is considerable debate about the appropriateness of the ICT NC in general and the ICT curriculum in schools. Some viewpoints were:

- ICT changes rapidly. The current NC was published in 2007 and the NS in 2008 and they were thought to be out of date.
- The teaching of ICT in schools was thought to be boring. The Minister of Education was reported as stating that children were 'bored out of their minds being taught how to use Word and Excel by bored teachers' (Vasagar, 2012).
- There was a feeling that 'a change in the ICT curriculum to give students more insight into programming and computer science would help businesses, which in turn would help the UK economy' (Shah, 2012).
- The number of people employed in ICT-related jobs is predicted to grow at four times the rate of the overall UK workforce (BIS, 2010).
- The teaching of computing and programming in schools was seen as a solution. 'Imagine the dramatic change which could be possible in just a few years, once we remove the roadblock of the existing ICT curriculum . . . we could have 11-year-olds able to write simple 2D computer animations using an MIT tool called Scratch' (Vasagar, 2012).

Activity

Describe in detail how the ICT curriculum is delivered in a school you know well. How could the delivery of the ICT curriculum be improved?

Computing and Computer Science are usually understood to be the same subject but there is some vagueness about the particular meanings of the terms: ICT and Computing. The BCS (2011) considers ICT to be 'computer technologies and software used by industry and the public'; whereas Computing 'includes amongst other things the underpinning scientific and mathematical principles'. Even so, Computing is often confused with ICT (CAS, 2011).

CAS (2011) regard Computing as those deeper aspects of the subject domain. They state that: 'just as numeracy is not mathematics, ICT is not Computing, like mathematics,

Computing is a discipline.' Another helpful analogy is that of the relationship between the car driver (the ICT user) and the mechanic (the Computing specialist). Computing will be taken to include the broad themes of:

- programming languages, computing machines, and computation
- data and its representation;
- communication and coordination of distributed computers;
- abstraction and design;
- the role and value of computers in society.

(BCS, 2011)

ICT knowledge, skills and understanding are increasingly a prerequisite for engaging with everyday features of citizens' experience of the UK in the twenty-first century, for example in banking, shopping, accessing media, in education, and in telecommunications. In addition, it is almost a prerequisite for employment in many sectors of the economy, as around 27 per cent of UK employment is ICT-related and this is expected to grow much quicker than the overall UK workforce (BIS, 2010).

ICT and Computing are thought to be key components of present and future competitiveness and prosperity. The UK market is the largest in the EU with an estimated value of Euro70 billion in 2010. The UK video games and visual effects industries earned over £2 billion in global sales and earnings from digital entertainment and media and are predicted to reach $1.7 trillion by 2014 (CIHE, 2010). 'Computing and IT significantly contribute to the competitiveness of UK companies, and are important to increasing their future competitiveness' (BCS, 2011).

Many more, if not all, employees need ICT skills and some need a more advanced understanding of Computing. At present, schools tend to teach pupils how to use existing software but do not teach the principles of Computing. This may make it harder for pupils to adapt to future technologies (ibid.). Firms that use ICT intensively are more likely to grow and this suggests that 'the whole workforce require some understanding of how computers and software systems work beyond the immediate skills necessary in using specific existing technologies' (ibid.).

Current concerns focus on recent and significant falls in the number of students opting to study 'academic' qualifications in ICT and Computing, that is, GCSE and A-level. In 2012, '31,800 students attempted the [ICT GCSE] examination compared with 81,100 in 2007 – a reduction of 64 per cent' (Ofsted, 2012). The number of students studying GCSE ICT has fallen by a third in three years; A-level ICT by a third over six years; and A-level Computing by 57 per cent over eight years or approximately 7 per cent per annum (Rodeiro, 2010). Moreover, the number of students studying AS and A-level Computing courses is small (CAS, 2011). However, these numbers do not take into account the numbers studying 'vocational' and other ICT-related courses, for example, OCR/Cambridge Nationals and BTECs.

Analysis of the total entry for academic and vocational qualifications suggests a shift in entries from Computing to ICT and from academic to vocational qualifications rather than a continuous and sustained decline in the total number of students entered for ICT and Computing-related qualifications. Taken as a whole, the number of pupils entered for a qualification in an ICT-related subject by the end of Key Stage 4 was: 363,481 in 2007; 395,935 in 2008 and 375,910 in 2009 (Rodeiro, 2010). Entries for ICT-related subjects at the end of Key Stage 5 were: 81,462 in 2007; 81,008 in 2008; and 82,203 in 2009 (ibid.); and there was a considerable increase in the number of students completing vocational qualifications in ICT: in 2012, '212,900 students completed OCR Nationals, a popular suite of vocational qualifications, compared with 58,900 in 2008' (Ofsted, 2012).

The rapid shift from academic to vocational ICT qualifications may be due to several unrelated factors. There may be underlying changes in the nature of teaching and learning in English secondary schools that encourage teachers to select vocational qualifications that support step-by-step learning, are more practical; and where pupils can see and understand the progress they are making. In addition, vocational qualifications are thought to have equivalences in the school league tables that exceed their actual equivalence (Wolf, 2011), that is, they are easier for pupils to acquire than the equivalent GCSEs, and this may encourage schools to introduce these in order to improve their standing in the school league table. Perversely, the introduction of new GCSE ICT specifications for first teaching in September 2010 may have accelerated the shift from academic to vocational qualifications, as a change in specification is often the time when teachers re-evaluate their arrangements for external accreditation of the courses they teach.

Similarly, the number of students on Computer Science courses in universities has also fallen dramatically (CAS, 2011), by 23.3 per cent from 2002 to 2010, or approximately 2.9 per cent per annum (Next Gen Skills, 2012). These figures do not suggest a dramatic annual decline and would be consistent with a shift in interest to related subjects. There may not have been an overall decline if all ICT-related courses are taken into account, for example, degrees in gaming, media and film technology often have significant components of advanced ICT and Computing; and many degrees in computer gaming include significant components of software engineering. More research is needed here.

There are various explanations for the decline in interest in Computing at A-level. It has been suggested that current arrangements for teaching Computing in secondary schools do not engage students and inspire them to make their careers in Computing (CAS, 2011). Moreover, CAS (2011) believe that GCSE ICT is 'boring and demotivating' and that it omits 'many of the fundamentals that are required to develop and inspire a future cohort of A-level Computer Science students'. If there is 'boring' teaching of ICT in schools, the problem is likely to be in the implementation of the curriculum and the quality of teaching rather than the curriculum itself. Even so, where pupils have a choice, they tend to want to study an ICT-related subject other than Computing. This may be because the subject content of Computing courses is not perceived to be of immediate relevance by pupils.

The government's reaction to the observation that fewer pupils are studying Computing has been:

- To say 'ICT is boring' – it isn't. The ICT NC is so vague it does not unduly circumscribe what is taught. Most schools already teach multimedia applications and programming as well as office applications.
- To suggest that introducing 'programming' into the curriculum is innovative. Many schools already teach some of Scratch, GameMaker, Kodu Games Lab, Logo, etc. which are programming environments designed for schools. Real programming languages, for example, C++ and Visual Basic, require specialist skills which are difficult to develop and would be of interest to only a few pupils and teachers.

- To encourage courses in GCSE Computing. However, the reason for the decline in the number of pupils studying GCSE Computing has not been identified and so it is unclear whether the number will increase in the long term.
- To disapply the 2007 ICT NC at all four Key Stages, along with the statutory assessment arrangements at Key Stage 3, from September 2012 (DfE, 2012a). However, ICT remains a compulsory subject at all Key Stages, pending the outcome of the current review of the NC in England.

It is intended that disapplication will free up teachers to teach ICT in ways that are creative, innovative and inspirational. However, if they want to do this, they already can because the vagueness of the 2007 ICT NC allows them sufficient freedom to do so. If teachers are not doing so, it may be due to other factors. Unfortunately, disapplication could be misinterpreted as 'there is no need to do ICT' and the ICT curriculum could be curtailed, and provision for the teaching of ICT constrained. ICT is expensive to resource so there is always pressure to provide less and especially so when finances are constrained. As a result, some secondary schools can be expected to reduce ICT staffing levels.

The impact of disapplication of the ICT NC is likely to be:

- Some pupils will be disadvantaged as they may not receive a sufficiently comprehensive and rigorous experience of ICT.
- There will be no consistent, shared framework to assess pupils' ICT knowledge, skills and understanding within and between schools, locally and nationally.
- The ICT curriculum will be cropped. It is likely that in some schools only very basic ICT skills will be taught. ICT is an expensive subject to resource, and there is a shortage of specialist ICT teachers. These two factors can influence head teachers to reduce the ICT curriculum in schools to a minimum.
- Trainee teachers specializing in ICT will be less likely to be trained in schools with a substantial ICT curriculum and this may affect the quality of provision in the future.
- The job prospects of pupils leaving schools with good ICT skills will be better than for those pupils leaving schools where the ICT curriculum is very basic and there has been no opportunity for them to develop a sufficient level of skill.
- Disapplication is unlikely to lead to more widespread teaching of Computing as the demand from pupils is likely to decline as they are less likely to experience a rich ICT curriculum, and the narrowed curriculum may not justify the employment of the highly skilled teachers required.
- The hybrid model for delivering the ICT curriculum is well established. However, if there is less requirement to teach discrete ICT, then a greater proportion of resources will be directed to cross-curricular ICT.

The way forward

All secondary school pupils need a good understanding of ICT and the opportunity to develop an advanced understanding of Computing. While Ian Livingstone believes that 'current lessons are essentially irrelevant to today's generation of children who can learn

PowerPoint in a week' (quoted in Burns, 2012), many teachers do not accept this viewpoint, and some bloggers commented that:

- 'This is crazy. Using Word and Excel may be boring but that's what most people will need in the real world. Not many will become programmers in the future. Speaking as an ex-programmer, one needs a certain aptitude to do programming, and I foresee a lot of frustrated, upset kids who simply cannot get their heads around the principles. It should definitely be an option, not mandatory (Hambo, 16:02, 11 January 2012).
- ICT skills are invaluable; to use Windows is the ICT aspect of many jobs. Have programming as an option choice. I was taught Computer Science, I have never used it since. Students should be given the choice, this would enable them to develop their skills in whichever area. After all, do you really need to know how a program was built in order to use it? I drive but I am not a mechanic (DMJ1970, 15:14, 11 January 2012).

Even so, programming should be taught in Key Stages 3, 4 and 5. It is a 'core activity of Computing' (Woolard, 2009, p. 3) and should be more widely taught. Currently, programming is not always taught in schools although the ICT NC did not exclude this and many schools teach simple programming using Scratch, GameMaker or Kodu Games Lab in KS 3 and KS4. Programming languages, such as Visual Basic, Java or C++, are most commonly studied by students following courses in A-level Computing.

Programming is important because pupils gain some control over technology and learn problem solving in relation to it. The use of technology is not unproblematic, however, and to make effective use of it, it is necessary to have the knowledge and confidence to solve problems that arise when using it. Programming facilitates the development of problem-solving skills and enables the user to access and release the potential of the technology they are using. Moreover, the problem-solving skills and attitudes learnt are generally applicable. Programming 'promotes intellectual development and the development of problem-solving skills in a way that is [also] applicable to many other subjects and in many other areas of life' (ibid., p. 4).

In addition, programming promotes other important skills that are relevant to the effective use of technology and in general. These include (ibid.):

- accuracy, for example, of sequence and syntax;
- completing a larger task by carrying out smaller instructions step by step;
- the analysis of tasks and the design of ways of doing them;
- representing tasks and sequences of tasks in different ways. for example, flowcharts and system diagrams; pseudocode; and storyboards;
- consistency in recording data and information so that it can more easily be accessed and analysed;
- logical thinking and action.

The ICT curriculum in schools should ensure that pupils leave school with broad experience and skills with a wide range of ICTs. Programming is an important part of the skill set of digital competencies that pupils should study and should be part of a broad and balanced ICT curriculum.

Activity

Discuss:

- Should all pupils be taught how to use email, web browsers, messaging and social networking software or should this be optional?
- Should all pupils be taught how to use office software, including word processors, spreadsheets and databases or should this be optional?
- Should all pupils be taught how to use multimedia software, including graphics, presentation, animation, recording and sound and video editing software or should this be optional?
- Should all pupils be taught computer programming or should this be optional?

Summary

- A revised National Curriculum (NC) will be introduced and apply from September 2014. It will set out a minimum national entitlement organized around subject disciplines.
- ICT will remain a compulsory subject at all Key Stages at least until September 2014.
- From September 2012, the ICT NC has been disapplied along with the statutory assessment arrangements at KS3.
- The 2007 ICT NC is described in separate PoS for KS3 (QCA, 2007a) and KS4 (QCA, 2007b). The KS3 ICT Attainment Target (AT) consists of level descriptions stating what pupils are expected to achieve at each of levels 4–8 (the highest). Above level 8, pupils are said to have achieved 'exceptional performance'.
- The 2007 ICT NC is well organized but sometimes vague, and this is not especially helpful to teachers planning detailed schemes of work.
- The ICT National Strategy (NS) has extensive and detailed resources for teaching and learning for KS3 which could be adapted for a wide range of pupils and includes:

  o a framework and teaching objectives for years 7 to 11;
  o a scheme of work for ICT organized into units with all the resources needed to teach the lessons, including presentations and worksheets;
  o sample teaching units, including lesson plans and resources in electronic form;
  o advice on how to organize the delivery of ICT in the school curriculum, including the recommendation that pupils study ICT for approximately 1 hour each week.

- When planning a curriculum for ICT in KS3, the NS lesson plans and resources are a good starting point.
- The ICT curriculum at KS4 and KS5 is dominated by external qualifications. At KS4, these qualifications include: GCSE and IGCSE; and Cambridge Nationals (for more detail, see Appendix 1).
- GCSE specifications exert a major influence on teaching in KS4. All GCSE syllabuses conform to the mandatory code of practice (Ofqual, 2011a) and are based on the GCSE subject criteria for ICT (Ofqual, 2011b). They all have similar aims,

objectives and subject content; however, assessment methodologies may differ (see Appendix 1).

- Schools choose to organize the delivery of the ICT curriculum in a variety of different ways. In practice, there are three basic models. These are referred to as:

  o Discrete ICT – ICT is taught as a separate subject.
  o Cross-curricular ICT – ICT is taught and used only in other subjects.
  o Hybrid ICT – ICT is taught and assessed by ICT specialists in separate ICT subject classes, and used across the curriculum wherever possible. The hybrid model for delivering the ICT curriculum is well established and known to be effective.

- In 2012, there was considerable debate about the appropriateness of the NC in general and the ICT curriculum in schools. Some viewpoints were:

  o The NC and NS are out of date.
  o The Minister for Education was reported as stating that children were 'bored out of their minds being taught how to use Word and Excel by bored teachers' (Vasagar, 2012).
  o There was a feeling that 'a change in the ICT curriculum to give students more insight into programming and computer science would help businesses, which in turn would help the UK economy' (Shah, 2012).

- The impact of disapplication of the ICT NC is likely to be:

  o Some pupils will be disadvantaged as they may not receive a sufficiently comprehensive and rigorous experience of ICT.
  o There will be no consistent, shared framework to assess pupils' ICT knowledge, skills and understanding within and between schools, locally and nationally.
  o It is likely that in some schools only very basic ICT skills will be taught.
  o Trainee ICT teachers will be less likely to be trained in schools with a substantial and varied ICT curriculum and this may affect the quality of provision in the future.
  o The job prospects of pupils leaving school with good ICT skills will be better than for those pupils leaving schools where the ICT curriculum is very basic.
  o Disapplication is unlikely to lead to more widespread teaching of Computing as the demand from pupils is likely to decline and the narrowed curriculum may not justify the employment of the highly skilled teachers needed.

- Current concerns focus on recent and significant falls in the number of students opting to study ICT and Computing at GCSE and A-level. Analysis of the entry data suggests a shift from Computing to ICT and from academic to vocational qualifications rather than a reduction in the total number of students entered for all ICT and Computing-related qualifications.

- All pupils need a good understanding of ICT and the opportunity to develop an advanced understanding of Computing:

  o ICT knowledge, skills and understanding are increasingly a prerequisite for engaging with everyday life.
  o ICT and Computing are thought to be key components of present and future competitiveness and prosperity.

o   All employees need ICT skills and some need a more advanced understanding of Computing.

o   Programming should be taught in schools as a component of a rich and balanced ICT curriculum.

Further reading

DfE (2012) *Removing the Duty on Maintained Schools to Follow the ICT Programmes of Study, Attainment Targets and Statutory Assessment Arrangements*, available at: http://www.education.gov.uk/consultations/index.cfm?actionconsultationDetails&consultationId1802&externalno&menu1 (accessed 4 April 2012).

Next Gen Skills (2012) *A Consultation Response to the DfE: Removing the Duty on Maintained Schools to Follow the ICT POS, ATS and Statutory Assessment Arrangements*, Next Gen Skills. Available at: www.nextgenskills.com.

Ofsted (2012) 'Young people are not being sufficiently chanllenged in ICT lessons', available at: http://www.ofsted.gov.uk/news/young-people-are-not-being-sufficiently-challenged-ict-lessons (accessed 2 July 2012).

Chapter 3

Assessment

Introduction

Assessment is an essential part of good teaching and can help improve learning (Crawford, 2012), and it is one of the most powerful educational tools for promoting effective learning (ARG, 1999). This chapter discusses:

- what is meant by Assessment for Learning (AfL) and Assessment of Learning (AoL) and a consideration of some of the advantages and disadvantages of both;
- recording and reporting, and eportfolios;
- moderation, controlled assessment and marking external examinations;
- the equivalence between vocational and academic qualifications.

Assessment for Learning (AfL) and Assessment of Learning (AoL)

Assessment for Learning (AfL) is the day-to-day assessment that helps teachers judge the progress pupils have made so that they can modify teaching and plan to focus more on what pupils need to learn. AfL is also known as *formative assessment*.

AfL can have different degrees of formality and scope, for example, a conversation with a pupil may help a teacher assess that pupil's understanding; in contrast, a test at the end of a unit of work, marked in detail and analysed by the teacher, could yield more accurate information on the progress of the whole class and each individual pupil.

AfL should include pupils in the assessment process so that they know what they can do and where they need to concentrate their efforts to learn. It is essential that pupils judge their own progress (self-assessment) so that they can have confidence in their learning and focus their efforts on further improvement. However, accurate self-assessment is difficult. When pupils are shown how to assess each other's work (peer assessment) and practise this, they become better at self-assessment. Peer assessment also helps pupils consider others and is a rich source of ideas.

Assessment of Learning (AoL) is *summative assessment*. It is a snapshot of pupils' skills, knowledge and understanding, for example, schools may have internal assessments, such as annual examinations or end of unit tests or teacher-set coursework, which lead to pupils being assigned a National Curriculum (NC) level or a grade or percentage mark. For example, school reports for parents often include each pupil's NC level in ICT at the end of Key Stage 3 (KS3). External assessments, such as GCSEs and A-levels, are well-known examples of AoL (see Appendix 1) and these lead to the award of a grade. These levels, marks or grades may be used to provide a snapshot judgement of a person's capabilities and to screen them for employment. For example, applicants for teacher training must have a grade C or above in GCSE English and Mathematics.

The purposes of AfL and AoL are dissimilar but they are not necessarily entirely different and may overlap. After an end of unit test in school, teachers will summarize the standard each pupil has achieved, perhaps producing a National Curriculum level or a percentage mark or grade, with a comment, to go into a report to parents. However, teachers may also look at pupils' performance in specific questions and use this to analyse what pupils understand and decide whether to modify what they were planning to teach so that concepts which are not well understood can be revisited. Teachers may also provide diagnostic comments on pupils' work to indicate how they can improve their work and encourage pupils to 'correct' their work in response to these.

Recording and reporting, and eportfolios

There should be regular assessment, recording and reporting of pupils' progress. Progress should be recorded in such a way that it is clear how the whole assessment process leads to the summative assessments reported to parents. Each school's approach to assessment, recording and reporting should be described in detail in the relevant policy documents and teachers should be aware of these for the school in which they are working.

Schools should have a system for tracking and recording pupils' progress and attainment across all subjects, including in ICT. Often this will include setting targets for each pupil's attainment in each subject and some means of tracking their actual progress relative to these targets. Schools and teachers often devise their own tracking and recording systems, for example, resources shared on the TES website include a 'progress report' tool uploaded by Sabeena Kauser and this has been downloaded more than 10,000 times (TES, 2011b). In addition, tracking and recording software is often an integral part of a school's management information system. In the UK, SIMS software (www.capita-cs .co.uk) includes facilities for assessment, tracking, recording and reporting as a part of an integrated school information management system. In contrast, Pupil Tracking software (www.pupiltracking.com) provides standalone tracking and reporting software which can be integrated with SIMS. Internationally, there is a wide variety of school administration software available and there are comparison websites, for example, www.capterra.com.

The way in which secondary schools organize the ICT curriculum (discrete, across the curriculum, or a hybrid version of these, see Chapter 2) will have an impact on the processes and effectiveness of assessment, recording and reporting systems.

Key Stage 3

It is reasonable to expect that all of a pupil's work using ICT and all the relevant evidence a pupil has produced in all subjects will be collected before a summative assessment of their level of attainment is made. Organizing the collection of the evidence to be assessed, and its summative assessment are relatively straightforward when ICT is taught as a discrete subject. In this case, ICT will be taught and assessed by a specialist ICT teacher. This teacher can reasonably be expected to take responsibility for the assessment and the recording and reporting requirements of the classes taught as most of the evidence to be assessed will be the work pupils will do in their ICT class. The process of assessment, recording and reporting is likely to be similar to that carried out by other subject departments, such as Mathematics.

If ICT is taught across the curriculum, pupils may be taught, use or be assessed in ICT in almost any NC subject. If all the evidence pupils generate is to be assessed, there will need to be procedures for collecting it for each pupil, assessing it, and recording and summarizing the assessments made, and tracking progress. This must be done thoroughly and systematically if pupils are to be credited with all the work they have successfully completed in all subjects and curriculum-related activities.

Eportfolios

Pupils may need to take responsibility for collecting their own evidence and there will need to be systematic procedures for teachers to check that this is being done. Pupils could be asked to record their experiences throughout the curriculum using a personal log available on the school's ICT network and put all their work in an eportfolio. However, not all pupils can be relied on to do this thoroughly and systematically.

Consequently, schools may adopt procedures that involve teachers in checking that the assessment evidence has been assembled and making sure that pupils provide all the required evidence for their eportfolios. This process can easily become complex, laborious and time-consuming. For example, suppose a pupil learns to use spreadsheet software in Mathematics. Evidence of this achievement will need to be assessed, and the pupil's achievements recorded and summarized, for both ICT and Mathematics. Either the Mathematics teacher will need to assess pupils' progress in both ICT and Mathematics, or the evidence will need to be accessible to both the ICT coordinator and the Mathematics teacher.

Even if pupils' work is present in their eportfolios, it may not provide the appropriate evidence of achievement needed by the ICT coordinator because it has been produced in order to meet the requirements of the Mathematics teacher. Moreover, a pupil's work may not be present in their eportfolio, so that the ICT coordinator will have responsibility for assessing the ICT, but has little control over whether that work has been done and is available for assessment.

The advantage of an on-line eportfolio is that the evidence available is accessible to all teachers. The disadvantages are: (1) consistent assessment is difficult because as pupils progressively update their eportfolios, the evidence available could change; (2) many teachers will be involved; and (3) not all the teachers involved in assessing the evidence will be specialist ICT teachers.

As there will be many items of evidence per pupil per year drawn from a variety of subjects, the task of collecting, assessing and summarizing all the evidence for every pupil in the school could be burdensome. It is almost always easier to collect and summarize teachers' assessments of pupils' ICT capability in a narrow range of subjects than to collect all the assessment evidence they have produced in all subjects and assess it.

The task of collecting pupils' work, assessing it and summarizing and reporting teachers' assessments could be significantly more manageable if specialist eportfolio software designed for the task and integrated with the school management information system is used. As pupils complete their work, they could upload it to their eportfolios on the network and this could be organized so that the presence or otherwise of particular pieces of work is obvious to teachers. The work could be viewed and assessed online, and teachers' grades and comments recorded and aggregated automatically for reporting to parents.

Specialist eportfolio software is more widely available for further and higher education than for secondary schools. Even so, eportfolios are not yet well used in further and higher education. Eportfolios are more likely to be used for specific vocational qualifications than assembling all of secondary school pupils' work across a wide range of subjects over an extended period of time. In addition, commercially available eportfolio software has associated set-up, licensing or subscription costs, and is often inflexible and has restricted functionality. It is not always possible for users to have ownership of the whole of their eportfolio, for example, some eportfolio software allows users to take copies of their files but removes the organizational features of the eportfolio, which can leave users unable to navigate or locate their work. A simpler solution is to use file management software which is readily available, for example, Microsoft Windows Explorer, and design and publish a hierarchical folder structure that meets the requirements of the school. This should be entirely flexible, appropriate and low cost, and can be adapted as requirements change. However, such a solution may not be integrated with software for tracking and recording pupils' progress.

Activity

Consider whether a fair assessment of each pupil's ICT capability is possible if the evidence is:

- collected in some subjects and not others;
- assessed by several teachers with expertise in different subjects.

Assessing Pupils' Progress (APP)

Considerable effort has been made at the national level to produce consistent, reliable assessment at the end of KS3 in ICT. A national online test in ICT was developed and it was intended that this would be compulsory for every pupil from 2008. However, despite a four-year pilot programme when the developing software was rolled out to secondary schools, there were problems implementing this in all schools and it was abandoned in 2007.

The APP materials were introduced as a part of the National Strategies programme in 2009. These support systematic, structured formative and summative assessment in KS3. They enable diagnosis of what pupils can and cannot do so that teachers can modify their teaching plans to focus on the topics pupils find difficult; and help teachers assess an overall NC level for each pupil. APP helps establish national standards and improves the consistency of teachers' assessments. The APP materials include detailed assessment criteria for each level of the NC; assessment guidelines that help teachers assess pupils' work (see Figure 3.1); and standards files which contain useful examples of pupils' work at different levels of the NC. This approach can be adapted to suit the ICT curriculum in individual schools and is a good starting point when designing an assessment framework for KS3.

Whichever system of record keeping is adopted, it should be both manageable and realistic. Assessment and record keeping should not become an intolerable burden to

ICT assessment guidelines: Levels 5 and 6
Pupil name:.................

	AF1 – Planning, developing and evaluating	AF2 – Handling date, sequencing instructions and modelling	AF3 – Finding, using and communicating information
L6	**Across a range of contexts pupils:** • Plan and develop solutions which show efficiency and integration of ICT tools and techniques • Use criteria and feedback to improve the effectiveness and efficiency of solutions • Explore the impacts of the use of ICT in work, leisure and home ☐	**Across a range of contexts pupils:** • Devise a data handling solution to test hypotheses that uses techniques to reduce input errors • Create efficient sequences of instructions including the use of subroutines • Test predictions by varying rules in models and assess the validity of the conclusions ☐	**Across a range of contexts pupils:** • Use complex lines of enquiry efficiently to interrogate information • Explain choices when presenting information for different purposes and wider or remote audiences ☐
L5	**Across a range of contexts pupils:** • Plan and develop structured solutions to problems which use a combination of ICT tools and techniques • Use criteria to evaluate the quality of solutions, identifying improvements and refining their work • Identify benefits and limitations of using ICT both inside and outside school ☐	**Across a range of contexts pupils:** • Use logical and appropriate structures to organise and process date • Create precise and accurate sequences of instructions • Change variables within models and explain the impact ☐	**Across a range of contexts pupils:** • Take account of accuracy and potential bias when searching for and selecting information • Present information in a range of forms for specific purposes and familiar audiences • Use ICT safely and responsibly ☐
BL	☐	☐	☐
IE	☐	☐	☐

Key: BL–Below Level; IE–Insufficient Evidence
Overall assessment (tick one box only)   Low 5 ☐   Secure 5 ☐   High 5 ☐   Low 6 ☐   Secure 6 ☐   High 6 ☐

Figure 3.1 Part of the assessment guidelines from the APP materials (The National Strategies, 2009b, p. 3)

teachers and schools. Effective assessment and record-keeping systems devised for the cross-curricular ICT approach are likely to be more complex, laborious and time-consuming than those for the discrete ICT approach. Consequently, many schools have found it difficult to meet their responsibilities with regard to assessment, recording and reporting pupils' levels of attainment in ICT where the cross-curricular ICT approach has been adopted. The hybrid ICT approach straddles both discrete ICT and cross-curricular ICT approaches. Procedures for assessment, recording and reporting are likely to be determined by the particular curricular hybrid constructed, and will have some of the advantages and disadvantages of each.

Key Stages 4 and 5

Procedures for assessment, recording and reporting in KS3 could be carried forward into Key Stage 4 (KS4). However, conformity with the requirements of the external examinations that pupils will be entered for at the end of KS4 and Key Stage 5 (KS5) is of great importance to teachers and pupils. Parents are likely to expect pupils to acquire qualifications in ICT or Computing before leaving school as this will help their future careers. It would therefore seem sensible to design a record-keeping system, which relates closely to that required by the chosen Awarding Organization (AO) for the external qualifications. However, the assessment and record-keeping methodologies for these external qualifications can be radically different and unlike those used in KS3.

Following the methodology of the AO is particularly important for work which is assessed in school, for example, work produced during controlled assessment. AOs require that records of the assessment of pupils' work should be sent to them in the format they specify. Such records are unlikely to show progression or relate directly to the organization of the curriculum in school. Pupils do the work in school and it is assessed by their teachers who record their pupils' results on the forms provided by the AO. Teachers' marking is moderated in school and then by the AO. The mark is later combined with the mark for other units of the qualification, for example, the written examinations, in order to arrive at an overall grade.

Reporting to parents during KS4 and KS5 is likely to reflect the estimated outcomes following external assessment. For example, pupils entered for GCSE will ultimately be awarded one of grades A* to G and the school's assessment of their potential grade is likely to be reported to parents along with an assessment of their progress towards this target.

Moderation

Moderation (also known as standardization) is essential if pupils' work is to be consistently assessed. Whichever strategy is used for collecting and assessing pupils' work, there will need to be some well-understood mechanism for moderation. Moderation is necessary as different teachers will be involved in the assessment of pupils' work. It is a means of ensuring that all teachers apply assessment criteria in the same way, producing reliable, consistent judgements of the standards pupils achieve.

At KS3, whether or not the APP materials are used, there will need to be some process that ensures teachers' judgements are consistent and reliable. At Key Stages 4 and 5, pupils' work submitted for assessment for GCSE or A-level must be internally moderated in each school before being moderated by the relevant AO. This ensures that standards in schools are consistent and in line with the standard set by the AO. Further inter-board moderation helps ensure consistency at a national level. Other assessments that are internal to the school should also be internally moderated to ensure consistent standards. A methodology for the moderation of coursework within the school should be agreed. If this includes the methodology that must be adopted to meet the requirements of the AO, there will be no need to have a range of different methodologies for different purposes.

Moderation involves teachers looking at each other's assessments of pupils' work, and agreeing that they too would have assessed the work as being of the same standard. A common methodology involves teachers re-marking a sample of each other's assessments (i.e. cross-marking). Having discussed any discrepancies, they then arrive at agreed standards. This discussion takes place in a moderation meeting involving all those teachers who have assessed pupils' work. Cross-marking may be carried out before or during the meeting. Discussion at the moderation meeting is likely to focus on resolving the discrepancies that have arisen during cross-marking. Teachers later adjust their initial assessments of all the work they have marked to make them consistent with the standards agreed during the moderation meeting.

A similar process may take place when pupils' work that has been internally moderated is externally moderated. For example, samples of pupils' work produced during controlled assessment are marked and moderated by the school, then sent to an external moderator appointed by the AO. The external moderator has three options: (1) agree with the school's marks; (2) apply an adjustment to the school's marks; or (3) request a re-mark. External moderators will have attended a moderation meeting arranged by the AO at an earlier date where the marking of moderators is aligned with the marking of the Principal Moderator.

However, there are different methods of ensuring pupils' work for external qualifications is in line with national standards, for example, a school representative may take samples of internally moderated assessments to an area moderation meeting where regional agreement is reached. Similarly, representatives from the area meeting may attend a national moderation meeting. In this way, consistent standards can be achieved in and between schools at a national level.

Another option replaces the area moderation meeting with a regional moderator who is responsible for ensuring that all schools in the region are making assessments that are consistent with national standards. Alternatively, the regional moderator may visit schools. Schools are then informed if their assessments conform to national standards, or must be adjusted to be in line with them.

Internal moderation is likely to be more complex and time-consuming where the cross- curricular ICT approach is adopted in a school, as substantially more teachers, from a variety of different subject areas may be involved in assessing pupils' work. There is often less likelihood of immediate agreement between teachers from different subject backgrounds, as the cultures of their own subjects will influence their assessments of pupils' attainment in ICT. In this case, moderation meetings may need to be held for each subject grouping, for example, there may need to be separate moderation meetings for ICT in English, ICT in Mathematics, and ICT in Technology before the school moderation meeting can take place.

Moderation is easiest where only a few teachers are involved and these teachers are specialists in the subject being assessed. The discrete ICT and hybrid ICT approaches lead to relatively straightforward moderation as all the assessment can be done by a few specialist ICT teachers. Where only one teacher in the school is involved in marking all the assessments, no in-school moderation is necessary.

Moderation will be made easier if there are examples of pupils' work available that represent agreed standards at different levels of achievement. For example, in KS3, the APP standards files could be used (DCSF, 2008). These are samples of pupils' work representative of attainment at the different levels of the NC. Otherwise, a school portfolio of pupils' work might be assembled. Brief explanatory notes accompanying the school portfolio could describe how the standards recorded in school relate to externally moderated standards year on year. This could include feedback from external moderators. Such a portfolio could help the school set appropriate standards during moderation and be powerful evidence that the school is achieving, maintaining or improving standards of achievement in ICT.

Activity

1   Write a test and the mark scheme.
2   Set the test for your class.
3   Mark pupils' work.
4   Select three examples of pupils' work that represent the full range of work produced by the class.
5   Give the test and the mark scheme and the three examples of pupils' work to a colleague and ask him/her to mark them. Do not discuss this process or the outcomes with your colleague.
6   Compare your marking with your colleague and discuss the marks or grades you have each awarded.

Controlled assessment

Since September 2010, controlled assessment has replaced coursework in new specifications for GCSE ICT. Before this date, GCSE coursework was authenticated as the candidate's work by the teacher but the coursework was not always done while pupils were being supervised by teachers, and, as a result, this authentication was not entirely reliable. Controlled assessment is completed only when pupils are supervised by teachers. Preparatory research can still be unsupervised and analysis of the task to be done can be informally supervised but completion of the controlled assessment task is supervised by teachers. Pupils' work may be internally assessed and moderated before being externally moderated; or externally assessed and moderated only.

Marking external examinations

In recent years, the process of marking written examination papers has changed. In the past, the external marking of examination papers was carried out in much the same way as teachers mark internal examination papers. In the past, a GCSE ICT written paper would be completed by a candidate during an examination and sent to the marker. The marker then marked the script using a red pen. Each marker received several hundred complete scripts and applied the same mark scheme as other markers. Being human, they made occasional errors. Occasionally multiple choice questions would be wrongly marked. Where candidates wrote prose answers, particularly if this was a short essay, consistency of marking by the same marker and between different markers could be difficult to achieve. A process similar to moderation would be carried out to help ensure that all markers marked at the same standard. The marking of individual markers was checked initially and during the marking process to ensure that they maintained the standard. Nevertheless, some variation was inevitable. However, as grades are awarded, not marks, a slight discrepancy in the mark would not necessarily lead to a change of grade. Further examination of scripts at grade boundaries helped ensure candidates were awarded the correct grade. This process ensured reasonable accuracy, and candidates could appeal. This ensured a review of the marking where candidates felt the grade awarded did not reflect their ability.

Most AOs now mark written examinations online, and many are moving towards online examinations, particularly in ICT. Typically, when written examination papers are marked online, they have been scanned and are distributed as clips which are images of the answers to individual questions. Markers work at a computer and are presented with candidates' answers to the same question one after the other. The marking scheme for the question is also available onscreen. Because markers are marking hundreds of answers to the same question over and over again, marking is much more consistent. In addition, after markers log on and before they are allowed to mark, they have to confirm the standard of their marking by remarking several exemplar clips. As a result, the standard of marking is being repeatedly checked. Multiple choice questions are marked automatically so that thousands of answers can be marked in a few minutes. Consequently, marking is much more reliable and consistent, and can be completed much quicker. There are also cost savings for the AO: distributing clips over computer networks tends to be less expensive than posting heavy parcels containing thousands of scripts. Markers do not have to physically meet to agree standards as this can also be done online so that the cost of hotel accommodation and travel is also reduced.

On balance, AOs, schools and pupils all benefit from the introduction of online examinations and assessment as the accuracy of marking and the speed at which it is carried out do improve. However, there can be disadvantages for schools and pupils:

- The school has to ensure that each pupil has access to a networked computer for the duration of an online examination which may last for 2 or 3 hours. Providing networked computers is expensive, and the computers used in the examination will be unavailable for teaching the normal curriculum.
- If a large number of pupils are sitting an online examination and there are insufficient computers available, pupils will have to sit the examination in groups at different times during the day and possibly on different days. The school may need to make arrangements so that the examination remains secure and pupils cannot confer with each other. Several AOs are intending to introduce online examinations that can be taken at any time on demand. Ensuring the security of these could be problematic.
- Computer rooms may need rearrangement and this may cause difficulties as computers are often secured to benching and cannot be moved easily.
- Pupils who cannot use a keyboard to enter data quickly and accurately will have less time to spend on attempting questions during the examination.

- The AO will almost certainly restrict the types of file that it will accept from pupils following the examination or will ask for printouts of pupils' work. This means that either pupils or teachers have to convert the files pupils produce so that they are of an acceptable type; or the work has to be printed out. This could be time-consuming. If it is done during the examination, the time spent on file conversion or printing detracts from the time available to spend on attempting the examination questions.

Equivalence between vocational and academic qualifications

In the school league tables, schools are ranked by the percentage of pupils gaining the number of points equivalent to at least five A*–C grades.

Prior to recent revisions in the number of school league table points given for vocational qualifications, it was thought that schools had been tempted to teach qualifications which attracted the most points in the school league tables instead of the qualifications that would most help pupils. Some vocational qualifications attracted four times the number of points given for a GCSE grade C and it was thought that this was inflating the school's ranking. Some 73 per cent of teachers believed that schools were using vocational qualifications to manipulate the secondary school league tables (TES, 2011a, p. 5). In 2009/10, 462,182 students achieved Level 2 (grades A*–C) in equivalent qualifications, up from 1882 in 2003/04 (DfE, 2011b). Many teachers believed this equivalence between academic and vocational qualifications was unsound (Mansell, 2010). Pupils might have been encouraged to take vocational qualifications in several subjects and were awarded qualifications stated to be equivalent to a large number of GCSEs. This was good for the school as its performance in the league tables considerably improved. However, there was concern that pupils were being steered into qualifications which may not have helped them in work or higher education and that more than half of 15- to 16-year-olds did not achieve good GCSEs in English and Maths (Wolf, 2011).

Even so, it may be that good results in vocational qualifications are because they suit different styles of learning and engage learners in different ways. A pupil who is not suited to GCSE ICT may well find the style of learning and assessment of vocational qualifications in ICT more interesting and engaging, and consequently achieve at a higher level.

The Wolf Report (Wolf, 2011) reviewed academic and vocational education and qualifications for 11- to 19-year-olds and considered ways to improve provision. Following this report, vocational qualifications were reviewed and new specifications were produced. These have more rigorous assessment, including a substantial proportion of external assessment. They attract a more appropriate number of points in the school league tables and make a more balanced contribution. Only two non-GCSEs count towards the five A*–C indicators in the school league tables. As a result, pupils tend to study an academic core which may be enriched with vocational qualifications.

Summary

- Assessment is an essential part of good teaching and learning.
- Assessment for Learning (AfL) is the day-to-day assessment that helps teachers judge the progress pupils have made so that they can modify their teaching plans.
- AfL should include pupils in the assessment process so that they know what they can do and where they need to concentrate their efforts to learn.

- Assessment of Learning (AoL) is summative assessment. It is a snapshot of pupils' skills, knowledge and understanding.
- There should be regular assessment, recording and reporting of pupils' progress. Many schools use software to keep a record of this.
- The advantage of an online eportfolio is that the evidence available is accessible to all teachers. The disadvantage is that consistent assessment can be difficult because pupils progressively update their eportfolios.
- The Assessing Pupils' Progress (APP) materials support systematic, structured formative and summative assessment in KS3.
- The record-keeping requirements of external examinations are of great importance to teachers and pupils in Years 10 and 11, and 12 and 13, and this has considerable influence on how progress is reported to parents.
- Moderation is a means of ensuring that all teachers apply assessment criteria in the same way, producing consistent judgements of the standards pupils achieve.
- Moderation involves teachers looking at each other's assessments of pupils' work, and agreeing that they too would have assessed the work as being of the same standard.
- Moderation will be easier if there are examples of pupils' work available that represent agreed standards at different levels of achievement.
- Since September 2010, controlled assessment has replaced coursework in new specifications for GCSE ICT. During controlled assessment pupils are supervised by teachers.
- Most AOs now mark written examinations online, and many are moving towards online examinations particularly in ICT.
- The Wolf Report (Wolf, 2011) reviewed academic and vocational education and qualifications for 11- to 19-year-olds and considered ways to improve provision. As a result, the academic equivalence of vocational qualifications has been adjusted so that they make a more balanced contribution to the school league tables.

Further reading

Assessment Reform Group (2002) *AfL: 10 Principles*, available at: http://assessment-reform-group.org/publications/ (accessed 4 January 2013).

Association for Achievement and Improvement through Assessment (n.d.) Report, available at: http://www.aaia.org.uk (accessed 23 September 2011).

Crawford, R. (2012) 'Understanding and using assessment and delivering feedback', in N. Denby (ed.) *Training to Teach*, London: Sage.

Chapter 4

Hardware and software

Dave Luke

Introduction

This chapter raises key questions that should be asked when acquiring and managing hardware and software in schools. The first section will consider the type of hardware available to schools and how it might be best employed. Hardware security is then discussed. This is followed by a section considering the range of software available to schools, reviewing the options that are available and suggesting some strategies for deciding on the appropriate software to obtain.

Hardware

Setting the economic background

Spending on ICT in schools is falling and pupil:computer ratios are only just being maintained. The total amount of spending on computers in all schools for 2010 was £537 million, a reduction of £40 million from 2009. The projected figure for 2011 is £502 million (BESA, 2010). This is based on primary schools cutting their budgets by 6 per cent and secondary schools by 7 per cent, resulting in the average primary budget being £12,200 and the average secondary budget being £56,200. The pupil:computer ratio in schools in 2010 was 3:1 in secondary schools and 7:1 in primary schools (Becta, 2010). This was the same as the 2009 ratios and is likely to be maintained. Some 72 per cent of secondary schools are reporting that they have 200 or more computers in school, with almost all of them having at least 50 computers.

The number of interactive whiteboards (IWBs) in schools has increased rapidly. In 2010, 87 per cent of primary schools indicated that they were well equipped with IWBs compared to 25 per cent in 2005; in secondary schools this figure was 64 per cent in 2010 from 18 per cent in 2005 (BESA, 2010).

Networks

The robustness and speed of the network infrastructure will directly impact on the effectiveness of the implementation of ICT in the classroom. Slow network speeds and high downtimes will negatively impact on teachers' and pupils' experiences of using ICT at school and could demotivate pupils and lead to teachers being wary of using the ICT facilities in the classroom.

Improving the capability of the network can be expensive and it is essential that the most appropriate and cost-effective networking systems are deployed. There are ways of saving money and creating a more effective network that involve a change in established approaches.

Virtual servers

In schools where there are multiple physical servers for various uses and sections of the network, it may well be worth considering virtualizing the majority of servers while upgrading one server to ensure it has the capacity to store the partitioned virtual servers. The overall impact is lower operating costs, reduced power consumption and greater reliability. There are other advantages, including allowing different operating systems to access the same data, and speeding up login times. A key advantage is that much of this can be achieved using open source server software, leading to additional savings (Sirius Corporation, 2011).

Virtual desktops

Up to 30 workstations can be created, each workstation consisting of the monitor, mouse and keyboard. The workstations are linked to one reasonably high-powered computer in the room, which acts as a local server and can be linked to the main school server. When the pupils log on, they each receive their own virtual desktop from the local server. The impacts are a reduction in the cost of the local network; a reduction in energy costs; a reduction of heat and sound in ICT rooms; and an increase in speed (NComputing, 2009).

Essential hardware to provide a good experience of ICT

Neither the National Curriculum (NC) nor ICT I/GCSE and vocational specifications specifically list the hardware required, but on reading the specifications and examples of activities, hardware requirements can be deduced.

In order to fulfil the ICT NC and meet the requirements of I/GCSE and vocational specifications by the end of KS4, pupils should have the knowledge and understanding to make use of a wide range of hardware including:

- desktop computers, and their component parts, including a monitor, mouse, processor, keyboard, DVD drives and hard disk;
- laptops, netbooks and tablet PCs;
- USB memory sticks, SD cards, and other portable backing storage devices;
- printers;
- scanners;
- webcams;
- headsets, microphones and earphones;
- digital cameras and camcorders;
- digital sound recorders;
- interactive whiteboard;
- LANs, and WANs, including hardware for Internet access such as modems and routers.

Knowledge and understanding to make use of the following would also be useful:

- PDAs, and mobile phones, especially smart phones;
- graphics tablets;
- interactive voting systems;
- touch pads and screens;
- games consoles;
- media players, e.g. iPod;
- navigation aids, e.g. SatNav;
- home entertainment systems;
- computers with midi capability for control of synthesizers and drum machines;
- graphical calculators.

The following hardware would be useful in some courses at KS4, but is no longer required in ICT at KS3 as control is now a part of the Design Technology curriculum:

- sensors, including those for temperature, pressure, light, and sound;
- actuators, including motors, heaters, lights, and fans;
- models to demonstrate computer control of washing machines, cranes, robots, greenhouses, or traffic lights;
- computer-controlled sewing machines or lathes.

With the introduction of KS4 courses that include multimedia and the development of similar courses in KS3, the need for a range of digital devices to be available to pupils has increased. It is essential that devices such as digital cameras, camcorders and voice recorders are available in schools. Schools are also developing games-related projects in which pupils are required to review and create their own games, so systems that support these activities should be available. Global Positioning System (GPS) activities are an effective method of developing learning in many curricular areas, and devices that support this would be a useful addition to a school's ICT resources.

Desktops, laptops, netbooks, tablets and hand-held computers

The appropriate mix of desktops, laptops, netbooks, tablets or hand-held computers is one of the most difficult decisions for schools. What are the needs of the different subjects and how would they be best met? The answer to this question is likely to be that the school will need mixed provision, and each subject department needs to know the capabilities and uses of each type of device. The following summary of their capabilities and potential uses will help in choosing the most appropriate provision.

Desktops have been the standard type of PC used in schools for many years, consisting of a system unit, monitor, mouse and keyboard. A hard disk drive, DVD drive or Blu-ray drive, microphone and webcam, and a card reader for memory cards, such as micro SD cards are likely to be built into the system unit. Connectivity may include USB, firewire, ethernet and jack ports for headphones. Many systems now have HDMI connections as well as the standard SVGA for connection to digital LCD screens. Integrated systems, some with touch screens, are now available, but they are more expensive and harder to upgrade. Desktop PCs are suitable for ICT rooms, and for specialist applications in curricular areas such as Music and Science.

Laptops consist of the same elements as a desktop PC, but have integrated keyboards, touchpads and a screen. They often have wireless connectivity built in which makes them suitable for use in classrooms and specialist areas with wireless connection to the school network. They are battery-powered and can be used for fieldwork.

Netbooks are smaller and lighter than laptops with a longer battery life. Suitability is similar to laptops, but only a restricted range of software is acceptable, that is, standard office applications and Internet search.

Hand-helds include a range of devices, for example, PDAs, smart phones, iPads, and Android tablets. Compared with laptops and netbooks, hand-helds have small screens; backing storage can be limited; there is no built-in keyboard; and they do not always use a standard Windows operating system, which limits compatibility with other software used in schools. However, they are very portable and have much longer battery life. Use in schools is at present in the experimental stage and much of it focuses on the use of Web 2.0 applications, such as Google docs, and Internet research. As Web 2.0 and 3.0 applications develop, these devices could become more widely used and cheaper. Schools have been discussing the use of pupils' own handheld devices which could open up opportunities to achieve the aim of having one device per pupil.

Activity

Many schools ban pupils from using their own mobile phones, including smart phones. What would be the advantages and disadvantages of letting pupils use these in school?

Activity

Consider whether schools need to provide a full range of desktop PCs, laptops, netbooks and hand-helds (Table 4.1).

Which subjects would use these and what uses would be made of each?

Table 4.1 A comparison of desktops, laptops, netbooks and hand-held computers

Desktop PC	Laptops	Netbooks	Hand-helds including smartphones and tablets
Bulky and sits on desktop. More robust which suits heavy usage	Smaller and not as robust as desktop PC	Lighter and smaller than laptop	Lighter and smaller than netbooks
Generally cheaper for higher specification. More processing power	Price depends on specification. Generally more expensive than desktop PC	Cheaper than laptop	Usually more expensive than a netbook

(Continued)

Table 4.1 Continued

Desktop PC	Laptops	Netbooks	Hand-helds including smartphones and tablets
Not portable. Fixed location often in ICT rooms	Portable – they can go where the learning is taking place. Can be used outside	Portable – they can go where the learning is taking place. Can be used outside	Very portable – they can go where the learning is taking place. Can be used outside
Uses mains power. No battery	Battery life can be limited and long recharging time	Longer battery life than laptop	Longer battery life than netbooks
Wide range of software	Can utilize the same range of software as a desktop PC	Can utilize the same range of software as a desktop PC but will often run slower and lack features	Restricted range of software, mainly Apps. Installation of software only via downloads
Large screen size. Can have several screens and these can be changed	Screen size usually smaller than desktop. One fixed screen	Screen size usually smaller than laptop. One fixed screen	Screen size usually 10.1″ or less, smaller than a netbook. One fixed screen
Uses full-size keyboard often with additional number pad	Uses smaller keyboard	Uses very small keyboard	Uses touch screen technology
Good quality external speakers, microphone and earphones	Built-in speakers and microphone with external earphones	Built-in speakers and microphone with external earphones	Built-in speakers and microphone. External earphones often used
External or built-in webcam	Built-in webcam	Built in webcam	Built in webcams, sometimes two
Connectivity usually wired. Access to the network and Internet is faster because of wired connection. Can have Wireless and Bluetooth connection to external devices. Multiple connections for external drives and other peripherals	Connectivity can be wired but usually wireless. Fewer ports for connecting external drives and peripherals. Wireless connection to Internet and Bluetooth to external devices. Network speed usually slower than desktop PC	Connectivity can be wired but usually wireless connection to Internet and Bluetooth to external devices. Network speed usually slower than laptop	Wireless and Bluetooth connection to Internet and external devices. Usually uses SD cards. Many devices have GPS
Larger HD and RAM	Internal storage capacity equivalent to desktop PC	Internal storage capacity less than laptop	Internal storage capacity less than netbook
CD/DVD drives	CD/DVD drive	No CD/DVD drive	No CD/DVD drive
Main component parts can be replaced. Easy to upgrade, e.g. graphics cards can be installed	Not easy to replace main component parts or upgrade, except for RAM and HD	Not easy to replace main component parts or upgrade	Replacement or upgrades impractical
Usually Windows, Linux or Apple OS	Usually Windows, Linux or Apple OS	Usually Windows, Linux or Apple OS	Usually Apple or Android OS

Hardware security

Hardware is attractive to thieves and should be secured using a variety of different and independent strategies. The following should be considered:

- Hardware should not be kept where it is visible and accessible to potential thieves, for example, in ground floor classrooms. Consider very carefully whether access is possible through walls or ceilings.
- Classrooms where hardware is kept should be locked when not supervised. Access may need to be regulated using identification systems, such as swipe cards, biometrics, key pads, etc.
- Windows should be reinforced with netting, bars or security foil. Security foil can be reflective and can help reduce problems with excessive light and heat.
- Desktop PCs should be physically attached to the bench with a steel cable.
- Security alarms should be independently activated when hardware is moved outside an ICT room or a designated area. These should be in addition to the security alarm for the whole building.
- There should be CCTV in rooms where hardware is kept, and outside the rooms, including in corridors.
- Computers should have internal identification devices fitted.
- Tracking software should be installed in all portable computers and this should identify the location of a computer when it connects to the Internet.

Software

The software required by schools so that they can provide pupils with a satisfactory experience of ICT is not summarized in the NC. However, its characteristics can be deduced from the Programmes of Study (PoS) that pupils must follow, and an understanding of the curriculum contexts used to deliver them. Many pupils will follow a curriculum based on I/GCSE ICT or other external specifications during KS4. Similarly, these do not always clearly specify which software is required but a careful reading of them will also indicate the software required.

Software may be purchased online and downloaded or may be available on DVD. Most schools now have virtual learning environments (VLEs) and many suppliers have SCORM-compliant (Sharable Content Object Reference Model) versions of their software, which can be imported into a VLE and linked to the MIS system for assessment purposes. Open source and free Web 2.0 applications are also widely available and many of the applications are very sophisticated and can replace standard office applications.

In order to meet the requirements of the NC and I/GCSE and vocational specifications, by the end of KS4, pupils should have been taught to use a wide range of software, including:

- different types of operating systems (e.g. Graphics User Interface and command line);
- word processors and desk top publishing (DTP) software;
- presentation software;
- website design software;

- graphics and image manipulation;
- spreadsheets and modelling;
- databases;
- concept mapping software;
- software to support collaborative working;
- web browsers;
- email;
- blogs and other social networking applications;
- video and audio editing, and media players;
- data logging;
- programming and games making, e.g. Scratch and Python.

Curricular-specific software

There is an extensive range of this type of software, and it would be impossible to list them all. However, they can be broken down into two categories: (1) support for teachers; and (2) activities for pupils, although in some cases this distinction is blurred. Many of the resources that can be purchased to support lesson delivery are intended to be used with IWBs and a number of companies have specialized in this area. Resources are now usually created for both installation on networks and hosting on a VLE, allowing schools a choice in the way that pupils access the resources. A number of publishing houses have created full courses for various subjects, with both teacher and pupil materials. This type of material is often used to support a specific Key Stage or designed to meet the needs of a specific KS4 course, such as Cambridge Nationals.

Open source software

Open source software is free and licences also allow users to alter and add to the underlying code if they wish to do so. This means that the software can be adapted to suit the needs of a school. Open source software is designed to be continually developed by both the original designer and the users of the software, so there are continual updates.

Careful consideration should be given to the opportunities provided by open source software and 'free' software. There is a range of web, office and graphics applications which could be used alongside or instead of standard office software, saving money on licences, or it can be used to supplement existing software and provide opportunities for pupils to compare and contrast different software, for example, Open Office.

Activity

Download and install Open Office. Available on www.theopendisc.com/education/ and http://sourceforge.net/projects/opendisc/files/.

What are the advantages and disadvantages of using Open Office in comparison with Microsoft Office?

Virtual Learning Environments (VLEs)

VLEs are best described as software-based hosting systems, which can be internal or external to the school, with built-in tools to support collaborative working, such as email, chat, forums and blogs. They include facilities teachers can use to create e-learning courses and also include tools to allow assessment of pupils' work, teacher feedback and record keeping. Their principal advantage is that they allow education to take place anywhere and at any time, at school or from home, but there are other ways they can support learning especially the effective use of the collaborative tools. To obtain the greatest impact, careful thought has to be given to the design of an e-learning course, especially how assessment and feedback are built into the system. E-learning courses which are just the online organization of worksheets that would have normally been used in the classroom are rarely the most attractive to learners. Audiovisual resources and the opportunity to talk to real people, using, for example, chat and forums, are essential in creating an effective online course.

Web 2.0

The increased range of Web 2.0 applications and the development of their functionality have opened other ways of creating documents online and sharing with colleagues and pupils. The development of Google docs in particular has widened the range of online tools. Among its features are: a blogging tool; the ability to create discussion groups; a calendar; email; image editing and sharing; an RSS reader; website and wiki design tools; sketchup for designing 3D models; chat facilities; and social networking. There are many other online tools, for example, image, audio and video editing; file conversion; and creating wikis, quizzes and presentations.

Software selection

A list of the software that pupils should or might make use of is a helpful starting point when purchasing new software or reassessing the adequacy of the existing range of software available in a school. Reference to such a list will help schools ensure they have a sufficiently wide range of software available for pupils to use. Some considerations that affect the selection of software are reviewed below.

Software should be easy to use. It should be simple for both pupils and teachers to learn how to operate the software, so that the complexity of the software does not prevent them making effective use of ICT. It should aid pupils with their learning and not be a barrier.

As software is improved from one version to the next, developers try to make the software easier for users to understand and operate, in addition, they also attempt to incorporate more functionality. These objectives may conflict and, unfortunately, on occasions, increased functionality leads to increased complexity. Where software is produced mainly for commercial use, schools may find that they do not need the increased functionality that accompanies new versions of software.

Cut-down versions of software are sometimes available. These are often cheaper versions of current software with the less frequently used functions removed. These cut-down versions may be much easier to use than the full version and still incorporate all the functions that schools require. Schools should consider purchasing cut-down versions of current software if these are suitable. For example, Adobe Premier Elements is a much less expensive version of the popular Adobe Premier video editing software. It has reduced functionality but is more than adequate for use in the classroom. Consideration should also be given to open source or free software which may have limited functionality, but can be easier to use.

The software used in schools should provide a differentiated experience of ICT for pupils at different levels of ability. It is unlikely that one piece of software of a particular type will allow for progression from the lowest levels of attainment to the highest. Thus, a complete version of an industry standard word processor that gives pupils access to a full range of functions is unlikely to be entirely suitable for all pupils. Younger pupils and the less able will need access to software that is appropriate to their level of development. Such software should be easy to understand and use, with a much reduced range of functions. As pupils develop, their understanding of the operation of ICT software and hardware will grow, so that they can be expected to make greater use of increasingly complex functions with a wider range of options. The best software allows pupils to access it at a level appropriate to their abilities. A number of applications allow users to change the toolbar and menu contents, so that some features are turned off for the least able and more can be turned on for the more able.

Software should be robust and otherwise usable within a school environment. Software that ceases to work effectively without warning for whatever reason is particularly unsuitable for use in schools. When pupils are learning to use software, they will make mistakes. User-friendly software that responds to pupils' mistakes by displaying a meaningful message describing the error and suggesting what should be done helps pupils' learning. Software that crashes in response to user errors or displays cryptic messages that are difficult for pupils to understand and with no indication of what they should do restricts progress and inhibits learning.

Software licensing

The owners of software restrict its distribution and sale by licensing it. A software licence gives users the rights to run software under the specific conditions and restrictions stated. Users should conform to the conditions and restrictions specified in their licence when they use the associated software. If a user does not possess a licence for the software, then the user's use of it is illegal. It is assumed that if software is installed on a hard disk or there is a copy of it on a CD, then it is in use. Schools should not use any software that is not licensed to them.

There are five general categories of software with distinct licensing arrangements. These are commonly known as:

1   licensed software
2   public domain software
3   open source
4   shareware
5   Creative Commons.

Licensed software

Licensed software is sold and purchasers buy the rights to use the software. These rights are typically one or more of the following:

- *A volume licence*, for example, from Microsoft is for organizations that require five or more licences, but do not need multiple copies of the media and the documentation and wish to have one single licence agreement. Microsoft has Volume Licensing programs that are tailored to the specific needs of its customers, based on program type, the size of the organization, and the market segment. Software is discounted to educational users.
- *A full-time equivalence (FTE) licence* covers all employees within a school who use a suite of software.
- *A site licence*, giving the right to distribute and use the software on any computer on a particular site.
- *A network licence*, that is, the right to distribute the software over a network for use on a specified number of network stations.
- *The right to use the software on one or more standalone computers.*
- *An OEM (Original Equipment Manufacturers) licence* is for software that is already installed when the hardware is purchased.

The cost of acquiring a software licence is usually at its highest per user when the right to use a single copy of the software is purchased. It is usual for the cost of individual usage to be at its lowest when a site licence is purchased. However, a site licence may be considerably more expensive than the licence for a single user. Consequently, when purchasing software, schools should consider the extent to which the software will be used. Site licences are preferable where the software will be in widespread use throughout the school, as a site licence has the advantage that it covers all the computers on the site, consequently, no further rights to use the software are needed for any additional hardware that may be purchased. However, the expense of a site licence may not be justified if only very limited use of the software is anticipated.

Public domain software

Public domain software is free software. The owners of the software make it available to anyone who wants to use it, or specific groups of users, at zero purchase cost. Owners may place any restriction on the use of the software that they wish. Even so, most public domain software carries no restrictions on its use. Schools wanting to investigate the range of public domain software available should look for suppliers' advertisements on the Web and elsewhere. The mirror service at http://www.mirrorservice.org is a useful source of public domain software.

Open source

An open source software licence makes the source code available for anyone to modify and reuse. Open source licences are usually free and allow users to modify and distribute the software to anyone they wish. A number of applications used in schools, such as Open Office, are in this category and many of these applications are appropriate for school use and provide alternatives to commercial applications.

Shareware

Shareware is licensed software that is initially distributed freely in the manner of public domain software. Users may install the software and try it out. However, if they decide to make regular use of the software, they must pay a licence fee. Users sometimes receive improved versions of the software when the licence fee is paid.

Creative Commons

Creative Commons licences help those who produce software communicate to users in a straightforward way the rights they keep for themselves and the rights they give others. Different licences are available. For example, an attribution licence lets others copy, modify and distribute the copyrighted work and other work based on it, even for commercial gain, provided the original authors are credited in the way they ask.

Whichever type of licence is chosen, care should be taken to ensure that all the software in use in the school is legally covered and that the functionality and cost of each type of licence have been compared with the alternatives. Choosing the right type of licence from the outset will save time and money in the long run.

Activity

- Name five pieces of software used in your school and describe the type of licence that covers each.
- For each different type of licence described above, name an example of a piece of software that is covered by that type of licence.

Software and data security

All users need to protect themselves against the loss of software. This is especially so in schools where many users of different status have access to the software. Some protection is achieved by requiring users to enter a user identification number and a password before they can use ICT resources.

Even so, not all users will make use of the available software and hardware in sensible or ethical ways. Loss of software can be caused by theft of the software or damage to it. Software can be stolen by the removal of CDs or DVDs, or by users copying it illegally. Damage to software can be caused by physical damage to the media it is stored on, or by the corruption or deletion of all or part of the software while it is stored. This may occur as a result of malfunction of the computer system, or be done inadvertently or maliciously by users. Software stored on CD or DVD is extremely vulnerable and should be locked in a secure cabinet when not in use and product keys, also known as a software keys, should be stored separately.

Viruses can cause extensive damage to computer systems. The damaging impact of viruses can be limited by using software that will detect and kill viruses. Viruses infect a computer system when they are transferred onto the system from an infected source. Many virus infections are caused by the use of infected software downloaded from the Internet. Most schools use virus protection software that automatically checks emails as they arrive; files as they are downloaded; and scans the entire system at least once a day. Virus protection software should be set to automatically update itself at least once each day. Viruses should be automatically quarantined or deleted. It is often wise to quarantine viruses rather than delete them immediately as some of the files picked up by virus protection software may be legitimate.

Backing up the system ensures that software and data are not lost. Back-ups of servers should be made automatically and can be done while the computer system is in use. Magnetic tape systems were commonly used for back-ups, but as servers have improved over the years it is now increasingly common to see hard disk backup capacity built in using a redundant array of independent disks (RAID) system. Data is constantly backed up to a second set of hard disks. The server switches to these drives automatically should the original hard disks fail. In addition, as software is usually installed on the hard disks of individual PCs, it is also common to make an image of a hard drive once all the software has been installed. This image can then be used to restore a PC quickly, should it crash. External hard disks containing the images should be stored safely and securely to avoid theft or damage by fire. They should be stored in fireproof safes on and off the premises. As an alternative, a number of companies provide systems which allow all data and software to be backed up online and stored offsite on their remote servers.

If external drives or tapes are used to store the back-ups, then a routine should be created, for example, tape or disk A is used on Monday; tape or disk B is used on Tuesday; tape or disk C is used on Wednesday, etc., so that there is one tape or disk per day. This routine is repeated the following week, which means any data loss is a maximum of one day old. This, coupled with a RAID system, ensures data loss is minimal. Data storage should always comply with the Data Protection Act and personal data should always be encrypted.

Summary

- Schools should have a mix of desktop PCs, laptops, netbooks, tablets and hand-held devices. These have different capabilities and uses.
- Hardware should be secured using a variety of different and independent strategies.
- Schools need a variety of software to provide pupils with a satisfactory experience of ICT.
- Online applications can replace or supplement existing applications installed on local networks.
- Software should be easy to use; it should allow pupils to progress as they develop; and it should provide a differentiated experience of ICT for pupils at different levels of ability.
- Schools should consider using public domain software, open source or shareware as the cost of acquiring it is often lower.
- Schools should conform to the conditions specified in their software licences. Site licences are preferable where the software will be in use throughout the school. Unlicensed software should not be used.
- Schools need to protect themselves against software loss or damage. Some protection is achieved by requiring users to enter a user identification number and a password before they can use ICT resources, and by restricting what they are permitted to do.
- Viruses can cause extensive damage to computer systems. They should be automatically detected and quarantined through an efficient anti-virus program.
- The most effective precaution against permanent damage or loss of software or data is to make regular back-up copies.

Further reading

Becta (2010) *Harnessing Technology Schools Survey: 2010*, available at: http://dera.ioe.ac.uk/1544/1/becta_2010_htss_report.pdf (accessed 13 December 2011).

BESA (2010) *ICT Provision and Use in 2010/11*, available at: http://www.besa.org.uk (accessed 13 December 2011).

NComputing (2009) 'Case study: New College, Leicester', available at: http://www.ncomputing.com/docs/casestudies/education/en/casestudy_leicester_edu.pdf (accessed 6 January 2012).

Sirius Corporation (2011) 'Case study: Bishop Fox's Community School', available at: http://www.siriusit.co.uk/clients/education/bishop-foxs-community-school (accessed 13 December 2011).

Chapter 5

Safeguarding and inclusion

Introduction

Teachers have a professional duty to ensure the safety of the children in their care and should help them understand how to protect themselves. In a handbook for ICT teachers, there is a particular emphasis on the use of ICT; however, this should be understood within the context of ensuring the welfare of pupils more generally.

Effective behaviour management

Through effective behaviour management within the classroom you are managing pupils' well-being and safeguarding both the pupils and yourself.

Here are some strategies that work:

- Learn the names of all your pupils.
- Establish clear rules and routines.
- Record positive and negative behaviour.
- Tactically ignore low-grade bad behaviour while noticing good behaviour and avoid confrontation.
- Ask casual questions to refocus and establish working relationships, e.g. 'How's it going?', and use distractions or diversions to direct pupils back on task.
- Phone home if necessary, to give praise and as well as raise concerns.

Remember:

- You are the adult, while you should be friendly towards pupils, you are not their friend.
- Always discipline the action, not the pupil.
- Be fair and consistent.
- Always accept apologies and work to repair relations.

(Emma Little, teacher)

Effective behaviour management contributes significantly to developing a safer and more inclusive classroom climate. Even so, this chapter does not specifically consider those teaching skills and practices that make the classroom a safer place other than when these relate to the use of ICT. Behaviour management and other aspects of teaching are not mentioned again in this chapter except where relevant to pupils' use of ICT.

This chapter considers the following issues:

- social use of the web, grooming, cyberbullying, evaluating online content, pornography, and phishing;
- technical dangers, including viruses and pharming;
- illegal conduct;
- health and safety;
- inclusion;
- gender and ICT.

Social use of the Web

Most pupils use the Internet at least once each week. However, they tend to prefer using mobile phones and text messaging for contact with friends. Most online communication is with friends who are personally known, and being in constant contact is highly valued. Most children have very little interest in talking to strangers online and are wary of them. 'A quarter of children and young people identify significant advantages to online communication in terms of privacy (25%), confidence (25%) and intimacy (22%)' (Livingstone and Bober, 2005). Even so, both parents and children consider the Internet to be riskier than other media due to the range of content and increased opportunities for contact with strangers (ibid.).

Children should be strongly discouraged from giving out personal information. Some 46 per cent of young people say they have given out personal information online, such as their full names, ages, email addresses, phone numbers, hobbies or names of their schools, to someone they met on the Internet. Social networking sites often encourage young people to populate their pages with personal information and the default security settings may give access to everyone. However, sharing personal information can be unsafe as it may undermine personal security.

Children should never arrange a meeting with someone they have not previously met face-to-face. Knowing a victim's personal information helps paedophiles groom children. Grooming is conduct that gives reasonable suspicion that any face-to-face meeting with a child would be for unlawful purposes. This is illustrated by the video *Jenny's Story* (Childnet International, 2005). Typically, a paedophile will adopt a false identity that is attractive to the victim. If they know the victim's personal information, they can use this to reassure them that they are likely to have mutual friends so that a suggested face-to-face meeting seems less threatening. Older children and adults should avoid using Internet dating sites where the intended outcome is a face-to-face date and false identities are likely.

Cyberbullying is bullying carried out using ICT. For a child, the first step in dealing with cyberbullying is to talk to a teacher or other adult. Cyberbullying is more threatening than the bullying that can be an unfortunate feature of social interaction between pupils in schools and elsewhere. Cyberbullying requires the bully to know the victim's basic personal information, such as the email address or mobile phone number of the victim. The victim can be bombarded with intimidating or insulting emails, text messages and phone calls and this is upsetting and disrupts normal usage of their computer, mobile phone or other communications equipment. Sometimes victims are photographed or videoed being physically attacked or made to look ridiculous and these photos or videos may be posted on websites that make them available to everyone. This may be done by one person or by many. As a result, the bullying is magnified as it has a wider circulation and it is always accessible. Strategies to prevent bullying in schools are also applicable to cyberbullying. In addition, materials posted on websites can be removed and websites can identify the users who posted the photos and videos. Intimidating and offensive emails can become useful evidence that helps identify the perpetrator. A related video is *Joe's Story* (YouTube, n.d.).

Activity

Write a presentation on cyberbullying that could be used with a group of pupils. There should be two slides:

- Slide 1: What is meant by cyberbullying.
- Slide 2: How to deal with cyberbullying.

Children should be taught to be sceptical and evaluate all information whether on line or in newspapers and magazines or whatever the source as they may lack these skills. Some 38 per cent of children trust most of the information on the internet; 49 per cent trust some of it; but only 10 per cent are sceptical. Problems arise when information is inaccurate, and this may be deliberate with intent to deceive (Livingstone and Bober, 2005). Children may access misleading information on websites or be bombarded with advertising in the form of email spam. At best, advertising presents the positive aspects of a product or service but leaves the buyer to identify the downside. Some websites are set up by groups with a particular bias, for example, political or racist bias. The best protection is to teach children to be sceptical and evaluate all information. Structured approaches are helpful in encouraging thorough evaluation. For example, pupils can be taught to evaluate using the RAVEN process:

- **R**eputation – does the information provider have a good reputation?
- **A**bility to know – does the information provider have first-hand knowledge and experience, or access to good quality first-hand information?
- **V**ested interest – does the information provider have an incentive to be less than 100 per cent truthful? Will the provider give only the upside and omit the downside?
- **E**xpertise – does the information provider have sufficient skills, knowledge and understanding to supply accurate information?
- **N**eutrality – is the information provider likely to be biased?

Children need to know how to deal with incidental exposure to pornography and need to be able to discuss aspects which they find intimidating or frightening. Many young people have seen online pornography. Most is viewed unintentionally: 38 per cent have seen pornographic pop-up adverts while doing something else and 36 per cent have accidentally found themselves on a porn site when looking for something else (Livingstone and Bober, 2005). Pornography online is more accessible than printed pornography, especially in schools. It is more extensive and pervasive and accidental access to it is often difficult to avoid.

Filtering software should be used that blocks access to pornography and other undesirable material from particular computers or networks. Some Web browsers have tools that enable users to adjust security and privacy settings and block pop-ups. In addition, there are commercially available Web filters, which include CYBERsitter, Net Nanny and CyberPatrol.

Features of filtering or parental control software include:

- *Personal information blocking* – an effective filter will block personal information, such as addresses and phone numbers, from leaving the computer.
- *URL filtering* – the URL or web address of all the websites accessed is checked against a list of undesirable sites and access to these can be blocked, for example, children can be prevented from accessing adult websites. Alternatively, a list of permitted websites can be set up and access to other websites blocked.
- *Keyword filtering* – the content of web pages, chat rooms, email, newsgroups, bulletin boards, pop-up windows and other Internet content can be monitored against a list of undesirable key words and the communication can be blocked.
- *Activity reporting* – you can view a log of what each individual has been doing on the computer, which could include details of what they have accessed on the Internet and what has been said in chat rooms.
- *Notification capability* – unauthorized access or active blocking is reported by email.

While awareness of these filtering tools and their capabilities, and strategies to protect children and ensure they understand the risks are prevalent in English schools, parents tend to significantly underestimate their children's exposure to Internet pornography (Livingstone and Bober, 2005).

Children should be taught how to recognize and deal with phishing attacks. Phishing is an attempt to find out personal information. Most phishing attacks are attempts to find out adults' social security numbers, credit card numbers, or usernames and passwords for online banks. These are then used for identity theft and fraud. A phishing attack is often an email asking the recipient to log on to their online bank and enter their username and password. A hyperlink in the email appears to connect to the online bank's website; however, clicking on this takes the victim to a plausible but fraudulent website not to the bank's real website. When the victim enters their username and password, these are stolen and later used to steal money from the victim's bank account. Most banks do not send unsolicited emails to customers so that customers will know that a phishing attack is underway when they receive an email claiming to be from a bank. Other phishing attacks may appeal to the victim's vanity. For example, they may be told they have won a prize in a competition but need to enter their personal details to collect it. Children are less at risk from this type of attack than adults as they are much less likely to have online bank accounts; nevertheless, they are still likely to receive phishing emails and may do so in the future when they are older. They need to know how to recognize and respond to them.

You can recognize and deal with phishing attacks like this:

- Look for spelling and grammar errors in the email. A reputable bank is unlikely to make such errors.

- If you are worried your bank might really be trying to contact you, then contact them directly but don't click on the hyperlink in the email. Break your connection with the email and separately logon to your bank through its website or telephone them.
- Check that you have an account with the bank named in the phishing email.
- Remember that you are unlikely to win a competition if you haven't entered it!

Risks of social networking sites

Emma Little notes the importance of making the pupils aware of the risks of using social networking sites. Discuss and advise pupils of the risks and what to be aware of when using social networking sites such as Facebook. It is imperative that the teacher emphasizes the dangers so that the pupils are aware of the potential problems and risks.

Technical dangers

Technical dangers affect all Internet users and include viruses and pharming. A virus is software that is designed to be secretly loaded onto a computer without the user's knowledge usually with malicious intent. Viruses can attach themselves to emails and infect a computer when the email is opened. They can also be transmitted by downloading programs or accessing portable back-up storage devices, such as memory sticks. Viruses have many forms, and can do many things, such as type the same character no matter what key is pressed on the keyboard, and can even delete all the data on a hard disk. Anti-virus software can automatically check a computer for viruses and remove them, for example, McAfee VirusScan.

Pharming is an attempt to collect personal information from users when they connect to a legitimate website. Unknown to the user, they have previously downloaded malicious software, that is, spyware, and this is running on their computer. The software either records any information they enter while connected to the legitimate site, or when they enter the web address of a legitimate website they are re-directed to a fraudulent website. Software such as: Spybot Search and Destroy (free download from www.safer-networking.org), can help find and remove spyware.

Illegal conduct

Most Internet users have downloaded software, music, video, images or text. Some of this is freely and legally available. However, illegal downloading is widespread in the UK and it is estimated that half the population have engaged in some kind of illegal downloading in the past five years. For example, RnBxclusive.com, a prominent music file-sharing website, had around 250,000 subscribers on Facebook and up to 70,000 visitors per day when it was shut down. A file may be available to download but this does not mean it is legal to download it as much of the material that can be downloaded is protected by copyright law.

The penalties for copyright offences depend on their seriousness. People who distribute and download copyrighted materials without permission face civil actions for thousands of pounds in damages. Serious cases may be sent to the Crown Court, which has the power to impose an unlimited fine and up to 10 years' imprisonment. Those downloaders who can show that all the music and films they copied from the Internet are only for personal use may escape the full weight of the criminal law; however, all users who download illegal content from the Web may have their Internet connection disabled. There is no general 'fair use' exception.

The dangers of downloading and file sharing are:

- *Technical dangers* – illegally downloaded files or software are more likely to have malicious software such as viruses and spyware attached, and there is no guarantee the song or video you think you're downloading is what it claims to be.
- *Data theft* – peer-to-peer file sharing can allow other computers to view all the files on your computer and this means that your personal information and privacy are at risk.
- *Unsuitable material* – users of illegal download websites risk exposure to pornographic, violent or age-inappropriate content.

Activity

Register with www.safeguardingchildren.co.uk/basic-awareness.html and complete the online course. This is an excellent basic safeguarding course for those working with children and young people. There are four sections: The Basics; Recognising Abuse; What Action to Take; Guidelines for Good Practice. There's a test at the end of each section with helpful feedback.

It takes around 15 minutes to an hour to complete the course and you can print a certificate when you have completed it.

Health and safety issues

An environment that is good for computers is usually good for people. A clean, dust-free, dry, warm, well-ventilated environment is good for ICT equipment and good for pupils and teachers. However, there are a number of health problems that have been associated with using computers. Very often the association is speculative not proven. Most health problems occur when users regularly and intensively use computers. In general, teachers and pupils make relatively low use of computers; however, it is prudent to be aware of the possible impact of using computers as existing health problems may be exacerbated.

The extensive use of a monitor screen may cause headaches and eye strain, and induce photosensitive (flicker-induced) epilepsy (HSE, 2006). Headaches and eyestrain may be caused by a poor quality monitor display and intensive computer usage over a long period of time. A poor quality monitor display may be due to the use of old equipment; purchasing a new monitor of inferior quality; or locating the monitor in a position where there is too much light falling on the screen. A good quality monitor should present a stable, flicker-free screen image. Reading the screen should be nearly as comfortable as reading a book.

Old monitors that are unsatisfactory should be replaced. You should test new monitors with a variety of text-based and graphics software before purchase so that the stability of the screen display can be assessed. Monitors should be located so that they face away from bright electric lights and windows or there should be effective blinds on the windows. Otherwise, light will be reflected onto the screen, making it difficult to read.

Rashes, skin problems and headaches are particularly associated with excessive screen static when using older monitors. To test for excessive screen static, after the monitor has been switched on for 15 minutes or more, touch the screen with your fingertips. If you receive a static shock, the screen is unsuitable for continuous use.

Headaches and eyestrain caused by intensive computer usage over a long period of time are not usually a problem for pupils as they are unlikely to use computers at school for long periods of time without interruption. Those pupils who regularly use home computers, and office staff and teachers who make extensive use of ICT throughout the school day, could be affected. Headaches and eyestrain can be reduced by taking regular breaks. For example, a break of ten minutes in every hour spent away from the computer can help reduce these symptoms and may also improve concentration.

Photosensitive epilepsy will not be caused by using a monitor but it may be induced in people who already suffer from it. Photosensitive epilepsy is very rare. Pupils will be affected by looking at a monitor screen to the same extent that they are affected by watching television. Schools should identify pupils likely to be at risk. Some schools ask all parents whether their child has photosensitive epilepsy during the initial information gathering exercise undertaken when pupils start at the school. This is to be recommended. If pupils are found to be susceptible, their doctor should be consulted so that the extent of the risk and its effects on a particular child can be assessed. If necessary, pupils with this condition should be withdrawn from lessons where problems are likely to arise. However, adverse reactions are not entirely predictable. Some sufferers find that they can use monitors without provoking an attack.

It is sometimes suggested that other possible consequences of the excessive use of monitors are reduced fertility, a higher likelihood of pregnant women having a miscarriage, and harm to the unborn child. However, there is little hard evidence that this is the case (HSE, 2006). The radiation emitted by monitors is normally very much less than that from natural sources such as the sun or other people. It is well below the levels considered harmful by responsible expert bodies such as the National Radiological Board.

There is an increased risk of electrical shock and fire as rooms where computers are used often have unusually high concentrations of electrical equipment, wiring, plugs and sockets, and may have printer paper on desks near printers. To reduce this risk, ICT equipment should be checked by an electrician or a suitably trained member of staff each year (HSE, n.d.). The impact on pupils or staff of an electrical shock can be minimized by the use of circuit breakers. Circuit breakers or residual current devices (RCDs) are tripped by a 30 mA leakage to earth. They can be purchased for use on an individual socket or built into the mains electrical circuit in a computer room when it is installed. When an electrical shock is experienced, current flows to earth and the circuit breaker is tripped, turning off the electric current. The use of circuit breakers is an important safety feature when ICT equipment is in use.

Static electricity can also cause electric shock. A severe static shock can be experience in some instances by touching the screen of an old CRT monitor or the prongs on an electrical plug just after it has been removed from a socket. This can be painful and should be avoided.

An ICT room with 30 computers, being used by 30 pupils, can become too hot and stuffy very quickly indeed. Computers and their associated peripherals generate heat and pupils generate heat. Consequently, it is important that there is adequate ventilation, preferably fan-assisted cooling.

Schools should take the health and safety of teachers and pupils using computer equipment very seriously. Some recommendations are:

- Characters on the monitor screen should be large enough to read, and clearly defined.
- The screen image should be stable, with adjustable brightness and contrast.
- Screens should easily tilt and swivel.
- There should be no reflective glare from artificial or natural light on the screen.
- Keyboards should be easy to use with clear and contrasting symbols.
- Chairs should be comfortable and stable, with positional adjustments, preferably a standard five-point chair with height, back and seat adjustment.
- Wrist supports and footrests should be available.
- There should be adequate space to allow users to change posture and position.
- The level of noise should not interfere with thought or conversation.
- There should be adequate ventilation.
- There should be regular and frequent breaks.
- Electric and other cables should be hidden but there should be easy access to standard wall sockets so that laptops and other portable equipment can be plugged in without the need for teachers to crawl under benches, etc.
- Use RCDs wherever there are accessible electrics.

Computer room safety tips

Emma Little gives the following advice.

- ICT rooms should be locked when not in use.
- Check the room for safety well before the start of the lesson. In one lesson there was a problem because the air conditioning caused a ceiling tile to fall down, leaving an open space where water was dripping through. This made a puddle on a desk close to some computers. Water and electricity are a dangerous combination. The HoD and the caretaker were informed, an alternative room found and notices were printed advising pupils of the room change. The caretaker isolated the equipment and organized the repair.
- Due to the inquisitive nature of children, there is always a great risk that some pupils in your class will fiddle with the computers. Prior to every lesson you should ensure that all computers are in full working order, all peripherals are plugged into the correct ports, the screens are switched on and there are no wires or other live connections exposed.

Inclusion

Inclusion means making sure that every child has the opportunity to achieve their full potential. This includes children with Special Educational Needs (SEN); children who speak English as an Additional Language (EAL); Gifted and Talented (G&T) pupils; and both girls and boys.

Schools should consider whether ICT can help pupils achieve their full potential. Many children will have some barriers to learning during their school career: some of these will be relatively mild and some will present more severe difficulties. ICT can help ensure that pupils' barriers to learning, including disabilities, do not prevent them learning. ICT can support pupils with SEN in their learning in similar ways to those in which all pupils' learning needs are supported but can be adjusted to their own specific individual needs and abilities. ICT can motivate by providing highly differentiated learning, incremental success, and apparently infinite patience. Pupils with poor concentration can be prompted or stimulated using sound or images following predefined or random schedules so that their attention is returned to the task in hand. In addition, pupils with specific disabilities can use ICT to help overcome them. Moreover, ICT can provide access for everyone to advanced knowledge at a level appropriate to them.

Particular ICT resources may be useful to many pupils with a wide range of different needs. The following list is grouped into broad categories of need with some suggestions as to how ICT may be helpful to pupils,

Pupils who have difficulties with basic literacy and numeracy

- May have their learning needs assessed using diagnostic software.
- Can draft and redraft their work using ICT, for example, using a word processor.
- Can concentrate on the content of their written work rather than the act of writing it, knowing that the product of their work will be neatly printed.
- Can use software to practise basic numeracy and literacy skills.
- Can access and manipulate information through images and sound, text, speech and pictures.
- Can listen to the computer 'speaking' their work as they read it on the screen, or can read 'talking books'.
- Can use touch screens to operate the computer, or keyboard overlays with pictures that correspond to images on the screen.

Pupils with language or speech difficulties, including EAL and dyslexia

- May have their learning needs assessed using diagnostic software.
- Can articulate text by entering it in a word processor that can 'read' it using speech synthesis software. This can be done as a word is entered, or the whole document can be read back.
- Can speak into voice recognition software, perhaps embedded in a word processor, and observe the accuracy of their pronunciation.
- Can use a spelling checker to identify and correct incorrect words.
- Can use grammar checkers to identify and correct incorrect phrases, and words with similar pronunciations but different meanings.
- Can use a computer-based thesaurus to select different words with similar meaning.
- Can improve their language capability using in combination speech recognition software, spelling and grammar checkers, and speech synthesis.
- Can use language translation software, such as Google Translator.

Pupils with emotional and behavioural difficulties

- Can receive consistent, non-judgmental feedback.
- Can interact with others using ICT to neutralize negative responses and prejudice.
- Can practise decision-making using adventure games.

Pupils with physical disabilities, very poor movement or coordination

- Can use ICT for writing and drawing using keyboard guards and overlays, and touch screens.
- Can select words and sentences that are 'spoken', helping them communicate with others, for example, on mobile devices, Apps such as Help Talk, present a set of icons that when tapped express basic needs, such as 'I'm thirsty.'
- Can use word predictors to suggest the next word or phrase.
- Can concentrate on the content of their work rather than the act of writing knowing that the product of their work will be neatly printed.
- Can play computer games that help improve hand–eye coordination.
- May personalize their computers, for example, setting the key repeat speed to slow.
- May find non-standard keyboards useful, for example, miniature and ergonomic keyboards, or keyboards with enlarged keys.
- May find alternatives to mouse controls useful, for example, switches instead of buttons; a drag latch instead of keeping a mouse button depressed; head-operated controls; and voice control systems.
- Can use ICT to control their environment, for example, to answer the door using CCTV to see who has called and a control switch to admit them.
- Can use virtual reality systems to extend their experience and understanding of the wider social context by 'visiting' supermarkets, shops, towns and cities.

Visually impaired pupils

- Can enlarge text and images on-screen, and quickly reverse the process. Similarly, teachers can prepare worksheets using enlarged fonts.
- Can re-size the mouse pointer, and set trails and direction indicators to help locate it.
- Can adjust screen colours, brightness and contrast to suit their own needs.
- Can use speech synthesis to keep track of what is being written.
- Can use a Braille keyboard and a Braille printer. Similarly, teachers can output their worksheets in Braille.
- Can use mobile Apps, such as, the Big Launcher and Zoom Plus Magnifier, to adjust the size of icons and text so that they can use smartphones and tablets more easily.

Pupils with impaired hearing

- Can use ICT for talking, by typing words into a speaking word processor.
- Can communicate quickly over long distances using email instead of a telephone.
- Can use video conferencing to communicate over long distances by signing.

Pupils with profound and multiple learning difficulties

- Can use combinations of the software and hardware listed above to support their individual needs.

Pupils with SEN should participate in mainstream lessons with other pupils. However, some pupils may find it difficult to acknowledge their SEN in these circumstances. Where special hardware adaptation is needed to help them use ICT, this potential reluctance should be taken into account. If possible, standard computer equipment should be customized to meet their needs. It may be possible to re-program a standard keyboard rather than installing a specialist keyboard and using overlays. Some pupils have their own specialist hardware or software and where possible these should be quickly and easily used with a standard classroom computer.

Some pupils with SEN find portable computers useful. These can be set up with appropriate software and any special hardware. They can accompany and support pupils throughout the school day and at home. A broadband connection at home can help pupils establish and sustain social relationships. If a portable computer is not suitable, a specially adapted desk top computer can be made more portable if it is installed on a trolley that can be moved from room to room. Some pupils will need help in moving their ICT equipment. Others may need physical adaptations to wheelchairs to facilitate both using and moving their ICT equipment. Schools should consider organizing training for all those who may be called on to support pupils with SEN when they are using ICT. Parents and teachers will need to be familiar with what is possible so that they can be of assistance when necessary.

Where schools have set up ICT hardware and software to support the particular needs of a pupil with SEN, this may be useful to that pupil on leaving school. It may be helpful if schools are able to offer such pupils the possibility of acquiring the ICT equipment they have been using at school so that they can make use of it in the longer term. This may be especially useful where pupils are moving on to Further or Higher Education. Access to ICT resources and the ability to use them effectively may improve employment prospects for pupils with SEN.

The needs of Gifted and Talented (G&T) pupils are similar to those of every pupil but they can be at an advanced level in some skills and abilities. Depending on their particular talents, G&T pupils can advance their learning by accessing advanced skills and knowledge using the Internet. For example, they can do the following:

- Improve their foreign language skills by talking to native speakers across the world using programs such as Skype.
- Study courses leading to advanced qualifications and read research papers. These are freely available from universities throughout the world, for example, the Massachusetts Institute of Technology (MIT) provides free access to advanced courses in a very wide range of subjects (http://ocw.mit.edu/).
- Travel the world virtually using programs such as Google Earth with Streetview.

Gender and ICT

Personal and social prejudices that are generally evident in relationships in the wider community may be expressed by pupils in schools, and gender-related stereotypes and expectations can have a significant impact on boys' and girls' attitudes towards ICT. For example, it is thought that boys tend to be interested in ICT for its own sake and are better at games and programming whereas girls see ICT as a means of pursuing their interests and furthering their learning and are better with email and social media. However, girls' interest in ICT tends to decline as they progress through school and fewer girls have qualifications in ICT and follow a career in the industry (Becta, 2008; Volman *et al.*, 2005).

School timetables should be constructed so that they do not encourage pupils to make selections that reinforce social and cultural stereotypes. Careers advice, text books, videos and other materials shown in schools should not confirm traditional stereotypes. Pupils' disengagement with subjects according to gender stereotypes is not only a problem in ICT. Culley (1986) recommends that, in order to encourage more girls to study ICT, it should not be closely linked with other subjects. In particular, it should not be closely linked with subjects that are known to have existing problems of a similar kind with equal opportunities, for example, Mathematics and Design Technology.

Monitoring

In tackling inequality and discrimination, accurate, quantitative information is essential (Culley, 1986). This is useful in identifying what ameliorative action needs to be taken. While the information that will be needed will vary from school to school, the indicators of gender bias described below are a good starting point (adapted from Milner, 1989; see also Culley, 1986):

- Where there is a choice, pupils will segregate themselves by their selection of ICT and related subjects. When making optional subject choices, boys will choose to study ICT whereas girls will choose subjects such as History.
- Boys generally achieve better results than girls in ICT and related subjects in school assessments and in external examinations such as I/GCSE.
- In class, when boys and girls are asked to use the computers, more boys than girls will usually operate the computers. If there are mixed groups using the computers, in most groups, a boy is operating the computer.
- When boys and girls have a choice whether to use computers or not, more boys than girls will choose to do so. Pupils turning up for the optional ICT programming club are nearly all boys.
- Boys compete more for access to ICT resources. If pupils have to queue for the lunchtime ICT club to open, the pupils at the front of the queue are usually boys. Boys will skip lunch to be first in the queue.
- When the teacher asks the class an ICT-orientated question, more boys than girls respond.
- Women and girls are under-represented in text books and other materials used in the classroom and elsewhere in the school. Careers literature reinforces traditional stereotypes, showing men in control of computers and related technology, with women in a supporting role.
- When ICT is employed as a cross-curricula resource, it is mainly used in subjects which are also known to have problems with gender bias, for example, in Physics and Design Technology.
- There is a general assumption that computers are 'toys for boys'.

It is important that information on ICT and gender is collected regularly and recorded. In the case of I/GCSE and other examination statistics, this will be done annually. Quantitative measures of most of the other indicators can be recorded as thought necessary.

Access

It may be thought that in order to achieve equality of access it is sufficient simply to give all pupils the same chances to make use of ICT resources. However, this is not necessarily so. If pupils' access to ICT resources is not carefully supervised, then the discriminatory behaviour of some pupils will exclude others. For example, if access to the lunchtime ICT club is on a 'first come, first served' basis, then it is likely that one group will tend to dominate; most probably these will be the stronger boys. The dominant group may arrive first, gain access and monopolize all the ICT resources, thus blocking the access of other groups. Even where initial access to the ICT rooms is controlled, if supervision is not maintained, the dominant group will tend to evict other pupils. In order to ensure equal access and, hence, equal opportunities, it is necessary to supervise very carefully all access to ICT resources and the continuing use of these resources (Culley, 1986).

A strategy often employed as a means of moving towards equal opportunities for all is that of positive discrimination. The intention is to redress known discrimination by making more resources more easily available to the disadvantaged group. In schools, positive discrimination might lead to ICT resources being made available for use only by girls, or only by girls at certain times. For example, girls could be given exclusive access to specific ICT resources at a particular time each day or each week. It might be considered necessary to establish girls' only classes or groups of girls who usually work together in mixed classes.

There can be disadvantages when positive discrimination is adopted in coeducational secondary schools. Making specific ICT resources available only to girls, or to girls at particular times, may exacerbate resentment on the part of boys, especially if girls do not make full use of the ICT resources reserved for them. A better alternative is to give girls first priority usage of some ICT resources at all times. This gives girls access to ICT resources at all times but does not prevent the use of these resources by boys at other times.

Single sex groups or classes are especially noticeable in mixed schools. As a result, the girls in these classes are likely to be subjected to increased levels of personal abuse and bullying. This is regrettable and should be firmly resisted by teachers. However, it may be better to avoid potential harassment by improving girls' access to ICT resources in other ways.

When positive discrimination strategies are used, it is essential to have overt rules defining the circumstances when particular groups of pupils are given priority use of ICT resources. This reduces conflict by setting clear guidelines that all pupils must follow. Overt rules can be a useful focus for discussion with pupils about the reasonableness of the rules within the general context of equal opportunities. This promotes all pupils' awareness of others' needs and provides opportunities for them to express their sensitivity towards them in particular circumstances.

The discriminatory attitudes that pupils bring with them to school tend to find their expression where there is a lack of effective supervision. Continuous supervision of pupils following clearly defined and overt rules will help ensure that all groups of pupils can gain access to ICT resources when it is appropriate for them to do so.

Positive discrimination can be effective but should be implemented with care as it can give rise to counter-productive resentment and hostility. Overt rules governing pupils' access to ICT, and careful supervision, are essential means of ensuring that disadvantaged groups feel sufficiently safe to take advantage of the resources reserved for their use. These overt rules may act as a useful focus for discussion of the underlying issues.

Role models

It is generally thought that boys respond best to adult male role models and girls respond most to adult female role models (Volman *et al.*, 2005). If this is the case, then it provides an explanation of how gender stereotypical behaviour is perpetuated in schools. Put simplistically, we might expect pupils to show more interest in and be most influenced by those lessons where they are taught by a teacher of the same sex. As some subjects are traditionally taught mainly by male or female teachers, these subjects are correspondingly more popular with boys or girls. Pupils thus make choices that confirm traditional stereotypes.

Strategies to encourage the equal development of all pupils in all areas of the curriculum have sometimes involved attempts to manipulate pupils' choices and attitudes by providing male or female role models in specific subjects where boys or girls are under-represented. As many ICT teachers are male, in order to provide encouragement for girls, female teachers may be appointed to teach ICT.

A teacher who does not believe that some pupils can learn certain skills is unlikely to be an effective teacher of those skills. A competent, effective female teacher who believes that all pupils can and should learn ICT skills is probably the best role model for girls. However, a male teacher who is competent and effective, with similar beliefs, may also be effective in encouraging girls to study ICT.

The selection of teachers as role models is further complicated by the covert nature of sexist prejudice. Adults with discriminatory attitudes are often unaware that they are prejudiced. The common belief that 'a woman's place is in the home' is almost entirely due to the historical subdivision of domestic labour and child rearing, and the importance of the relatively greater physical strength of many males in a traditional economy dominated by manual labour. However, while these historical conditions are on the whole no longer evident, the social beliefs and prejudices which they gave rise to have persisted. These tend to be transmitted through socialization in the family and elsewhere. As a result, both children and adults may express these attitudes in their speech and behaviour without previous reflection on their validity. Consequently, it can be expected that some teachers will unconsciously communicate discriminatory attitudes. In addition, when discriminatory beliefs are conscious, if they are held to be true, they are likely to be concealed in a professional setting in education.

To summarize, perceived competency and supportive attitudes towards the development of all learners are especially important for teachers of ICT. A female teacher is probably the best role model for girls and a male teacher is probably the best role model for boys, so it is appropriate to ensure that both male and female teachers have responsibility for delivering ICT. However, competency and high expectation for all are more important than the gender of the teacher. A school's ICT staff should be a mix of male and female teachers so that both boys and girls have appropriate role models.

Activity

Read this quote from the Educational Technology Debate:

> Look at any ICT-enabled school classroom, and there is often a greater excitement for the technology with boys than girls, which by middle or secondary school, can translate into ICT tools being an exclusive domain of boys, excluding half the learning population from their benefit. How can technologists and educators design more gender neutral, or pro-female ICT-enabled learning experiences? And from these experiences, can we hope to also change the gender balance in the ICT industry? Or will ICT, as an industry, always be mainly male?
>
> (http://edutechdebate.org/gender-equality-in-ict-education/)

In a small group, consider the following points:

- Should teachers try to achieve equal outcomes for boys and girls?
- What action could teachers take to promote gender equality?

Summary

- Teachers have a professional duty to ensure the safety of the children in their care.
- Professional and moral imperatives demand that every teacher should ensure that all pupils have equal opportunities to develop their full potential.
- Social use of the Web:
  - Most online communication is with friends who are known face-to-face. Most children have very little interest in talking to strangers online and are wary of them.
  - Parents and children consider the Internet to be riskier than other media.
  - Sharing personal information can be unsafe as it may undermine personal security.
  - Children should never arrange a meeting with someone they have not previously met face-to-face.
  - Cyberbullying is bullying carried out using ICT. For a child, the first step in dealing with cyberbullying is to talk to a teacher or other adult.
  - Children should be taught to be sceptical and evaluate all information on the Internet.
  - Children need to know how to deal with incidental exposure to pornography.
  - Parents tend to significantly underestimate their children's exposure to Internet pornography.
  - Filtering software should be used that blocks access to pornography and other undesirable material, for example, CYBERsitter, Net Nanny and CyberPatrol.
  - Children should be taught how to recognize and deal with phishing attacks. Phishing is an attempt to find out personal information.

- Technical dangers affect all Internet users:

  o A virus is software secretly installed with malicious intent. Anti-virus software, such as McAffee VirusScan, can automatically check for viruses and remove them.

  o Pharming is an attempt to collect personal information from users when they connect to a legitimate website. Remove such spyware using software such as Spybot Search and Destroy.

- Illegal conduct:

  o Most Internet users have illegally downloaded software, music, video, images or text.

  o The penalties for copyright offences depend on their seriousness.

  o Illegally downloaded files or software are more likely to have malicious software such as viruses attached.

  o Your personal information and privacy are at risk especially using peer-to-peer file sharing.

  o Users of illegal download websites risk exposure to pornographic content.

- Health and safety problems associated with using computers:

  o Headaches and eye strain.

  o Photosensitive (flicker-induced) epilepsy.

  o Rashes or skin problems.

  o Electrical shock and fire.

  o Hot and stuffy ICT rooms.

- Inclusion: Every child should have the opportunity to achieve their full potential. ICT can help pupils with difficulties:

  o Pupils who have difficulties with basic literacy and numeracy.

  o Pupils with language or speech difficulties, including EAL and dyslexia.

  o Pupils with emotional and behavioural difficulties.

  o Pupils with physical disabilities, very poor movement or coordination.

  o Visually impaired pupils.

  o Pupils with impaired hearing.

  o Pupils with profound and multiple learning difficulties.

  o Gifted and talented pupils.

- Gender stereotypes can have an impact on boys' and girls' attitudes towards ICT:

  o School timetables should be constructed so that they do not encourage pupils to make selections that reinforce social and cultural stereotypes.

  o Schools should monitor indicators of gender inequality and keep records.

  o A school's ICT staff should be a mix of male and female teachers so that both boys and girls have appropriate role models.

Further reading

Childnet International (n.d.) *Why is e-Safety Important?*, available at: http://childnet.com/kia/trainee-teachers/why.aspx (accessed 17 March 2012).

DCSF (2007) *Cyberbullying*, available at: http://www.digizen.org/downloads/CYBERBULLYING. pdf (accessed 15 March 2012).

Volman, M., van Eck, E., Heemskerk, I. and Kuiper, E. (2005) 'New technologies, new differences: gender and ethnic differences in pupils' use of ICT in primary and secondary education', *Journal of Computers and Education*, 45: 35–55.

YouTube (n.d.) *Joe's Story*, available at: http://www.youtube.com/watch?v=cJAYMaT5BJg (accessed 7 March 2012).

Chapter 6

Training to teach ICT and Computing

Introduction

Training to teach means achieving Qualified Teacher Status (QTS). QTS qualifies you to teach in state-maintained schools in England (and Wales but not Scotland or Northern Ireland). QTS is acquired by completing a programme of Initial Teacher Training (ITT).

As a newly qualified teacher (NQT), you complete an induction year before becoming fully qualified. Many trainees will already aspire to take on a subject leader role, perhaps as a Head of Department (HoD). Promotion can be facilitated by taking on a variety of roles in school and studying for related qualifications. Promoted posts beyond this tend to focus more on general management and less on teaching ICT, and are beyond the scope of this book. Chapter 7 discusses your career in teaching ICT.

This chapter covers:

- Preparing yourself before applying for teacher training.
- Different types of teacher training.
- Whether to train to teach only ICT or Computing or with another subject.
- Where to find information about courses and apply for training.
- The application.
- Financial support.
- Your interview for teacher training.
- What teacher training involves.
- An example of a teacher training course – case study.
- Applying for a teaching post.
- Your interview for a teaching post.

Preparing yourself before applying for teacher training

Teaching is a popular and rewarding career. Many people choose to teach because they consider helping young people learn to be intrinsically more rewarding than, for example, manufacturing sports clothing more cost effectively or working in a call centre. Teaching, manufacturing and other employment sectors are each important in different ways and all sectors contribute to our well-being and social progress. However, if you enjoy using your ICT skills, knowledge and understanding and helping young people to learn similar skills, then you may find teaching more rewarding.

If you wish to train as a teacher for maintained secondary schools in England, you should prepare carefully well in advance of application. Making sure you are well prepared will: (1) help you complete your application; (2) maximize the likelihood of being invited for interview; (3) increase the possibility of being offered a place on a training course; (4) help you successfully complete your training; (5) improve your chances of being appointed to a teaching post; and (6) underpin your later development.

If you are intending to apply for postgraduate teacher training, you should make sure that:

- *You are well qualified in your subject.* Qualification requirements differ slightly between different types of teacher training and different teacher training organizations, so check out requirements before application. You should have at a minimum an honours degree at 2:2 or above from an English university and GCSE Mathematics and English at grade C or above. If you intend to apply for Teach First (see p. 71), you will need BBB at A-level excluding General Studies and an honours degree at 2:1 or better. Your profile will be enhanced significantly if your degree is in an ICT-related subject or includes many modules in ICT-related subjects. For example, if your degree is in Fine Art, it is unlikely that you will be accepted for training as an ICT teacher. Your chances would be improved, if you have GCSE and A-level ICT or similar and ICT-related modules in your degree. The reason for this is that if you are going to teach any subject, not only must you be competent in the subject, you must also be able to convince others that you are competent. If you are unable to do this, you could consider completing a one-year full-time Master's degree in Computing or ICT or a related subject that is suitable for applicants who are well qualified in another subject but are planning to work in the ICT sector. Several universities offer suitable courses. If you have not already passed GCSE Mathematics and English at grade C or above, then you should do so. Many ITT courses offer equivalency tests but these are usually not certificated or accepted by other providers so that equivalency may need to be demonstrated repeatedly if you have applied to more than one provider. You may also find in the future that prospective employers ask for similar evidence that you have adequate literacy and numeracy.
- *You are highly committed to a career in teaching.* If you have not made sure that you know what is involved in teaching ICT, then you will not have demonstrated a sufficiently robust commitment. You should have experience in a secondary school observing ICT teachers at work. To gain this experience, you may find it more useful to visit a school other than the one you attended as a pupil. At a minimum, this experience should be sufficient to help you understand what is involved in teaching ICT in a maintained secondary school. You could also attend a taster course, or while you are at university, get involved in programmes similar to the Undergraduate Ambassador Scheme which awards module credits for undergraduates working with teachers in secondary schools (more details on www.uas.ac.uk).
- *You can demonstrate that you will be a responsible employee.* Any previous employment you have had, whether full or part-time, over several years in any role could demonstrate that you are reliable and know what employers require of a diligent employee. Preferably, you will have been employed in an ICT-related job for several years since completing your degree. Employment as an ICT technician or teaching assistant in a

secondary school is ideal. If you are applying immediately after completing your degree, then experience of part-time work to help support yourself throughout your degree can help your application even though this is in, for example, fast food or retail.

- *You are familiar with the ICT taught in schools.* You should you know what topics the ICT curriculum is likely to cover and be familiar with more general information about the education system, such as: types of school; the Key Stages; the external examinations available; and current issues in ICT in education. You could learn about these by browsing awarding body websites and downloading A-level and I/GCSE specifications; reading a textbook for pupils studying for I/GCSE (Crawford, 2010) or A-level; browsing the DfE website; and reading the *Times Educational Supplement* (TES) which is available in newsagents every Friday. Do not assume that because you recently attended a secondary school and studied ICT that you are familiar with the ICT taught in schools. Your experience as a pupil will have been very specific to your needs and abilities and the school you attended. Your future career as a teacher means that you will have a different viewpoint and this will take in the needs and abilities of all pupils of whatever gender, ethnicity, age, sexuality or disability and in a range of different types of schools.

- *You have passed the skills tests in numeracy and literacy.* The Teaching Agency (TA) requires that applicants for teacher training have passed a skills test in each of numeracy and literacy. These tests cover the core skills teachers need to fulfil their professional role in schools. If you start teacher training on or after September 2013, you are required to pass these skills tests before starting a course. You have to submit an application form for an ITT course before you can register for the tests; however, you can be interviewed for a place on a course before passing the tests. Even so, it may be prudent to prepare for the tests prior to applying for teacher training as many providers will want to know whether you have passed the tests or see evidence that you are likely to pass before arranging an interview. Interviews could follow quickly after application; consequently, it is recommended that you attempt the tests as soon as possible after application. You can book the skills tests via the DfE website (www.education.gov.uk). You are allowed only three attempts at each test. The first attempt is free of charge. If you fail on all attempts in either test, you are not allowed to take resits for 24 months from the date of the failed resit. Skills tests are only available in the UK. Prior to September 2012, you could only register for the tests after you had started an ITT course and there was also an ICT skills test which has been discontinued. For trainees on courses from September 2012 to September 2013 transitional arrangements apply.

If you are applying for undergraduate teacher training, you should read the above section on postgraduate application but also note that:

- *You should be well qualified but at a different level.* Check requirements on the UCAS website (www.ucas.com). Typically, you should have: 260 UCAS points which include at least two A-levels or equivalent, of which 80 points (grade C) are in ICT or a related subject; and GCSE Maths, English and Science at grade C or above, for example, the BSc in ICT Secondary Education with QTS at Edge Hill University.

- *You should demonstrate that you are committed to a career in teaching.* Talk to your ICT teacher about ways of gaining appropriate experience while you are still at school. And look for opportunities during your undergraduate degree.
- *You should demonstrate that you will be a responsible employee.* If you intend to train immediately after completing your degree, a part-time job for a few hours each week could help.
- *You are familiar with the ICT taught in schools.* Don't assume that all schools are similar to the school you attended. Find out about how ICT is taught in a range of different types of school.

Activity

Audit your qualifications and current experience. Consider:

- your qualifications and evidence that you achieved these;
- evidence of your commitment;
- evidence that you will be a responsible employee;
- your familiarity with the ICT taught in schools.

Identify areas that need improvement; plan how you will improve; carry out your plan.

Different types of teacher training

Qualified teachers have qualified teacher status (QTS). This qualifies you to teach in state-maintained schools in England (and Wales but not Scotland or Northern Ireland). QTS is acquired by completing a programme of initial teacher training (ITT). ITT tends to be specific to an age group or subject, for example, you could complete a PGCE in ICT and Computer Science preparing you to teach secondary school pupils aged 11–18. Similar courses might prepare you for teaching different age groups, for example, 11–16, or different subjects, for example, Music. All courses will prepare you to teach and will include teaching placements in more than one school.

The main routes to achieving QTS are:

- postgraduate
- undergraduate
- employment-based.

Most initial teacher education inspected by Ofsted is good or outstanding. There is more outstanding provision in secondary partnerships led by universities and other institutes of higher education than in school-centred partnerships or employment-based routes. Currently, around 78 per cent of trainees follow training programmes offered by a university or other institute of higher education; approximately 4 per cent train in School Centred Initial Teacher Training (SCITT); and 18 per cent of trainees follow employment-based routes (Ofsted, 2011). At the time of writing, the government intends to train more teachers in school-based provision.

Postgraduate

A postgraduate ITT course at a university or institute of higher education leads to a Professional Graduate Certificate in Education or a Postgraduate Certificate in Education (PGCE). Both courses lead to QTS but the PGCE will include modules at Master's level whereas the Professional Graduate Certificate will not. As a result, the PGCE may be a better choice if you are interested in your personal, educational and career development. Notice that it would be easy to confuse the Professional Graduate Certificate in Education and the Postgraduate Certificate in Education and you should check carefully whether a course includes Master's level modules. In this book, PGCE is taken to mean the Postgraduate Certificate in Education.

A PGCE specializing in ICT and Computer Science takes around a year to complete and will include at least 120 days teaching placement in a secondary school. The course will focus on developing your teaching but not significantly develop your in-depth subject knowledge. This is why you must have a degree in an ICT-related subject. Even so, you will be expected to develop your subject knowledge across the broad range of topics you will teach. At the end of the course, assuming you meet the standards, you will be awarded a PGCE and qualified teacher status (QTS) and become an NQT ready to undertake your induction year. A PGCE is currently the most popular route to QTS. Currently around 80 per cent of trainees follow training programmes offered by an HEI (Ofsted, 2011; Smithers and Robinson, 2011) and 83 per cent of Newly Qualified Teachers (NQTs) qualify in this way (DfE, 2011c).

You can also be awarded QTS by completing a programme of School Centred Initial Teacher Training (SCITT). This route is school-centred but you are not employed by the school. SCITT training programmes are designed and delivered by consortia of schools and colleges. At the end of a one-year course, you are awarded QTS, and SCITTs that work with a university or other institute of higher education may also award a PGCE. You are not employed by a school and do not receive a salary; however, you are normally based in one school and complete teaching placements at other schools in the consortium.

It may also be possible to complete ITT via flexible distance learning, for example, the Open University (www.open.ac.uk) offers a Professional Graduate Certificate in Education to teach the 11–16 age range but not specifically in ICT.

Undergraduate

An undergraduate degree course with teacher training at a university or institute of higher education leads to a Bachelor's degree with QTS. These may take two to four years to complete depending on the course. These are not widely available and you will need to search the UCAS website very carefully before applying through UCAS. There are full-time three-year degree courses where you specialize in ICT only, for example, the BSc in ICT Secondary Education with QTS at Edge Hill University. However, many of the courses available provide training to teach ICT with another subject, for example, the two-year full-time ordinary BSc at the University of Wales in Mathematics with ICT. Between 4–5 per cent of all secondary NQTs complete an undergraduate degree with QTS (Smithers and Robinson, 2011).

Employment-based courses

A popular employment-based route is the graduate teacher programme (GTP). Around 18 per cent of NQTs train through an employment-based route (DfE, 2011; Ofsted, 2011). You obtain QTS while working as an unqualified teacher. Trainees completing some, but not all, GTP courses are awarded a PGCE. The school employs you and pays you as you train. Training is usually for one year full-time. The school is responsible for arranging the training although this is often done in partnership with other institutions, such as universities or colleges of further education. Training providers are usually centred on a Local Authority, e.g. the Kirklees Partnership, or a university, e.g. Sheffield Hallam University. Some training providers will help you find a school to train in but some will expect you to find a school to sponsor you before applying. The application process, application deadlines and starting dates vary between training providers.

School Direct is a new teacher training route available from September 2013 and it is intended that this will replace GTP (Gove, 2012). As this is a new course, you should check out the details on www.dfe.gov.uk. All trainees completing School Direct training success-fully will be awarded QTS and some will also be awarded a PGCE validated by a university or institute of higher education. Courses are expected to last one year and there is an expecta-tion that trainees will go on to work in the school that recruited them although this is not guaranteed. Graduates with three or more years' career experience will be eligible for School Direct (salaried) and trainees on this route will be employed as an unqualified teacher.

Teach First (TF) is also an employment-based route. Trainees are employed by their placement school. In the first year they are paid as an unqualified teacher and in the second year as a qualified teacher. TF specifically aims to address educational disadvantage by placing graduates with good degrees in schools in challenging circumstances. The training begins with an intensive six-week residential course prior to placement. During the first year trainees have full responsibility for their classes, teaching a full NQT timetable, that is, teaching 80 per cent of the timetable a fully qualified teacher would have. Placement schools work in partnership with a university so that trainees work towards a PGCE and QTS, and become qualified teachers by the end of the first year. In the second year, trai-nees continue to work in their placement school as an NQT. Some 90 per cent of trainees stay for a minimum of two years and over 50 per cent stay longer (www.teachfirst.org.uk).

The *registered teacher programme* is an employment-based route suitable for you if you have only completed the equivalent of two years of higher education, for example, those with foundation degrees or HNDs. Trainees are employed by the school as an unquali-fied teacher and sometimes enhance their subject knowledge by completing an honours degree during their training. The training usually takes place over two years. The regis-tered teacher programme is not as widely available as other employment-based routes.

Troops to Teachers courses

Troops to Teachers is also a new teacher training route introduced in 2012 and at the time of writing full details are not available. You should check out the details on http://www.education.gov.uk/. Former members of the armed forces are welcome on all tea-cher training courses and are not excluded from other arrangements for ITT provided they meet the same admission conditions that are required of other applicants.

Whether to train to teach only ICT and/or Computer Science or with another subject

Experience of teaching another subject can enhance your training. For example, if you have a degree in ICT or Computing or a closely related subject, you may be more interested in applying for a PGCE ICT and Computer Science and you will probably want to specialize in teaching these and closely related subjects. During your training you will mainly teach ICT and Computing but there may be the opportunity to teach some other subjects. Taking the opportunity to teach another subject for a few lessons each week can enhance your training, for example, if you have a degree in an ICT-related subject with some Psychology modules and would like to teach Psychology, you may have the opportunity to teach this subject for one or two lessons each week. This could enhance your training as you will find, for example, that teachers of different subjects tend to use different teaching strategies.

Experience teaching another subject may also help you find a teaching post. Secondary schools tend to offer subjects such as Psychology to a very limited extent, perhaps only at A-level to a small group of post-16 pupils, and may not want to employ a teacher only to do this. In this circumstance, an applicant for a post as an ICT teacher might well be more attractive because they are able to teach Psychology. In similar circumstances, appropriate qualifications and experience in, for example, Drama, Beauty, Dance, Mathematics, or Business Studies can also be helpful.

Some teacher training includes ICT as a second subject, such as the PGCE in Business with ICT Education at Manchester Metropolitan University. Teacher training in two subjects could enhance your training and improve your employment prospects for a teaching post where you are expected to teach Business and ICT. However, as a newly qualified teacher (NQT), you would be less likely to be appointed to a teaching post advertised as specializing in ICT only, as you would be in competition with NQTs who are likely to have specialist ICT qualifications and more experience teaching ICT.

Where to find information about courses and apply for training

Where to find information about courses and apply for training is shown in Table 6.1. The current application system is complex and the government intends to introduce a simplified application system for those applying for postgraduate and employment-based ITT starting in September 2014 and beyond. There is more information about applying for teacher training on: http://www.education.gov.uk/get-into-teaching/apply-for-teacher-training/apply-now.

Your application

Read the section above entitled 'Preparing yourself before applying for teacher training'. In your application, make sure it is clear that you are well qualified; highly committed to teaching; will be a responsible employee; and are familiar with the ICT taught in schools. Make sure your spelling, punctuation and grammar are accurate.

Financial support

The financial support available to teacher trainees tends to vary from year to year and you should check this out very carefully on the DFE website. At the time of writing, the financial support that may be available is shown in Table 6.2 on page 74.

Table 6.1 Where to find information and apply for training

Type of teacher training	Where to find information about courses and apply for training
Postgraduate courses	Visit the GTTR website for more information about PGCE courses and SCITTs (www.gttr.ac.uk). You can search by age range and subject to be taught, and provider. There is detailed information about the courses and whether there are vacancies. You also apply through this website.
Undergraduate courses	Visit the UCAS website for more information (www.ucas.com). You can search for a suitable degree course by course type, institution and whether the course leads to QTS. There is detailed information about the courses and whether there are vacancies. You also apply through this website.
Employment-based	You can search for a GTP training provider through: http://www.education.gov.uk/get-into-teaching/teacher-training-options/gtp/. You can also search through agencies, such as:www.gtpteachers.co.uk There is information about Schools Direct on: http://www.education. gov.uk/get-into-teaching/teacher-training-options/school-based-training/ school-direct. There is more information about Teach First on their website: http:// graduates.teachfirst.org.uk/. You can apply through the website. For the registered teacher programme – apply directly to your local employment-based initial teacher training provider.

Activity

- Make a list of the advantages and disadvantages of each type of teacher training.
- Decide what type of teacher training you are interested in.
- Check out the financial support you would receive.
- Decide when you would like to begin teacher training.
- Apply for teacher training (around 10 months before you want to start).

Your interview for teacher training

You are likely to be invited for interview on a specific date. The interview may involve several professionals from different institutions. An interview for a PGCE ICT and Computer Science at a university could involve lecturers and school teachers. Because of the difficult of arranging for everyone to attend, there will only be a few dates when your interview can take place. If you cannot attend on one day, you can ask for another date; however, there may not be alternative dates available.

Interviews for teacher training posts usually take place over one day, and for a PGCE ICT, may include: a presentation about the course and the financial support available; an interview with a university lecturer and a school teacher; a presentation to a group of applicants and an observer; the completion of tests of your literacy, numeracy and subject knowledge; inspection of your original qualification certificates; an application for a Criminal Records Bureau (CRB) check.

Table 6.2 The financial support available to teacher trainees

Type of teacher training	Financial support
Postgraduate courses	For students on a PGCE ICT in 2012/13, the financial support package consists of: • Bursary – ICT attracts a bursary of £9,000 for a first class honours degree; £5,000 for a 2:1; and £0 for a 2:2. This is not repayable. Bursaries are paid in 10 equal monthly instalments. • A means-tested maintenance grant is paid if family income is up to £25,000 and the grant is £3,250. This is not repayable. There is a sliding scale up to a family income of £42,600 when no grant is available. • A loan to pay the tuition fees. This is repayable after the course and repayments are based on what you earn and not on what you borrow. Repayment is 9 per cent of salary over £21,000 p.a. which means that an NQT could repay almost nothing in the first year of teaching but this would slowly increase as salary increases. A teacher earning £31,000 would repay around £75 per month. Payments cease when the loan is written off after 30 years or when the loan has been fully repaid, whichever is the sooner. • A maintenance loan to help with living costs of up to £5,500 if not living at home; and £4,375 if living at home. This is repayable and is aggregated with the tuition fee loan.
Undergraduate courses	Financial arrangements for undergraduate teacher training are the same as for most other undergraduate courses. Different providers charge different tuition fees and tuition fees can be up to £9,000 each year depending on where you study. To cover the costs of undergraduate study you can apply for: • A means-tested maintenance grant. This is only available to full-time students and the details are the same as for postgraduate teacher training (see above). • A tuition fee loan to cover your tuition fees in full (see above). • A maintenance loan for living costs for full-time students only (see above). • Scholarships and bursaries from colleges and universities. • Extra financial help if you have a disability or dependants. Grants and bursaries do not have to be repaid but you have to pay back any loans (see above).
Employment-based	Trainees on employment-based courses are paid a salary by the school. This can vary between schools and should be checked with the training provider. During the first year of your training you are likely to be paid a salary on the unqualified teacher scale (see http://www.education.gov.uk/get-into-teaching/salary.aspx). Where you fit into these scales will depend on your post, previous experience, location and on your individual school. Unqualified teachers' salaries in 2012 were: • London fringe: £16,856–£26,052 • Outer London: £18,789–£27,992 • Inner London: £19,893–£29,088 • Rest of England and Wales: £15,817–£25,010.

Table 6.2 Continued

Type of teacher training	Financial support
	Teach First trainees continue to work in their placement school after they have qualified for at least a further year. They are paid on the qualified teacher scale which is the same for all NQTs appointed to a teaching post. Starting salaries in 2012 were: • London fringe: £22,626 • Outer London: £25,117 • Inner London: £27,000 • Rest of England and Wales: £21,588.

You should prepare thoroughly before the interview. Make sure you know where the interview is being held and that you can get there on time. Check out your travel plans carefully. Read your application again and take a copy with you. Take your original qualification certificates and do not forget basic equipment such as pens and a notepad. You will probably be asked to complete a pre-interview task and you should take this with you. You may also want to take examples of your previous work.

Make sure you are well presented at interview. Teachers are expected to be clean and dress professionally. If you do not dress appropriately for an interview for teacher training, it may be assumed that you will not dress appropriately when you are on teaching placement in a secondary school.

One mistake that applicants sometimes make is not to act on feedback. For example, suppose an earlier application was rejected and you apply again the following year to the same institution. If during the first interview, it was suggested that you should pass GCSE Mathematics and English at grade C or above, you will be expected to have done this. If you re-apply and have not done this, you will need to be able to explain this omission.

How will you get to know the outcome of the interview? Different routes into teacher training do this in different ways and you should ask about this at the interview. Make sure you get the telephone number or email address of those who will know what offer has been made so that you can follow this up quickly if there is a delay. The offer you receive might be conditional on your achievements. For example, if you are just completing your degree, an offer might be conditional on you achieving a 2:2 or above. If you are unsuccessful, you should ask for feedback as this can help you prepare for your next interview or an application in future years.

What teacher training involves

Training to be an ICT teacher involves:

• the general professional duties and responsibilities of a teacher;
• ICT subject studies, that is, pedagogy and curriculum;
• ICT subject knowledge, skills and understanding.

You will study initial professional development (IPD). These studies may be in lectures to large groups of trainees; or seminars, tutorials, workshops or similar in much smaller groups. Professional development will focus on topics such as: lesson planning; classroom and behaviour management; assessment; inclusion; and career development.

In ICT subject studies, you will learn ICT pedagogy, that is, how to teach ICT and you will learn about the ICT curriculum. Many of the topics you begin to study in IPD will be revisited in the context of teaching ICT. For example, some behaviour management issues are specific to ICT, access to ICT resources engages pupils but it can also distract them. You will be shown simple techniques to ensure pupils listen to you when you are teaching, perhaps using software such as NetSupport School (www.netsup portschool.com). Similarly, while the general principles of assessment are likely to be discussed in IPD, the actual assessment of samples of pupils' work using ICT in relation to the levels of the ICT National Curriculum or I/GCSE ICT mark schemes will take place in ICT subject studies. You can also expect to consider how access to ICT resources can help support pupils who have barriers to learning, that is, learning difficulties; special educational needs; or limited understanding of English. You should expect to: discuss issues; deliver short presentations; collaborate and cooperate with other trainees to complete tasks; watch videos; listen to lectures; take notes; ask questions; investigate new technology; and take part in role play, simulations and learning games.

Teacher training in ICT and Computer Science is not usually designed to teach you these subjects because, unless you are on an undergraduate programme, you will have an honours degree in a related discipline. However, it is likely that your degree will be relatively specialized and to teach in schools you will need to have a wider knowledge of ICT and Computing. Consequently, you should expect to be asked to audit the range of your skills at a level above the age range you expect to teach. This audit will identify the areas you need to develop. Some of these areas will be developed while you research what you will teach; even so, you may need to independently study those areas that you have not already covered and do not expect to teach during your training. This audit will be started after you have been accepted on a teacher training course and should continue throughout.

The acquisition of ICT skills, knowledge and understanding is essentially an active process. Learners must be actively engaged otherwise they are unlikely to acquire skills. They may need access to reference manuals, learning guides, help sheets, tutorial exercises, and online help and other resources, and advice from an expert. The acquisition of ICT skills is often a time-consuming process so that learners must find sufficient time to devote to learning. However, the most important aspects of ICT skills acquisition are the involvement and motivation of the learner. Trainee teachers are relatively well provided for. They are usually on full-time courses where they have some development time allocated, and will have access to expert help from lecturers and mentors with specialist skills. Their motivation is high as they are focused on successfully completing their teacher training.

Teacher trainers are usually skilled practitioners with many years' experience in schools and other educational institutions. Trainees can expect to participate in a range and variety of activities that are designed to engage them and extend their skills, knowledge and understanding. Some example activities follow.

The 'ICT across the curriculum' game

An example of a typical activity in ICT subject studies that is designed to engage trainees is the 'ICT across the curriculum' game. The framework of the game could be used by an individual to inform the organization of the ICT curriculum or the content could be delivered as a lecture; however, this is likely to be much less engaging. The content is presented as a game to encourage trainees to become familiar with and discuss different ICT-based activities in a range of different subjects appropriate for the 11–16 age range. The game helps participants develop an understanding of the cross-curricular nature of ICT and appreciate its uses in all subjects of the curriculum.

The game is best organized in groups of five participants. The game will last a minimum of three-quarters of an hour but can last much longer. The curriculum board (see Figure 6.1) is a grid with Years 7 to 11 across the top and different subjects down the side. If desired, these could be changed to show, for example, Key Stage 3, Key Stage 4 and Post-16 along the top and different subjects down the side, depending on the context in which the game is played. Trainee teachers may find it helpful to have their specialist subject included even though it may not be central to the National Curriculum. The Activity cards (see Figure 6.2) could also be changed to take into account participants' subject backgrounds, or particular concerns, such as the use of ICT in Music. It may also be desirable to adjust the rules to achieve particular training objectives. For example, rule 7 ensures a good distribution of activities throughout the curriculum. However, it rules out one possible outcome of the game, that is, the identification of those subjects which could be given extensive responsibilities for the development of pupils' ICT capability. Suitably adjusted to the context in which it is to be played, the 'ICT across the Curriculum' game is a useful training activity. Stripped of its rules, it is also a good framework for planning the ICT curriculum.

The resources needed to play the game are:

- The Curriculum board (see Figure 6.1).
- The Activity cards (see Figure 6.2), cut up separately.
- ICT curriculum documents for KS3 and KS4.
- Relevant external assessment syllabuses or specifications for I/GCSE ICT.

The rules of the game are:

1 The game is played in groups of five players.
2 Deal out the Activity cards equally, discarding the remainder.
3 Starting at the dealer's left, in turn, each player places an Activity card on the Curriculum board.
4 When an Activity card has been placed by a player, the group decides whether it has been placed in an appropriate cell on the Curriculum board.
5 If the Activity card has not been placed in an appropriate cell on the Curriculum board, the Activity card is returned to the player who placed it. Otherwise, the Activity card remains on the Curriculum board and the game moves on to the next player.
6 If an Activity card is placed on an ICT cell, the player misses a turn.
7 If an Activity card is placed on a cell that already has an Activity card on it, the player misses a turn.
8 The winner is the player to discard all their Activity cards first.

Year 7	Year 8	Year 9	Year 10	Year 11	
					English
					Maths
					Science
					ICT
					Design & Technology
					PE
					Modern Languages
					History
					Music
					Other

Figure 6.1 The Curriculum board

Set up a database of the names and addresses of pupils in their class.	Use a word processor to write a letter to a friend.	Write a computer game in Scratch.	Describe how hospitals and GPs use ICT to handle medical records.	Use a spreadsheet to work out percentage discounts on a range of goods.	Use search conditions with AND, OR and NOT operators to search a database.
Measure and record the temperature every hour for one month.	Participate in an online discussion using Skype.	Send personalized letters to sponsors of the football team.	Use different fonts, sizes and styles of text.	Use clip art to illustrate an advert for a sports shop.	Describe the uses of a supermarket stock control system based on bar codes.
Model the growth of bacteria using a spreadsheet.	Delete a file on a hard disk.	Use a spelling checker to help eliminate spelling mistakes.	Scan a photograph of themselves and include it in their CV.	Discuss problems associated with the storing of personal data on a computer.	Guide a Valiant turtle around an obstacle.
Analyse survey data collected using a questionnaire.	Draft and edit an article for the school newspaper using a word processor.	Set up a spreadsheet to work out the cost of making a bicycle.	Describe the ICT systems' life cycle and know why each stage is important.	Generate pie diagrams, bar charts and line graphs using a spreadsheet.	Describe how to use an ATM or a cashpoint.
Explain how an automatic door works.	Extract a list of books on horses from a library database.	Discuss the social, economic, ethical and moral issues related to illegal downloads.	Copy a file onto a hard disk from a memory stick.	Design a questionnaire so that it is easy to input the data collected into a computer.	Use a database to sort a list of names into alphabetical order.
Write a Logo procedure to draw a square on the screen.	Design and make flashing words for a website.	Create animations using shape and motion tweening in Flash.	Draw a wallpaper design with a repeated pattern.	Using ICT, compose a piece of music and print the score.	Use QR codes and know why they are used.
Using ICT, modify a recorded piece of music so that it is played on different 'instruments'.	Design a company logo, business card and headed note paper.	Get information from a database and import it into a word-processed essay.	Include a screen shot in an eportfolio.	Draw a picture and print it.	Recognize that poor quality data may give inaccurate results.
Explain the advantages and disadvantages of email in relation to texting.	Write an article about a dance, and design tickets and posters advertising it.	Use ICT to keep a record of the books they have read and their opinions of them.	Reorganize blocks of text to improve the sense of a report about the youth club.	Write an illustrated book to help young children learn to read.	Record a piece of music and play it through a synthesizer at a concert.
Convert a document to a pdf.	Scan part of a magazine article and include it in a word-processed essay.	Save a file on a hard disk and open it at a later date.	Set up a printer so that it is ready to be used.	Investigate how height is related to strength and speed.	Extract a list of books on cars by authors beginning with 'H' from a library catalogue.

(Continued)

Analyse census data and parish records on a database.	Lay out a page of text and graphics for the school newspaper using DTP software.	Use Teletext to find the position of a football team in the league tables.	Scan a picture and modify it using graphics software.	Explore how to control inflation using a computer-based model of the economy.	Manage a petrol refinery using a computer-based simulationUs.

Figure 6.2 Activity cards

Personal experiences of ICT in schools

It may seem somewhat trite to observe that teachers' and trainee teachers' collective experiences of schools are broader and more varied than those of an individual teacher or trainee teacher. However, it is undoubtedly true. Individual trainee teachers usually have little experience of what is happening in schools in general. They tend to assume that the one or two schools in which they are placed during their training course are typical of all schools. It is unlikely that they are. Similarly, individual teachers often spend a large proportion of their professional careers in no more than two or three schools. As a result, teachers may also have a narrow view of what is happening in schools in general. Moreover, the organization of individual schools often isolates teachers and trainee teachers within their subject departments and within their classrooms. It is not unusual for them to be unaware of what is happening elsewhere in the school in which they teach. This is particularly true of the use of ICT in schools. However, in order to understand the strengths and weaknesses of the ways in which ICT is used within their own school, it is important that teachers, trainee teachers and others are aware of the variety of different approaches to organizing ICT provision in schools and the diversity of provision.

This exercise seeks to broaden trainees' experience, building on their current experience by sharing it with others and listening to others' descriptions of what they have encountered. It also illustrates another means of structuring discussion between participants so that a useful exchange of views takes place within a short time. Initially, participants are asked to work in pairs with another trainee whom they do not know well. This ensures that pairs have a limited knowledge of each other's prior experiences. Each member of the pair is given an interview prompt sheet (see Figure 6.3) and asked to interview the other. After a short time, these pairs are then asked to join another pair. Each member of the group of four then describes the experiences of ICT of the person they have just interviewed. One of the group of four should act as a scribe and summarize the discussion on two or three PowerPoint slides. The groups of four can then present their findings to the whole class. This encourages participants to share their different experiences and, almost inevitably, leads to a useful exchange of views and opinions.

This exercise can make the sharing of experiences richer and more informed. It is a good 'ice breaker' as it encourages participants to get to know each other. When trainees are between teaching placements and have had opportunities to reflect on their own experiences of teaching ICT, it can help them prepare for the next placement. However, it can be a useful exercise at any stage of a course.

You are asked to interview a colleague about their experiences of ICT in secondary schools. You should be able to describe their experiences and discuss any significant issues, conflicts, contradictions, and good or bad ideas that are mentioned.

The following indicates some of the information you might wish to know:

Hardware

- What type of computers were used? Model? Features? Costs?
- Who supplied them? Who repairs them?
- Where were the computers located? Why?
- Were all the ICT rooms secure? Accessible? To everyone?
- When did pupils have access to the hardware? Was there enough hardware?
- What restrictions were placed on pupils' use of hardware? Why?
- How was printing organized? When could it be done?
- Were all the computers compatible? Did this cause any problems?

Software

- What type of software was available?
- Name all the software that was available and indicate its type.
- Why was that particular software available?
- Who was allowed to use the software? Where? When? Via the Internet?
- What restrictions were placed on access by pupils? By staff? By others?
- Was all the software easy to use?
- Were the files generated by one piece of software compatible with other software?
- Was the software integrated or were different pieces of software used?
- What ICT coursework projects were done? Why? By which pupils? In which subjects?
- How did the software provide for progression, continuity and differentiation of learning?

Supervision and control of ICT resources

- Who was responsible for ICT resources?
- Who controlled the use of ICT resources? Why? In what ways? For staff? For pupils? For others?
- How did you find out what ICT resources were available for your use?
- Who was allowed to use the ICT resources? When? Where?
- Was technical help available? From whom? When? Where? For staff? For pupils? For others?
- How were technicians trained? What qualifications did they have?
- What organizational structures were used to manage ICT technicians?

Teachers' attitudes and experiences

- Were all the teachers enthusiastic about ICT? Technophobic?
- Which teachers used ICT in teaching their subjects? Where? To which pupils?
- What teaching styles were used when teaching ICT?
- What provision did the school make for training staff in ICT?
- Were there ICT resources reserved for staff use? Were these sufficient?

Pupils' attitudes and experiences

- Were pupils well motivated in ICT? Boys? Girls?
- Were pupils well behaved in ICT? Boys? Girls?
- Did pupils believe ICT is relevant and useful?
- Did all pupils have equal access to ICT? During timetabled lessons? Outside timetabled lessons?
- Did pupils' experiences of ICT meet statutory requirements?

ICT policy and the curriculum

- Did the school have an ICT policy?
- Was the policy agreed? By whom? How?
- Do you have a copy of the ICT policy? Why not?
- Have you read the ICT policy? Why not?
- Was all the policy written or is some of it informal?
- Was the policy part of a school booklet? Which?
- Was ICT taught as a subject? Across the curriculum? Using a hybrid combination of these?
- In your opinion, was ICT used appropriately?
- How were assessments of pupils' ICT capability recorded and reported?

Administration

- Was ICT used for school administration? Departmental administration? Individual teachers' administration? What other administration tasks?
- Were senior management enthusiastic about the use of ICT for administration? Office staff? Year Heads? Subject HoDs? Teachers?
- Did the use of ICT for administration decrease or increase workloads?

The good and the bad

- What experiences of ICT were particularly successful? Disastrous?
- Identify any issues, conflicts or contradictions, and good or bad ideas.

Figure 6.3 ICT interview prompt sheet

An example of a teacher training course

Training courses vary considerably in structure and content. Some of the differences between courses are inconsequential but others are due to the provider's approach. For example, a PGCE will include two teaching placements which together total 120 days in school. Different training providers split the 120 days in different ways. At the University of Huddersfield, PGCE ICT students have a first placement of around 40 days which is completed by the end of term 1; and a second placement of around 80 days. The short first placement helps trainees become accustomed to the school environment before they tackle the more substantial second placement when they must demonstrate that they meet all the training standards.

The case study below describes the experiences of Daniel Midgley, a student on the PGCE ICT at the University of Huddersfield during the 2011–12 academic year. Daniel wrote this case study just after he had completed his teacher training and while working as an NQT.

Case study: Training to teach, by Daniel Midgley, PGCE ICT student

Undertaking a PGCE at the University of Huddersfield I had several initial expectations and concerns of both teaching and postgraduate study. Would I be able to adapt to a new profession and the professional lifestyle that went along with it? Training to teach is hard work; however, with smart choices and using all the support available it is the most rewarding process I have ever taken part in.

Why choose the PGCE route over the other routes into the teaching profession? I would recommend the PGCE route to people interested in teaching for many reasons. University is easy to settle into and gives a trainee the chance to study away from the classroom and their placement school. This helps the trainee reflect on their experiences on placement. PGCE courses have university-based mentors who are unbiased with their support and advice, whereas school-based mentors are understandably more focused on their pupils, department and school. The PGCE seems a less lonely route than other routes into teaching. You are placed on a course with many students going through similar experiences and challenges. It is extremely beneficial to compare your experiences with your fellow students on the PGCE course as you then don't feel quite as bad when things don't go to plan in the classroom! PGCE courses include Master's level assignments which not only help you research, experiment and reflect on new ideas in the classroom but you can also use them towards gaining a Master's level qualification to help support and advance your teaching career. A planned structure is an important part of a PGCE course with multiple assignments spread out over the year giving you the chance to reflect on and develop your teaching throughout the year. This helps build the confidence and morale of a trainee teacher as you can see from assignment feedbacks and lesson observations that you really are developing as a teacher.

The primary concern raised by friends, family and the media was: would a new teacher be able to handle the nasty and dangerous young adults that supposedly now inhabit UK schools? Within hours of speaking to children in the classroom it became evident that most people with the aforementioned extreme views of pupils in UK schools have most likely never actually spoken to a pupil. The pupils I have come into contact with have always been keen to demonstrate their skills and share their achievements, and I am yet to meet a pupil who is nasty or dangerous. I quickly realized that a teacher's duty extends far beyond teaching their subject and that the support and encouragement of growing children are at the core of a teacher's role.

The PGCE course is adapted to the needs of the trainee teacher in terms of support and pace, but every student must teach their first lesson and this is easily the hour of your life when you are most desperate to get it right first time and impress your placement mentor. This may not happen and you follow a route of practice, reflection and improvement. This process works, and by the time you start your second placement, you already feel more confident because you have some teaching experience and your abilities in the classroom have improved.

Adjusting to a changed pace of life, one where free time at work is non-existent, was not an easy change. Time management and planning were the two most frequently used skills during my PGCE year. Once you manage to map your teaching life out in your mind and stick to that map, planning, marking and reflection begin to become second nature, and automatically fits into your non-contact time at school. It really is possible to maintain an adequate level of teaching quality and do all the marking, marking, marking that teachers spend all their waking lives completing.

An expectation I had was that departments would have tightly mapped schemes of work, and that each lesson would have been planned, refined and taught many times by teachers in that department, and that teachers would not be allowed to deviate from this structure. What I found during my PGCE placements is that teachers are given much more control over their own lessons than I anticipated. Teachers are expected to collaborate and share; however, in the classroom they are free to adapt and refine lessons to fit both their own teaching styles and to meet the needs of the pupils in their classes.

Almost everyone in the UK has been to school and as such already has judgements and opinions of the teaching profession. I was braced to deal with comments such as, 'Teaching is easy, you only work 9 till 3!' and 'Look at all those holidays you get, teachers are hardly at work.' The reality of public opinion is quite different. Teaching is a respected profession, and one where people are aware of the large workload that extends beyond the classroom. Speaking to several parents during my PGCE year I have felt respect from parents who are extremely thankful for the commitment that teachers give to their children.

The reality of lesson planning is something that the trainee teacher must get to grips with quickly. There really is no such thing as a 'pick up and teach' lesson. Every single lesson requires planning, research and study. This needs to be followed by some kind of reflection on how that lesson or activity went. Do you need to do something different next time? Do you need to consult your mentor for support? During the first placement of my PGCE, each one-hour lesson needed at least two hours of research, planning and reflection and for some lessons this was much greater. Gradually throughout the year, lesson research, planning and reflection became much more efficient as I became much more practised in it.

Applying for a teaching post

Where to find a teaching post

There is no one single point of application and you need to watch out for adverts in a range of different media. Many teaching posts are now advertised online and you can apply online, for example, on the *Times Educational Supplement* (TES) website: www.tes.co.uk/jobs/. You can filter your search to focus on secondary schools, teaching ICT, and the distance from your postcode. You can register to be sent alerts when a job becomes available. Individual Local Authorities may recruit teachers through websites, for example, Bradford Council recruit teachers through www.prospectsonline.co.uk, and there are many recruitment agencies working with schools, such as www.hays.co.uk/job/education-jobs/. Don't forget to use search engines such as Google.

You will also find job adverts in national papers. *The Guardian* has adverts for jobs in education on Tuesdays; and the *TES* is published in printed form each Friday and is often composed mainly of job adverts. Local newspapers also have adverts for local teaching posts. You may find these papers and others in your placement school as it is not unusual for secondary schools to order copies for the school library or staff room.

Many schools now advertise teaching posts through their own websites and a direct approach to individual schools where you would like to teach should be considered. You could contact schools through their websites; email or post your CV with a covering letter and statement in support of your application to the head teacher; or turn up at reception looking smart and with your supporting documentation. You could make yourself available for supply teaching at the school. It is not unusual for supply teaching jobs to become more permanent. Remember that recruitment is not cheap and schools are short of finance. If you were a head teacher and there was a candidate who was smart, polite and well qualified for a teaching post you were struggling to fill, would you turn them away without consideration?

How to improve your chances

Be flexible. The more flexible you are, the more you will maximize the likelihood of being appointed to a teaching post during your training. If you are only prepared to accept a post in a school adjacent to where you live, you have narrowed your opportunities significantly. It is not unusual to find a glut of NQTs in one area but a shortage in another. Similarly, if you only want to teach in a maintained school or a sixth form college or a religious school, you have again narrowed your options. If you are using an online appointment service, set your filters well outside your preferences. If you set a filter to only find jobs in schools that are 30 miles from your home, then a job 31 miles away will be excluded. Relax your filters and decide for yourself whether jobs which do not meet your ideal criteria should nevertheless be considered. When you visit a school, it is often quite different from the expectations you have from the application pack or the website. You may find that a visit to a school you are not enthusiastic about beforehand can change your preconceptions of it. Even so, you need to be sure that your first appointment is in an institution that can help you complete your NQT year.

Practise applying. Don't wait until you are applying to a school where you really want to work before you fill in and submit an application. Send off for or download application packs so that you can practise completing them. You will get better at applications and these are likely to become more impressive as you develop your approach.

Enquiring about a teaching post that is available

When you are enquiring about a teaching post that is available, you do not need to provide much information about yourself. The purpose of a job enquiry is get access to the application process. This may be a printed application pack; a number of files attached to an email; or a hyperlink so you can download the application pack from a website. You need to provide your contact information and name but any other information you give is likely to be ignored. Moreover, you may not know what the job specification involves at this stage and may give information that disqualifies you from the post.

The process of finding a teaching post is time-consuming and you can significantly reduce the time you have to spend by making good use of a word processor. Prepare a short standard 'letter' on a word processor (see Figure 6.4) and fill in the gaps each time you apply for a post. This could be copied into an email or printed and posted to the school. Don't forget to replace the data that changes with each enquiry, that is, the name of the school.

Whether your enquiry is by email or post, follow it up if you do not get a reply. The school may have decided from your letter that they do not wish to employ you. At this stage, if there are a large number of enquiries, an enquiry that includes mistakes in the spelling and grammar, or casual writing and text speak, or that addresses the Head Teacher inappropriately, may well have been discarded.

```
                                                        9 Main Street
                                                        Ulverston
                                                        Cumbria
                                                        BF23 8SX

                                                        01279-184373
                                                        alan@mainstreet.com

                                                        10/01/13

Dear Head Teacher,

I am interested in the post of ICT teacher at Manor Academy and would be grateful if you would
send me an application form and further details or direct me to where these can be found.

    Yours sincerely,

    Alan Johnson
```

Figure 6.4 Example of an enquiry letter

The application pack

An application pack is likely to include:

- a description of the post giving essential and desirable characteristics;
- a description of the department and the school;
- an application form;
- other information.

   Before applying, do your research. Read the application pack carefully and make notes if necessary. Look at the school's website and note points that may influence your application. Look for particular ways in which you could contribute to the school. For example, if the school gives sport a high profile, and you are a qualified coach, don't forget to mention this. Similarly, you may have ICT skills that could help the school develop its ICT curriculum, for example, if you have written Apps for the iPad, would this be something pupils would be interested in? If so, mention it. The school is more likely to be interested in ways you can contribute to the school rather than being a suitable launch pad for your career.
   Your application is likely to consist of:

- *A covering letter or email.* This should be short and to the point. State which teaching post you are applying for and what is included in your application.
- The *application form.* Fill this in electronically if possible. If you have to write it by hand, photocopy it, fill in the photocopy and then copy across to the actual application form. A common complaint is that application forms do not have sufficient space in some sections and have too much in others. This is likely to be a more serious problem if the form has to be handwritten. You can get round this by referring the reader to your CV for more details when you run out of space.

- Another common complaint is that applications forms ask for obscure information or information that is not known at the time of application. A common example is your teacher reference number which is also known as the DfES number; GTC number, etc. depending on when the application form was last redesigned. Currently, the DfE which was previously the DCSF writes to trainees before they complete their training giving them this number. Confused? This frequent change of name occurs because governments frequently change the name of the Department for Education.

- When you fill in the form, be clear, especially about your qualifications. Leaving out your degree classification or A-level grades will simply irritate someone who is assessing your application and this is likely to reduce your chance of being invited for interview. You will need to provide at least two references. Make sure these are likely to support your application. Good referees could be: your personal tutor; your mentor. A good academic reference and a good school-based reference could be very helpful in securing an interview.

- *A statement in support of your application.* This should be one or two pages at most. A longer statement is unlikely to be read. This is your opportunity to sell yourself. Start by stating clearly and briefly how you can contribute to the school. This should be specific to the post and the school. General statements saying how well organized and ambitious you are will not impress. Next, make sure that you demonstrate you meet all the essential characteristics and some of the desirable. However, it is not necessary to repeat what is evident elsewhere in your application. For example, you may have stated that you have a BSc honours degree in Interactive Multimedia in your list of qualifications and it is not necessary to mention this again.

- Your statement is very important and it must be coherent and readable. If you are filling in an application form by hand, it is worth printing out your statement and stapling it to the application form next to the space provided.

- Preparing a statement in support of your application is likely to be the most time-consuming part of preparing your application and it may be worth considering whether you can adapt a previously prepared statement to meet the requirements of this post. However, be careful. Avoid leaving in the name of the school you applied to previously and irrelevant sections of the statement that do not apply to the current post.

- *Your Curriculum Vitae (CV).* Applications for some posts require only a CV. In contrast, some posts specifically prohibit sending a CV, and if so, do not send it. Make sure your CV is brief and well presented. Your CV should be one or two pages at most and should provide basic information such as: your name and contact details; the names of the schools and universities you attended; your qualifications with grades, including work-related qualifications; membership of professional societies, such as MBCS; the name and address of your previous employers, with the dates you were employed and a brief description of what the post involved; and the names and contact details of two referees. You should consider including at the top of the first page, a small colour photograph showing you looking happy, smart and professional, and a very brief overall summary of your CV.

Check your application before you send it off to make sure there are no mistakes in your expression, spelling, punctuation and grammar. This is most important and you should consider asking a friend or tutor or employment consultant to check your application. Poor expression, spelling, punctuation or grammar in your application are unlikely to recommend you to a school.

Keep a copy of your entire application. Reading this again can be helpful preparation for the interview.

Follow up your application to ensure it has been received. Whether your application is by email or post, follow it up if you do not get a reply. Schools are busy places and internal communications can be complex and as a result, email and the post can be mislaid. A polite enquiry by email a few days after sending in your application is acceptable.

Your interview for a teaching post

You are likely to be invited for interview on a specific date. If more than one applicant is being interviewed, this is likely to be the only date when interviews can take place. If you do not attend on that day, you are effectively withdrawing your application.

Interviews for NQT posts usually take place over one day. In the morning, you may be taken on a tour of the school. This is an opportunity to ask questions. Although the school is interviewing you, you are also interviewing the school to find out if it is one in which you would wish to teach. Engage with your tour guide and make a careful note of matters you may wish to raise during the formal interview. During the tour, you may meet members of the ICT department and other teachers. It is very likely that whoever takes you on the tour will feed their impressions of you into the interview process.

You might also be expected to give a presentation or mini-lesson or complete a task during the morning. You may be informed of the topic in advance or on the day. If you teach a mini-lesson even if it is very short, do a formal lesson plan and give observers a copy.

Everyone who attends during the morning may expect to be interviewed in the afternoon. However, it is not uncommon for some candidates to be asked to leave while the remainder have a formal interview in the afternoon.

You may be interviewed by a panel of four or five, possibly including: the Head Teacher, the Head of Department, the Chair of Governors, an LA representative, a teacher representative and a pupil. You can expect some of these to have a special interest in ICT. They may sit in a semicircle in front of you and ask you questions. Often, every candidate is asked the same questions so talking to other candidates before you are interviewed could give you time to think, but revealing too much after your interview could be a competitive disadvantage. You might find it useful to have a pen and paper handy to take brief notes during the interview.

You should prepare thoroughly for the interview. Make sure you know where the school is and can get there on time. Check out your travel plans carefully. Read your application again and take a copy with you. Make sure you are well presented at interview. Teachers are expected to be clean and dress professionally. Take evidence of your qualifications and show off what you are proud of, for example, your assignments; a curriculum package with resources and pupils' assessed work; a profile of your subject knowledge; and your mentors' lesson observations and other feedback. If you have an eportfolio, take it with you and show the interview panel perhaps on a laptop or tablet computer. Not many applicants will have a complete eportfolio with them. Don't forget basic equipment such as: pens, a notepad, a laptop, etc. A whiteboard pen may be useful and cables to connect your laptop may be needed.

How will the school let you know the outcome? This is often done by asking everyone who is interviewed in the afternoon to stay behind until a decision is made and communicated to the successful candidate. This has the advantage that other applicants can have feedback immediately and the appointment process is completed on the day. It has the disadvantage that the successful candidate may decline the offer and all the other candidates will be aware that they are not the first choice. Another approach is to telephone candidates later in the day.

Likely questions

Before the interview, prepare a list of likely questions and decide how you will answer these. Your answers should relate to the post you have applied for. You should expect questions about current issues in education generally and related to ICT in secondary schools. You could prepare by reading the *TES*. Write a list of the obvious questions, for example: 'Describe your best lesson'; and 'What is your approach to classroom and behaviour management?' Make sure that you are prepared for questions about your strengths and weaknesses and make them work for you. For example, your main weakness may be an over-fondness for chocolates but 'My main weakness is that I am too conscientious and prepare in too much detail' may be more appreciated by the interview panel. At the end of the interview, you are likely to be asked if you have any more questions. Prepare one or two uncontroversial questions that you can ask if necessary. A question such as: 'I've brought samples of my work, would you like to see them?' may be very productive. There are many extensive lists of such questions which you can find by typing 'teacher interview questions and answers' into a search engine.

Activity

Prepare a list of questions you are likely to be asked at interview and decide how you will answer them.

Summary

- Training to teach means achieving Qualified Teacher Status (QTS).
- Prepare yourself before applying for teacher training. Make sure:

   o You are well qualified (except for undergraduates, at a minimum: an honours degree at 2:2 or above in an ICT-related subject from a British university, and GCSE Mathematics and English at grade C or above, or equivalents).
   o You are highly committed to a career in teaching and have experience in a secondary school observing ICT teachers at work.
   o You can demonstrate that you will be a responsible employee.
   o You are familiar with the ICT curriculum in schools.

- There are different types of teacher training. The main routes to achieving QTS are: postgraduate (PGCE and SCITT); undergraduate; employment-based (GTP and Teach First); and Troops to Teachers.

- You can train to teach ICT and Computer Science only, or combine these with another subject.
- Applying for teacher training is usually online (for web addresses, see Table 6.1).
- After you have applied, you have to pass the TA's online tests in literacy and numeracy.
- Interviews usually take place over one day and can include:

  o an interview with a university lecturer and a school teacher;
  o making a presentation to a group of applicants and an observer;
  o checking your original qualification certificates;
  o applying for a Criminal Records Bureau (CRB) check.

- Training to be an ICT and Computer Science teacher involves:

  o the general professional duties and responsibilities of a teacher;
  o ICT and Computing subject studies, that is, pedagogy and the curriculum;
  o ICT and Computing subject knowledge, skills and understanding.

- When you apply for a teaching post:

  o Look for adverts in a range of different media, especially websites: the *TES*; LAs; recruitment agencies (for web addresses, see Table 6.1); and contact to individual schools.
  o Be flexible about the schools you consider.
  o Practise applying for jobs.

- Information about the post is likely to include:

  o a description of the post giving essential and desirable characteristics;
  o a description of the department and the school;
  o an application form.

- Your application is likely to consist of:

  o a covering letter or email;
  o the application form;
  o a statement in support of your application;
  o your Curriculum Vitae (CV).

- Interviews for first posts usually take place over one day and might include:

  o a tour of the school;
  o meeting members of the ICT department and other teachers;
  o giving a presentation or mini-lesson or completing a task;
  o a formal interview in the afternoon.

- Before the interview, prepare a list of likely questions and decide how you will answer them.

Further reading

Crawford, R.A. (2010) *Edexcel IGCSE ICT*, Harlow: Pearson.
Denby, N. (ed.) (2012) *Training to Teach*, London: Sage.
NUT (2012) *First Post*, available at: http://www.teachers.org.uk (accessed 16 February 2012).

Chapter 7

Your career

Introduction

This chapter follows on from Chapter 6 'Training to teach ICT' and addresses the concerns of NQTs and considers their terms and conditions during the induction year. A helpful format for organizing the wealth of resources that teachers produce is suggested so that this becomes a good evidence base to demonstrate achievement of the teaching standards. The characteristics of an effective teacher are described from the different viewpoints of teachers and pupils. Ways to prepare for promotion are suggested and there is consideration of ways to manage ICT in secondary schools.

Where should I start my career?

NQTs are often concerned about whether their first teaching post is an appropriate starting point for their career. It is likely that at any point in your career, your prior experience will influence what you want to do and can realistically expect to do in the immediate future. For example, if your first teaching post was mainly teaching A-level Computing and then you applied for a teaching post where you would mainly teach pupils with severe SEN, in competition with others with more experience of teaching SEN, you might be less likely to be successful. Prospective employers might wonder why you wanted to make such a dramatic change in the focus of your work and question whether you would already have the appropriate skills. Similarly, if you wanted to move from the maintained sector to the independent sector or vice versa, prospective employers might want to know whether you appreciated what this change entails.

When applying for a post, you should always show how you have prepared yourself for it. For example, if you want to move from teaching A-level Computing to teaching SEN pupils, if you have some special interest, have worked with pupils with SEN as a volunteer and have done related training, this would improve your prospects. Similarly, if you work mainly with SEN pupils and want to teach A-level Computing, you could improve your prospects by, for example, having good ICT/Computing qualifications and technical experience, and working as an A-level examiner for Computing for an Awarding Organization.

Think about your long-term ambitions but also bear in mind that it is not unlikely that you will change your ambitions as you gain more experience. It is not unusual for NQTs to want to be an outstanding teacher and to focus on this throughout their induction with the intention of being a classroom teacher throughout their careers. However, many quickly realize that more control over the curriculum that is taught and the context in which it is taught can help them provide a better experience for pupils and more professional satisfaction. This may lead to a willingness and a desire to take on more responsibility. It is not unusual to move from NQT to Head of ICT within five to ten years.

Activity

Discuss with others:

- What are your long-term ambitions?
- Does the job you are applying for fit in with your long-term ambitions?
- What do you need to do to prepare yourself for your next post?

Induction

As a newly qualified teacher (NQT) you must complete induction so that you can be employed as a fully qualified teacher in the maintained sector. The terms and conditions of employment for NQTs during the induction year are different from those of other teachers and tend to change from time to time. You should check out the details given below on the relevant websites.

Most trainees complete their initial teacher training (ITT) and begin teaching in a full-time post at the start of the next academic year. Induction can be full-time for one year or part-time (pro rata). Periods of teaching that count towards induction must be at least one term in duration in institutions with an academic year of three terms. You have only one chance to complete induction and you are not permitted to repeat it.

You should avoid delaying your induction even though there is no set time limit for starting an induction period. It is prudent to complete induction at the earliest opportunity after you have completed a programme of ITT and achieved QTS. For example, it would be prudent to complete induction before teaching overseas. You may be eager to travel the world following your training but when you return and want to start your induction, you will be in competition with those who have just completed their training and this will be seen as more up-to-date by prospective employers.

Before accepting a teaching post, always check whether statutory induction is possible. Some schools offer induction but some do not. For example, schools and colleges that have failed a recent Ofsted inspection cannot offer induction and there are British schools overseas which can offer induction but some do not. Even so, there is no legal requirement to complete induction if you intend to work only in an independent school, academy, free school, or in further education (FE) even though it is possible to do your induction in some of these institutions.

If you are not appointed to a teaching post immediately following your ITT, you can work as a supply teacher for five years following the date when you first began supply teaching. You do not have to do all your induction in the same school or college but short-term supply teaching contracts of less than one term do not count towards induction. You can complete your induction part-time while working as a supply teacher.

Induction is a three-term period usually completed in a single school year. You can only begin induction when you have gained qualified teacher status (QTS). During induction you can expect:

- a 10 per cent reduction in your teaching timetable. This is in addition to your statutory 10 per cent planning, preparation and assessment time.
- an induction tutor who has QTS;
- a range of activities and tasks that enable you to complete the Teachers' Standards;
- to regularly teach the same classes;
- to teach the age range and subjects you were employed to teach;
- not to regularly encounter discipline problems that are unreasonably demanding;
- a personalized programme of training and support and professional dialogue that extends what you have already learnt during ITT;
- to take part in staff training activities where appropriate;
- to observe experienced teachers to help you develop good practice;
- a timetable of observations, reviews and assessment meetings;
- to be observed and receive feedback;
- assessment against the Teachers' Standards.

(DfE, 2012c)

The programme of training and support is personalized to help you develop. This is unique to each NQT and is designed to help you become an effective teacher and underpin your development throughout your career. It will be based on your action plan for your future development that you produce towards the end of your ITT which is also known as the career entry and development profile (CEDP). You should play an active part in identifying which aspects of your work you need to improve; discuss these with your mentors; decide how you will go about making improvements; and regularly evaluate your progress. This cycle of reflection, development and self-evaluation should be familiar to you from ITT. A good induction programme should provide you with opportunities to become a better teacher and show your potential for the future.

Support from an effective mentor is important throughout induction. If your mentor has good skills, knowledge and expertise as a teacher, mentor and assessor, and you have a good relationship which facilitates honest and robust communication and listen carefully to the advice you are given, then you are likely to know what you need to do to improve (Denby, 2012).

The programme of training and support should focus on the Teachers' Standards as you will be assessed against these. There are two parts to the standards: (1) Teaching; and (2) Personal and Professional Conduct. During training you should refer to the standards and make sure that you are able to produce evidence that you have met requirements. If you have developed a comprehensive portfolio of evidence during ITT, this could be a useful starting point for building a comprehensive evidence base that will be developed throughout your teaching career.

How you organize the evidence that you have met the Teachers' Standards should be discussed with your mentor. You could simply collect evidence that you have met each section of the standards, for example, you could collect evidence against Part 1, Section 4, that you can 'Plan and teach well-structured lessons'. This approach will help you check that you have sufficient evidence for each section of the standards and could help you focus on those aspects that you find more difficult. However, it is likely that you will have to accumulate this evidence separately from the way you organize your teaching and other resources. Annotate your evidence so that is clear to your assessors what the evidence proves.

Another approach is to organize the evidence in a way that supports your teaching and self-development. Often this is best done electronically as most teaching resources are now available in this way. You may have to scan those documents that are only available on paper.

A folder structure similar to Figure 7.1 could help you organize your work electronically and produce an eportfolio. When evidence is organized in this way, it is easy to

---

Your eportfolio
index.html – a web page giving access to the folders
standards.html – a web page giving access to evidence for each of the standards
user_guide.doc

Teaching folder
- Timetable
- Year 7
  - Class 7M
      Register
      Seating plan
      Record of assessments
      120321 Lesson
        Lesson plan
        Resources for the lesson
        Others' observations of the lesson
        Self-evaluation
        Examples of pupils' work (at different levels of ability)
      120328 Lesson
        Lesson plan
        Resources for the lesson
        Others' observations of the lesson
        Self-evaluation
        Examples of pupils' work (at different levels of ability)
- Year 8, etc.

Subject folder
- A collection of subject content resources in folders with names relating to the software used.
- A personal audit of subject knowledge against the different specifications taught, for example, I/GCSE ICT; Cambridge Nationals; A-level; etc.

Professional folder
- Curriculum Vitae
- Detailed record of the roles and the contexts in which you work, for example:
  - ✓ A record of all meetings between you and your mentor and others, whether formal or informal.
  - ✓ Observations made of you by others.
  - ✓ Your self-evaluations.
  - ✓ Records of your assessments with feedback from your mentors and others.
- Record of continuing professional development activities and events, for example:
  - ✓ Observation by you of others.
  - ✓ Training activities you participate in whether in school or elsewhere.

Figure 7.1 Structure of folders and files for an eportfolio

update it. You do this as a part of your ongoing work as you plan, teach and evaluate lessons; organize your resources and engage with your self-development. However, it is not always easy for others to access an eportfolio.

Your assessors may find it helpful if you use your ICT skills to provide easy access for them to your eportfolio. This could be done through a front end which is a web page (index.html) that provides hyperlinks to the Teaching, Subject and Professional Folders. In addition, you could provide a web page which replicates the organization of the Teachers' Standards and hyperlinks to the evidence for each standard (standards.html).

Don't forget to annotate the evidence so it is clear why it is included. You could do this using features such as tracking, comments, sticky notes, etc. which are found in most software. Don't forget to back up your eportfolio.

During induction you must achieve the Teachers' Standards and become an effective teacher. The standards apply to the majority of teachers throughout their careers. They describe the minimum expectations of teachers after they have been awarded QTS at the end of their training. They should be used to plan your development and assess your ongoing performance. You use the standards for self-assessment and self-evaluation of your progress and your mentors use the same standards to support and assess you.

Head teachers or other appraisers will assess you against the Teachers' Standards. This assessment takes into account what can reasonably be expected of an NQT during induction. As your career develops, you will be assessed against the same standards but more will be expected of you as you become more experienced. You will be expected to extend the depth and breadth of your knowledge, skill and understanding in relation to your professional roles and the contexts in which you work. Assessment against the Teachers' Standards is a part of the appraisal arrangements in many schools.

Induction is assessed across the equivalent of three full school terms, with assessment at the end of each term. Towards the end of each term, you should meet with your induction tutor or the head teacher for a formal observation and a discussion of your progress in relation to the Teachers' Standards. After each of the first two meetings, the head teacher reports to an appropriate body, for example: the Local Authority; the Independent Schools Council Teacher Induction Panel (ISCTIP); or a teaching school and records your progress towards meeting the standards. In addition, following the assessment at the end of your third term, the head teacher makes a recommendation about whether you have met all the Teachers' Standards. The appropriate body will decide whether you have met the requirements and successfully completed the induction period.

If you are unsuccessful because you do not meet requirements at the end of the third term, you have the right of appeal. However, if this assessment is upheld, you will not be allowed to repeat induction. You retain QTS but you are not allowed to work as a teacher in a maintained school.

Case study: The induction year, by Rebecca West, NQT

When you have been appointed to a teaching post, beginning at the start of the school year, give serious thought to spending some time in your new school in the weeks after you have finished your training and before the end of the summer term. This is invaluable. You can meet pupils, check out your teaching room (if you are lucky enough to have one), meet your colleagues and start planning for next year.

The first term is a challenge: new job, new school and the pupils are your responsibility. It's very easy to become insular in the first term: head down; trying to do everything and do it brilliantly; working long hours; fretting that you haven't got all the class behaving well; and feeling a little harassed. If you feel overwhelmed, talk to your mentor and other colleagues and get things in perspective. Remember all the successes you are having.

Establish behaviour management routines and boundaries at the start of the school year and persist with them. By Christmas younger pupils should be familiar with your routines but some older pupils may take longer. Eventually most will get tired of detention, litter duty and phone calls home. Remember that some pupils will not share your enthusiasm for ICT so try to work with them in other ways (for example, the school play; a sports club) as this may help to build relationships. Schools keep significant and detailed data about their students and this will also help you understand your pupils. Don't forget to praise pupils when they do something well–it really works! However, it is important to realize that some pupils might not respond. This could be for many reasons including external factors outside your control. So set your routines and boundaries, keep to them, aim to be fair and reasonable and give your pupils an interesting and supportive learning experience. If you are doing all of this, you are doing well!

As an NQT, you will need to keep a file of evidence to show you are meeting the teaching standards. Put all your evidence into a folder (electronic or paper) and review progress against the standards every month. This way you stay up-to-date and you can clearly see your progress.

Going into final term, you will feel much more confident. All the best with your teaching career; you are going to love it!

Activity

Check out the terms and conditions of service for NQTs on: http://www.education.gov.uk/schools/leadership/deployingstaff/b0066959/induction-newly-qualified-teachers (accessed 30 March 2012).

Becoming an effective teacher

Teachers really do make a difference. Within their classrooms, effective teachers create learning environments which foster pupil progress by deploying their teaching skills as well as a wide range of professional characteristics. Outstanding teachers create an excellent classroom climate and achieve superior pupil progress largely by displaying more professional characteristics at higher levels of sophistication within a very structured learning environment.

(Hay McBer, 2000, para 1.1.9)

Becoming an effective teacher means meeting the Teachers' Standards at an appropriate level for the stage of your career you are at and this is important if you are to make progress in your career. However, the standards which apply are altered by different governments and tend to reflect the political concerns of the moment. Being an effective teacher is related to the context in which you work and the different viewpoints of those who are describing your effectiveness. Researchers, teacher trainers, teachers, pupils and others tend to emphasize different characteristics from their different viewpoints.

From the viewpoint of researchers, teacher trainers, and teachers, an effective teacher should do the following (based on Crawford, 2012; Hay McBer, 2000; TTA, 1996):

- Have a professional manner and appearance.
- Maintain good working relationships with colleagues and pupils. Teaching is a cooperative, collaborative, team activity and an appreciation and acceptance of others' viewpoints are essential for effective team work and managing pupils.
- Be present, punctual, prepared. If you are not present, a colleague may have to do your teaching and they will not necessarily welcome this especially if you are absent frequently and they have planned to do other work. If you have not left your lesson plans and resources for the substitute teacher to use, this will impact on pupils' learning and leave the substitute teacher to sort out what needs to be done at short notice. If possible, always arrive early whether this is at the start of school or for each lesson. If you are not on time for a lesson, your pupils will be waiting for you, and may not be well behaved. This disorder may have to be controlled by others who have their own classes to teach. Forward planning is a very important aspect of teaching. Lesson plans should be prepared well in advance and, if required, sent to mentors, leaving sufficient time for them to feed back to you on the strengths and weakness of your planning so that you can review it. As a result, lack of forward planning can lead to less effective lessons.
- Create a secure, welcoming classroom climate.
- Be enthusiastic, interesting and engaged. You may not always be so, but if you make the effort, you will more often appear to be so.
- Be calm and consistent.
- Be clear what is expected. It is often helpful to pupils if you display the learning objectives throughout the lesson. In addition, when you give pupils instructions, you should not expect them to understand what they have to do immediately. Patiently read the instructions, display the instructions, and make them available for as long as pupils are working on the relevant tasks, and do this repeatedly.
- Maintain behaviour for learning, that is, an orderly classroom where pupils are well behaved and make progress with their learning. Ensure that you continue to develop your behaviour management (BM) techniques so that you understand what needs to be done to improve behaviour in your classes. Remember that the causes of inappropriate behaviour may be carried over from home, friends or other teachers' classes. However, your BM strategies should help you manage inappropriate behaviour, whatever the reasons for it.
- Support and encourage pupils and expect them to participate in the lesson. Involve pupils throughout the lesson. Questioning which uses pupils' answers to build understanding engages pupils; getting a pupil to demonstrate how to use software interests others; and using mini-whiteboards for feedback ensures that all pupils participate.
- Be fair and reasonable. You should not treat some pupils more favourably than others.

- Promote inclusion and differentiation. Everyone, whatever their background or barriers to learning, should be valued and helped to learn. Provide differentiated worksheets and avoid negative attitudes.
- Have high expectations but be realistic so that you expect the best from pupils whatever their level of ability.
- Practise assessment for learning (AfL). AfL will help you judge pupils' progress, and help pupils know what they know and what they do not know so that they can focus their learning and learn more efficiently and effectively. Self-assessment will help pupils develop the ability to learn independently and learn more quickly and efficiently; and peer assessment will help increase pupils' understanding of the assessment process.
- Develop a portfolio of teaching techniques and skills, and an understanding of how pupils learn. This will introduce variety into your lessons and make them more interesting.
- Demonstrate a good understanding of the subject at the level being taught. As an ICT teacher, you may be asked questions that you do not immediately know the answer to. Hardware and software are complex and extensive and it is unlikely that you will be familiar with all the questions pupils will ask. Be prepared to research these and direct pupils to a solution. You may find it helpful to have a strategy such as 3b4me. That is, before asking the teacher: try to work it out yourself; use online help; and ask a friend.
- Model those characteristics you expect of pupils. For example, if you insist that boys tuck their shirts into their trousers, you should not wear your shirt differently unless you can justify this with obvious fairness. Similarly, if you expect pupils to allow for occasional mishaps such as a temporary lack of Internet access, it will seem unreasonable if you do not make similar allowances for pupils if they do not always meet your expectations due to unforeseen events.
- Do all the routine tasks expected. Complete all the documentation and administration requested; respond to email promptly; and attend all meetings and parents' evenings.
- Do more than the minimum. For example, get involved in whole school activities beyond teaching ICT. If you can offer an extracurricular activity you will get to know colleagues and pupils in other settings. The range of possible extracurricular activities is wide: dance, beauty, outdoor pursuits, gym, football, etc.
- Manage time effectively. You are expected to achieve a good deal and to do this well, you need to make good use of a calendar or similar to plan how you will spend your time. Do not rely on your memory but enter appointments in your calendar.
- Uphold high standards of personal behaviour and ethics.
- Listen to advice and act on it as soon as possible. If you do not do this, your mentor will feel you are not making sufficient progress and not listening. If you do not respond to advice you should be able to explain why, and your unsatisfactory personal time management is not a reasonable explanation.

If you aspire to become an outstanding teacher, it is helpful to know how Ofsted describe outstanding teaching:

Teaching is at least good and much is outstanding, with the result that the pupils are making exceptional progress. It is highly effective in inspiring pupils and ensuring that they learn extremely well. Excellent subject knowledge is applied consistently to challenge and inspire pupils. Resources, including new technology, make a marked contribution to the quality of learning, as does the precisely targeted support provided by other adults. Teachers and other adults are acutely aware of their pupils' capabilities and of their prior learning and understanding, and plan very effectively to build on these. Marking and dialogue between teachers, other adults and pupils are consistently of a very high quality. Pupils understand in detail how to improve their work and are consistently supported in doing so. Teachers systematically and effectively check pupils' understanding throughout lessons, anticipating where they may need to intervene and doing so with striking impact on the quality of learning.

(Ofsted, 2010, p. 32)

In addition, it is also useful to understand pupils' viewpoints. It is interesting that pupils tend to emphasize personal characteristics. Pupils tend believe that a good teacher has the following characteristics (Hay McBer, 2000, p. 3):

- is kind;
- is generous;
- listens to you;
- encourages you;
- has faith in you;
- keeps confidences;
- likes teaching children;
- likes teaching their subject;
- takes time to explain things;
- helps you when you're stuck;
- tells you how you are doing;
- allows you to have your say;
- doesn't give up on you;
- cares for your opinion;
- makes you feel clever;
- treats people equally;
- stands up for you;
- makes allowances;
- tells the truth;
- is forgiving.

Becoming an outstanding teacher is demanding. It is a considerable but worthwhile challenge that contributes considerably to individual development and social welfare and brings many personal, professional and financial rewards. However, it is important to manage your time effectively so that you do not neglect your personal, domestic and social life. 'All work and no play...'? Being dull is not a characteristic of an effective teacher.

Activity

- From the viewpoint of the Teachers' Standards, consider what you need to do to become:

  o   an effective teacher;
  o   an outstanding teacher.
  o   Next consider what you need to do from the viewpoint of Ofsted.
  o   Next consider what you need to do from the viewpoint of your pupils.
  o   Are there differences in what is expected of you?

Preparing for promotion

If you are striving to become an outstanding teacher and are making good progress, you are already making good preparation for promotion. You should continue improving your teaching and your subject knowledge, skills and understanding. You should continue to reflect on your performance; engaging in self-evaluation; setting yourself demanding targets; and reviewing your progress regularly.

In addition, it may be helpful when planning your career to consider the areas of professional practice that contribute most to developing good teaching. These include (Coates, 2011, pp. 50, 52):

- coaching and mentoring (including sharing good practice);
- innovation and creativity;
- engagement with research;
- leading change and the development of innovative practice;
- higher level communication skills;
- data analysis;
- achievement of higher-level qualifications;
- enhanced use of ICT;
- the ability to be creative and innovative;
- cross-curricular learning;
- contributing to policy development.

It is important to take opportunities when these are offered as they may not be offered again. When you are offered further responsibility, or training or some other opportunity, try to say 'yes', not 'no' or 'maybe'. Such opportunities might range from running extra support sessions for I/GCSE ICT candidates to taking responsibility for the KS3 ICT curriculum. Even so, don't forget that you will be committing your time and check that what you undertake can be fitted within your time management schedule and that your personal, domestic and social life survives. It may be acceptable to you to put your social life on hold for a short time but doing this in the longer term will not help your mental health and you are likely to be less robust when there are difficulties. Teachers who neglect their personal and domestic responsibilities risk relationship difficulties, depression, divorce and suicide (Knowsley, 2012). Make sure you don't get overwhelmed by the demands of your career. Try to achieve a good work–life balance.

You may find waiting for opportunities tedious and decide to be more proactive. Look for opportunities and suggest ways forward for you, the ICT department and the school. Self-evaluate; set yourself demanding targets; and review your progress regularly as this will help you identify the many ways in which you can improve your own performance but you may find your efforts more widely appreciated if you look beyond your own self-development and consider how you can contribute to the wider community. Could you start an extra-curricular club or help with an existing club? This could be based on your current skills or provide an opportunity for you to develop new skills. Does the department need someone to organize the curriculum and teaching resources for pupils with EAL? Is there some wider need within the school or community? This does not have to be ICT-related. ICT teachers often have surprising talents which are not related to their subject teaching, such as, dance, beauty, drama and sport.

Find a mentor and share your ambitions; discuss what needs doing and ask for advice. This could be your induction tutor or could be a less formal arrangement. Mentors do not always have to know they are mentors: talk to a friend or colleague and ask for advice. You will quickly find which teachers you can ask for advice and who has particular expertise. A group of NQTs and other teachers could informally mentor each other. You could read Ofsted reports for your school and for other schools and discuss these. Working together preparing for your next inspection can help you improve and help you contribute to general improvement. Discussion with appropriate others will help you identify what needs to be done and whether there are initiatives that would contribute to school improvement. However, don't be too pushy or insist too hard; be assertive and polite and acknowledge others' contributions.

Networking is a good source of ideas and you may identify opportunities that are not available in your own school. You can network at Local Authority training days; by doing short courses; by attending the National College for School Leadership (NCSL) annual conference; by talking to parents and other stakeholders; by working as an examiner for an Awarding Organization, and online through social networking sites such as Twitter, Facebook, LinkedIn (http://uk.linkedin.com/) and the TES forums (http://www.tes.co.uk/).

Continuing professional development (CPD), education and training are good ways of preparing for leadership. Engaging with a range of learning opportunities will enhance your Curriculum Vitae and your chances of success. You could consider preparing for opportunities to develop new and interesting aspects of the ICT curriculum through personal study and short courses that enhance your technical expertise. Many potential teaching resources are free. For example:

- You could download Scratch (http://info.scratch.mit.edu/) and learn to program games using online resources for teaching and learning (http://learnscratch.org) before introducing games programming into the curriculum.
- Other games construction programs can also be downloaded and there are online resources for teaching, for example, GameMaker (http://www.yoyogames.com/gamemaker/); and Kodu Games Lab (http://www.microsoft.com/download/en/details.aspx?id=10056).
- There are online tutorials that will help you develop skills in programming in Visual Basic or variants (http://www.microsoft.com/visualstudio/en-us/products/2010-editions/express).

- You can download Visual Studio Express for the Windows Phone and develop mobile apps (http://www.microsoft.com/visualstudio/en-us/products/2010-editions/windows-phone-developer-tools).
- More formally, the IT Essentials course available through the CISCO Academy (http://cisco.netacad.net) provides an introduction to the computer hardware and software skills needed by ICT professionals. Students who complete the course will be able to describe the internal components of a computer, assemble a computer system, install an operating system, and troubleshoot using system tools and diagnostic software.

You could train others as well as yourself: engage in CPD, develop skills, and then help others develop those skills. Innovate, encourage others to take over, and then innovate again. You may have completed your degree relatively recently so that you may have a better knowledge of more recent technologies than many of your colleagues in the ICT department. There are almost always opportunities to train colleagues from other subject departments in the latest ICT software. Recently areas where training has been helpful are: animation in Flash; and how to use the school's VLE more effectively.

Safeguarding is an important issue in schools and there is concern for the safety of young people using the Internet, especially social networking sites. This is an area where you could make use of your advanced ICT knowledge, skills and understanding, and your understanding of young people and schools. You could train as a CEOPS (Child Exploitation and Online Protection Centre) ambassador for your school. This prepares you for talking to pupils, parents and other teachers about the possible dangers for young people and ways they can protect themselves (https://www.thinkuknow.co.uk/Teachers/).

You could develop opportunities for personal development through organizations such as the army cadets (http://armycadets.com/) and programmes such as Duke of Edinburgh's Award (http://www.dofe.org/). There are over 47,000 army cadets in almost 1,700 detachments throughout the UK and these provide opportunities for young people to take part in activities such as rock climbing, mountain biking and archery. Training is provided for adult volunteers and can lead to qualifications accredited by St John's Ambulance, Mountain Leadership training or the Duke of Edinburgh's Award (DofE). The DofE is a balanced programme for young people that develops the whole person and can include a wide range of activities and skills, and participation can help applicants applying through UCAS to UK universities.

You may find that continuing with your education will help your ambitions. Greater understanding of education and better ICT subject knowledge could help your ambitions. Studying for a Master's degree that builds on your first degree and your ITT will help increase the breadth and depth of your understanding of the education system and/or your subject. There are many options and you should consider a further degree that enhances your current qualifications and interests you. Studying for a Master's degree part-time is very hard work especially if you are also working full-time and in your induction year. Some Master's degrees will accredit some or all of the Master's level modules that are included in some ITT courses; and some can be studied by distance learning and are mainly online courses, whereas others require attendance ranging from one or two nights a week to occasional Saturdays. The topics that can be studied range from ICT-related Master's degrees to Master's degrees in Education, and there are hybrids that include elements of both ICT and education. With the growth of federations of schools it is not unlikely that leaders of these very large organizations would benefit from studying for an MBA or similar. You should check carefully that the degree you enrol for suits your requirements.

As examples, you could study for the following qualifications:

- MSc Information Technology at Anglia Ruskin University (http://www.rdi.co.uk/it-telecomms-pathway/60-msc-information-technology.html). This is an online distance learning course normally studied over a 24-month period. It is designed for Computing graduates to enable them to specialize in web development and computer networks. You will plan, manage and execute a large-scale IT project.
- MA Education with the Open University (http://www3.open.ac.uk/study/postgraduate/qualification/f01.htm). This is an online distance learning course. You study three modules and you complete the qualification within a maximum of six years. There is one compulsory module: Educational enquiry; and two optional modules.
- MSc Multimedia and E-learning at the University of Huddersfield (http://www.hud.ac.uk/courses/2012-13/part-time/postgraduate/multimedia-and-e-learning-msc/). This course can be studied full-time in one year or part-time in up to six years. All teaching is on Saturday or online so you can complete the course and work. The course helps you use, research and manage multimedia and e-learning effectively.
- MBA at Bradford University (http://www.rdi.co.uk/management-pathway/40-mba.html. You can vary the speed of progression through the programme to suit your own needs. Distance learning students usually study two modules every three months.
- The National Professional Qualification for Headship (NPQH) at the National College for School Leadership (NCSL) (www.nationalcollege.org.uk). This course is for school and academy leaders and those who aspire to be head teachers. It is modular and based on Master's level criteria. There are three essential modules covering core leadership knowledge, skills and qualities; and two elective modules.
- The Doctor of Education (EdD), for example, the EdD at Leeds University (http://www.education.leeds.ac.uk/postgraduate/research-postgraduates/edd). This can be studied full-time in up to four years or part-time in up to seven years. The EdD is for those who wish to become researching professional teachers. There is a programme of taught modules and a substantial research thesis. The course should help you carry out research in your own school. Such research helps schools adapt custom and practice and leads to school improvement.

You may need to consider whether you want to continue teaching ICT in the classroom or progress your career in other directions. Many experienced ICT teachers take on more responsibility for whole school and pastoral issues and this can lead to less ICT subject teaching. There are many pastoral roles available, such as primary school liaison; assistant or head of house; and assistant or head of year. Those teachers who are promoted within the ICT department may find that, having become HoD ICT, further promotion tends to lead to less responsibility for the subject of ICT and that they teach the subject less if promoted beyond this into an Assistant Head or Deputy Head or Head Teacher role. In addition, it is not uncommon for teachers to move into related sectors such as: teacher training in schools or Higher Education; Local Authorities; Ofsted or an inspection agency; and educational publishing. Employment in these sectors often requires substantial experience teaching in secondary schools but does not involve further direct teaching of pupils in the classroom.

The government intends to introduce the 'Master Teacher Standard' for those wishing to focus predominantly on classroom teaching. The Master Teacher Standard does not identify specific roles and tasks but shows how an outstanding teacher, working across the full breadth of the Teachers' Standards, might demonstrate consistently excellent practice. It recognizes that although Master Teachers may take on additional management and leadership responsibilities, they should be recognized principally for the excellence of their teaching and there is no presumption that they will move outside the classroom. The Master Teacher standard recognizes truly excellent teachers and provides a focal point for all good teachers to plan their professional and career development. The Master Teacher Standard was proposed by the government in December 2011 and replaces the previous Post-Threshold, Excellent Teacher and Advanced Skills Teacher grades. The Master Teacher Standard builds on the foundations of the Teachers' Standards introduced from September 2012.

The Master Teacher Standard describes a clear set of characteristics for high-performing teachers. They include:

- Deep and extensive knowledge of their specialism, going beyond the set programmes they teach.
- Command of the classroom, skilfully leading, encouraging and extending pupils. They will have the respect of both pupils and parents.
- Meticulous planning and organization to ensure pupils are well prepared for all forms of assessment.
- The class is one in which pupils feel welcome and valued. There is a stimulating culture of scholarship alongside a sense of mutual respect and good manners. The Master Teacher has an excellent rapport with classes and with individual pupils.
- They are highly regarded by colleagues, who want to learn from them. They play a role in the development of school policies and they engage with professional networks beyond the school.

You may need to investigate how much you will be paid when you achieve the promotion you seek. Teaching is generally regarded as a worthwhile and socially useful occupation. Even so, teachers have practical needs and families. At the time of writing there is a pay freeze as a part of austerity measures introduced by the UK government. In addition, academies and independent schools and some other schools do not have to pay national rates, and the government has stated its intention to move away from national salary scales to more local arrangements. You should carefully check how much you will be paid and the conditions under which this will be increased.

National salary rates from September 2011 were:

- Qualified teachers: £21,588 (bottom of scale in England and Wales) to £36,387 (top of scale, inner London)
- Post threshold: £34,181–£45,000
- Excellent teachers: £39,697–£60,993

- ASTs: £37,461–£64,036
- Head Teachers and Deputy Head Teachers: £42,379–£112,181.

It is intended that the Master Teacher Standard will replace Post-Threshold, Excellent Teacher and AST grades; however, at the time of writing, it is not known whether this will be linked to pay.

Managing ICT in secondary schools

The effectiveness of the ways in which ICT is delivered in English secondary schools may be influenced by different approaches to educational management. Traditional departmental management roles and organizational structures are unlikely to be effective as these are too restrictive (Owen, 1992).

In most English secondary schools, teachers are responsible to heads of department (middle management), who are answerable to senior managers. In general, the head of the mathematics department, for example, will have stable expectations regarding the amount of time that will be allocated to teaching mathematics each week; will produce programmes of work that enable the statutory curriculum or external examination syllabuses to be covered within the time available; will be allocated modest but consistent funds each year for spending on resources for teaching and learning; will allocate responsibilities for teaching particular classes to the minority of the school staff who are specialist teachers of mathematics; and will generally, though not entirely, ignore such matters in other subject departments, assuming that they are the responsibility of another head of department. Is such a relatively closed model of the scope of middle management responsibilities available to the HoD ICT, or are there factors that should result in the greater involvement of senior management?

Schools that assume that ICT can be implemented through traditional models of departmental management will not make the best use of ICT throughout the school (ibid.). Curriculum models for ICT in English secondary schools can be described as: (1) discrete ICT, where ICT appears in the school timetable, and is treated as a discrete subject similar to Mathematics; (2) cross-curricular ICT, where ICT is delivered entirely through the medium of other subjects, and the subject of ICT does not appear in the school timetable; and (3) hybrids of discrete and cross-curricular ICT (Crawford, 1997). The majority of English secondary schools deliver ICT as a hybrid and the deployment of ICT hardware and software is more often throughout the whole school rather than only within the ICT department. Consequently, pupils' experience of ICT is not limited to lessons delivered by a small number of ICT specialist teachers working within an ICT department, and there is unlikely to be a consistent experience of ICT for each pupil within or between schools. This contrasts markedly with the relative consistency and reliability of provision for well-established subjects, such as Mathematics.

ICT in secondary schools extends across traditional departmental boundaries, and, consequently, effective management of it is more appropriately the responsibility of senior management. Funding for the provision of ICT resources is likely to be of particular concern because of its magnitude in relation to the total school budget for teaching and learning resources. As there is unlikely to be ample finance, decisions will be made that prioritize spending, and as a result, what can be done is determined. In general, it is senior management that decides, or at least has a very strong influence on, how funding received by the school is spent by the school, and consequently determines the various activities carried out by the school. As a result, the budgetary decisions made by senior management affect the quantity and quality of the ICT resources available in a school.

Regular and adequate funding is necessary to ensure appropriate provision of ICT resources. Because of the rate of technological development, ICT hardware and software are generally considered obsolete after three to five years. Whether or not sufficient funding is consistently available each year is the responsibility of senior management, and the recognition of this responsibility is a major factor in determining the adequacy and availability of ICT resources.

Different approaches to educational management affect the delivery of ICT in English secondary schools. The adoption by a secondary school of a management strategy similar to that described below is one of the factors associated with high levels of ICT capability in 14- to 16-year-olds in English schools (Crawford, 2011; Crawford and Jenkins, 2001):

- The head teacher or a senior manager with positive attitudes towards ICT should have overall responsibility for the management of the delivery of ICT throughout the school. This emphasizes that successful implementation is important for the whole school.
- The senior manager in charge of the whole school delivery of ICT (often known as the ICT director or ICT coordinator) should have good ICT skills, and an understanding of technical issues. This makes it more likely that the practicalities of technical implementation will be integrated with educational strategy and policy; and that the different needs of ICT specialist teachers and the whole staff are taken into account.
- A formal, hierarchically organized management structure is preferable, but this should be relatively flat-topped. This ensures that it is clear who has overall responsibility; decisions can be made rapidly; and those teachers with expertise and interest are consulted.
- Consultation should be open and genuine and senior managers should be flexible and open to change.
- The HoD ICT should encourage colleagues to use ICT more widely for professional activities and to support teaching and learning, and should position ICT as a solution to a wide range of existing and potential problems.
- The HoD ICT should build coalitions among groups with similar interests in order to provide support for policy proposals. The HoD should seek to influence others by providing information, and by supporting colleagues' use of ICT, for example, in making use of the VLE.
- The different ways in which individual teachers value ICT and their motivations should be taken into account, and there should be an awareness that changing these is likely to be a slow process which can be supported by the provision of up-to-date ICT resources for teachers' use.
- ICT should become a part of the traditions and rituals of school culture. It must be overtly demonstrated that the school values and takes a pride in its financial and intellectual investment in ICT.
- Acquisition of ICT resources should be funded by the allocation of sufficient annual funding in the context of long-term developmental planning, so that teachers' efforts can concentrate on the integration and support of new and existing ICT resources rather than on the pursuit of one-off bids for financial support.

The HoD is central to improving teaching and learning in ICT. 'The personal qualities, leadership and management skills of middle leaders are often the most significant variables influencing departmental effectiveness' (NCSL, 2003, p. 4).The specific tasks undertaken by a HoD ICT vary but the characteristics of effective middle leaders can be summarized as follows (based on Emmerson *et al.*, 2006; NCSL, 2003):

- Leads by example.
- Distributes leadership. Trusts, consults and empowers colleagues and builds teams.
- Builds consensus. Is available for collaboration and makes time to do this.
- Includes teaching and non-teaching staff in decisions that affect them. This includes teaching assistants and technical support.
- Dialogue is continuous and develops and influences everyone's understanding.
- Generates positive relationships. Cares about colleagues and pupils.
- Shows a commitment to improving learning and teaching. Shares good practice.
- Consistent, has high expectations and a clear sense of direction.
- Improves the environment and the classroom climate.
- Planning is meticulous and detailed. Knows what is happening in the department and when.
- Organizes resources for teaching and learning and administration so that they are readily available when needed, including handbooks, schemes of work and the VLE.
- Ensures that ICT resources are sufficiently up-to-date.
- Evaluates progress against shared and well-understood criteria.
- Innovates.
- Engages with the community.

Activity

Consider what knowledge, understanding and skills you need to develop in order to become an effective HoD ICT.

Summary

- NQTs are often concerned about whether their first teaching post is an appropriate starting point for their career.
- Think about your long-term ambitions but also bear in mind that it is not unlikely that you will change your ambitions as you gain more experience.
- Induction is a three-term period usually completed in a single school year. It is prudent to complete induction at the earliest opportunity.
- Check that the school you will be working in can offer induction. NQTs must complete induction so that they can be employed as fully qualified teachers in the maintained sector.
- You can work as a supply teacher for five years but short-term supply teaching contracts of less than one term do not count towards induction.
- There is no legal requirement to complete induction if you intend to work only in an independent school, academy, free school, or in further education (FE).

- During induction you can expect:

  o   a 10 per cent reduction in your teaching timetable in addition to 10 per cent PPA time;
  o   not to regularly encounter discipline problems that are unreasonably demanding;
  o   a timetable of observations, reviews and assessment meetings;
  o   a personalized programme of training and support;
  o   assessment against the Teachers' Standards (DfE, 2012c).

- How you organize the evidence that you have met the Teachers' Standards should be discussed with your mentor. You could use your ICT skills to construct an eportfolio that gives easy access to all your work and helps you organize it.
- An effective teacher should:

  o   Have a professional manner and appearance.
  o   Maintain good working relationships with colleagues and pupils.
  o   Be present, punctual, prepared.
  o   Create a secure, welcoming classroom climate.
  o   Be enthusiastic, interesting and engaged.
  o   Be calm and consistent.
  o   Be clear what is expected.
  o   Maintain behaviour for learning.
  o   Support and encourage pupils and expect them to participate in the lesson.
  o   Be fair and reasonable.
  o   Promote inclusion and differentiation.
  o   Have high expectations but be realistic.
  o   Practice assessment for learning (AfL).
  o   Develop a portfolio of teaching techniques and skills, and an understanding of how pupils learn.
  o   Demonstrate a good understanding of the subject.
  o   Model those characteristics expected of pupils.
  o   Do all the routine tasks expected.
  o   Do more than the minimum.
  o   Manage time effectively.
  o   Uphold high standards of personal behaviour and ethics.
  o   Listen to advice and act on it as soon as possible.
  o   Manage time effectively.

- If you are striving to become an outstanding teacher and are making good progress, you are already making good preparation for promotion.
- Take opportunities when these are offered as they may not be offered again.
- Be more proactive. Look for opportunities.

  o   Find a mentor and share your ambitions.
  o   Network.
  o   Participate in and deliver CPD and other personal development programmes.
  o   Study for a Master's level qualification or an EdD.

- Consider whether you want to continue teaching ICT in the classroom. In some promoted posts you may not teach ICT to the same extent.

- The Master Teacher Standard focuses sharply on the very best quality classroom teaching. It recognizes that Master Teachers should be recognized for the excellence of their teaching.
- The effectiveness of the ways in which ICT is delivered in English secondary schools may be influenced by different approaches to educational management.
- Schools that assume that ICT can be implemented through traditional models of departmental management will not make the best use of ICT.
- Curriculum models for ICT in English secondary schools can be described as: discrete ICT; cross-curricular ICT and hybrids. The majority of English secondary schools deliver ICT as a hybrid.
- Effective management of ICT is the responsibility of senior management.
- The adoption of a management strategy similar to that described in this chapter is one of the factors associated with high levels of ICT capability in 14- to 16-year-olds in English schools (Crawford, 2011):
- The HoD is central to improving teaching and learning in ICT. The characteristics of effective middle leaders include:

   o   Leads by example.
   o   Distributes leadership.
   o   Builds consensus.
   o   Generates positive relationships.
   o   Is committed to improving learning and teaching.
   o   Meticulous and detailed planning and organization
   o   Evaluates progress against shared and well-understood criteria.
   o   Innovates.

Further reading

Crawford, R. (2011) *ICT Capability in English Schools*, Saarbrucken: Lambert Academic Publishing.

Emmerson, K., Paterson, F., Southworth, G. and West Burnham, J. (2006) *Making a Difference: A Study of Effective Middle Leadership in Schools Facing Challenging Circumstances*, National College for School Leadership. Available at: http://www.nationalcollege.org.uk.

Hay McBer (2000) *Research into Teacher Effectiveness: A Model of Teacher Effectiveness*, London: DfEE.

Chapter 8

Using ICT to support teaching and learning

John Higgins

Introduction

This chapter examines the role of ICT tools in improving the relationship between teaching and learning. Any ICT tool that does not contribute to improving learners' understanding of the curriculum has no role in the learning process.

The complex and delicate relationship between teaching and learning through technology faces many evolving obstacles. In recent years, new technologies have emerged which students find desirable, yet teachers do not or cannot use these in their teaching. Such technologies include but are by no means limited to: Virtual Learning Environments (VLEs), blogs, wikis, forums, podcasts, IWBs, collaboration tools, Skype, mind mapping tools, mobile devices (smartphones, tablets), and electronic textbooks. The deployment of such technologies may weaken the relationship between teaching and learning unless consideration is given at the outset to the way in which they are deployed.

Students adopt technology if it is socially desirable and serves their personal and social interests, and devote a considerable amount of their time to their use of technology especially if this promotes their social standing with their peers. In contrast, many teachers adopt technology in line with the ethos of the school they work; the curriculum they are following; and the time available to them. As a result, teachers tend to adopt new technology more slowly than students.

Moreover, while parents may perceive their children as being ICT literate, this literacy is often not relevant to curriculum requirements. Parents often wonder why their child's ICT grades are not better than reported when they spend hours and hours on the computer in their bedrooms (Bryant, 2010).

Different approaches to learning

Learning styles

Different learners have different styles of learning. Meeting the needs of all learners is difficult, if not impossible. For any teacher to plan 5–9 lessons a day which are tailored and customized to meet the individual needs of each student is almost impossible, given the numerous constraints, for example, quality issues, time and resource constraints and personal skills and knowledge. However, by ensuring that a variety of teaching styles are used, we hope we meet the different needs of all the class.

Regardless of the learning style preferred by students, an underlying assumption is that learners must be actively engaged in the lesson if effective learning is to occur (Anderson,

2008). Choosing a 'correct' technology to ensure that all learners are engaged in the lesson is difficult unless there is an understanding of the different ways learners learn.

Honey and Mumford (1992) grouped students in relation to their learning style:

- *Activist* – learns by doing. They like to learn by experience and are keen to 'have a go' at something in order to improve their knowledge.
- *Reflector* – learns by observing and thinking. They prefer to gather views and information from several sources and consider carefully before coming to any conclusions.
- *Theorist* – learns by constructing theories. They think problems through logically, following step-by-step sequences, and then organize their conclusions into a theory.
- *Pragmatist* – learns by trying out ideas. They tend to take what they know and try out the new learning in a variety of new situations.

Choosing one technology tool which will meet the learning needs of all groups may prove difficult, especially considering that different students can be in more than one group, or may change groups throughout the course of their schooling.

Student-centred learning

Student-centred learning approaches learning from the standpoint of the learner. E-learning serves this aim by enabling teachers to provide a variety of tasks for students to undertake and repeat at their own pace as often as the student deems necessary. Although this approach is can be used in face-to-face teaching, using a VLE brings the added benefit of independence from the teacher and the classroom. This approach can free up teachers' time and allow the student to take greater control of their own time management. Further, if such learning takes place in a synchronous interactive environment, student-centred learning via a VLE may benefit from instant feedback.

Blended learning

Blended learning is understood to mean a mixture of self-led, onscreen activities and face-to-face seminars, classes or workshops. This approach was developed in response to the recognition that virtual classrooms on their own are not a sufficient substitute for small group and one-to-one teaching. Blended learning is a hybrid model which attempts to create 'independence' from the traditional classroom environment whilst being supported by face-to-face contact (JISC, 2006).

Social learning

Students need to do some of their learning as a group. Concepts are more easily explored through discussion with others, receiving feedback and sharing the way forward. This social interaction can involve a variety of teaching and learning strategies, for example, Assessment for Learning which is the process of seeking and interpreting evidence for use by learners and their teachers to decide where the learners are in their learning, where they need to go and how best to get there. Although Web 2.0 components attached to the Internet or the Virtual Learning Environment (VLE) are able to deliver social learning strategies, they do not necessarily provide the social contact and interaction which are desirable.

Activity

- How many different styles of learning can you identify within a class you teach?
- To what extent does your use of ICT support these learning styles?
- In what way could you extend your use of ICT so that you improve your support for all these learning styles?

Matching learning and technology

Having identified various approaches to learning, the discussion now focuses on why it is important to ensure that the correct user and their preferred learning style are married up to the correct technological tool.

Curriculum alignment

English and Steffy (2001) break the curriculum into three components: written curriculum, taught curriculum and the assessed curriculum. Each individual component does not lead to the agreed learning without support from the other components. Learning can only occur if the teacher is teaching the agreed written curriculum and assessing the curriculum in a predefined and consistent manner. The better the synchronization of the three components, the greater the amount of learning that occurs. As the components of the curriculum increasingly overlap, the greater the frequency and volume of agreed learning that takes place. When the relationship between the components is not fully understood, the components drift apart, overlap becomes less, resulting in less agreed learning taking place. Consequently, a state of misalignment occurs.

Misalignment due to technology mismatch in schools

There are numerous causes of educational misalignment resulting from the introduction of ICTs in schools (Pelgrum, 2001). The most common causes are:

- Adopting the incorrect teaching or technology for the learner.
- Incorrect sequence of technological design and implementation to support learning.
- User needs are not recognized or prioritized.
- Training needs are assumed, not understood.
- Misunderstanding of the scope of the technology being deployed, for example:

  o Hardware and software capabilities are not understood.
  o Software and data are incompatible.
  o Back-up and archiving of resources and materials for potential future use are not done.

- No global ownership and adoption of the technology, for example:
  - There is no audit of user needs and these are neglected.
  - Misunderstanding of the translation between users' needs and technical implementation.

The four Ps of Web 2.0

In order to successfully engage and educate students using ICTs, attention should be given to the four Ps of Web 2.0: Personalization, Participation, Peer-to-Peer, and Predictive Modelling (Barkley, 2009).

- *Personalization*: e-learning methods give the teacher the ability to personalize and deliver an education to meet the specific needs of the individual as well as groups of students who share similar learning characteristics.
- *Participation*: with e-learning tools, the teacher is able to contribute to the specific needs of students by creating a steady stream of highly targeted content to meet their individual learning needs. Posting information on forums, updating blogs and creating links to relevant websites that support learning combine to increase participation and engagement which generates interest and promotes learning.
- *Peer-to-peer*: students are no longer isolated when working in or away from school. They interact, they communicate, they exchange impressions and they form a collective understanding about the course content and expectations. In practical terms, if a small number of students initially find the content of a component useful, then word is likely to spread throughout the student's community, and the number of hits can rise rapidly both in terms of volume, frequency and repeat visitors. This is easily monitored by the teacher who can add knowledge objects relevant to the specific content and sustain the positive momentum of interest in this curriculum area.
- *Predictive modelling*: this is how ideas, impressions and trends work in the e-learning enabled world. Through research with your student body, perhaps through the student council, it is possible to predict how students want their e-learning to evolve to meet their educational needs. Identifying and creating trends earlier in the development of e-learning tools and being able to react quickly to such trends, the teacher will be able to capitalize on securing targeted student traffic for the website through marrying up knowledge objects to the specific educational needs of the students.

E-learning

E-learning comprises all forms of electronically supported learning and teaching. E-learning is able to utilize Web 2.0 tools, for example, wikis and blogs. These are associated with web applications that aid information sharing and are centred on the user's specific needs, allowing for collaboration. Such collaboration may take place via the Internet, or may occur via an Intranet which uses the same technologies. However, an Intranet is confined to a specific organization, with all information securely shared behind various security measures away from the public gaze.

When considering using ICT to support learning, it is imperative that the learning objectives of the class are explicitly understood by all before lesson content or the method of delivery is considered, otherwise the tool drives the learning rather than vice versa. Constant review of the educational aims should contribute to minimizing the potential drift from learning to adopting 'unnecessary' e-tools.

A VLE houses several e-learning components and a collection of integrated tools that enable the management of online learning, and provide a delivery mechanism, student tracking, assessment and access to resources. A VLE should ensure that all parties involved in the learning process are able to access information that is relevant to them at a time that suits them and that is accompanied by appropriate and timely feedback. A VLE can include many tools including quizzes or tests, discussion boards or bulletin boards, learning objects and knowledge objects, together with multimedia elements and tutorials.

However, it may be that it is not appropriate to use particular elements of a VLE. Use of technology for the sake of it may be transparent to students, and may lead to them disengaging from the learning process. Caution needs to prevail to ensure that the VLE is strictly tied to the learning of the students so that students do not see such a tool as a 'gimmick'. In this case, the gimmick will be short-lived, contribute little to the learning process and make any further introduction of such technology more difficult for the next enthusiast.

E-learning consists of both asymmetric communication and symmetric communication methods. Asynchronous communication (discussion boards or bulletin boards), provides a forum where discussions are conducted in private possibly within a group which has been predefined through choice of course. Users post notes, comments or questions and at some point in the future a reply may be received. This reply will not 'directly' necessarily affect the next input; nonetheless a knowledge base (thread) is created which the user can scroll through to enhance their own understanding and appreciation of issues.

Synchronous communication is, for example, a chat room facility which acts as a 'substitute' for face-to-face meetings. Communication is in real time between two or more participants online at the same time, each input has the potential to receive immediate feedback. This form of communication tends to be less formal and is rarely assessed, instead serving to clarify and reaffirm understanding away from the pressures of the teacher's supervision and formal assessment.

Both learning objects and knowledge objects are able to exist in asynchronous and synchronous communication methods. For example, a knowledge object might take the form of a video clip from a speech or an extract from a newspaper. Such objects tend to be dissociated from an educational purpose unless they become part of a learning object, that is, adding them to a lesson or lesson objective gives the knowledge object purpose. Such knowledge objects can be stored and reused in other learning contexts so as to avoid unnecessary duplication of resources, in effect creating an e-catalogue of digital resources which can be accessed by content authors and students alike if permissions and access rights allow.

A common misconception with non-ICT specialists, including senior leadership teams (SLTs), is the assumption that all learning which is carried out using a computer is e-learning and as such offers the same support for the learning process as 'real' e-learning. This misconception leads to the educational potential of e-learning being missed, and obscures the paradigm shift that is occurring in education and training as a result of e-learning advancements. For example, the major difference between an interactive CD-ROM and a VLE is the communication element and the user's ability to receive real-time feedback from their unscripted input. With a CD-ROM, the user enters a response from a predefined list and the computer system responds correct, or not correct and provides a statement which may not take into account the initial incorrect selection, for example, the response may be 'try again'. However, a VLE is able to offer more than a nominal response, instead accepting a comment from the student which can be read and responded to by the teacher as opposed to a computer system. In short, e-learning encompasses both synchronous and asynchronous communication between the student and the teacher.

Advantages of e-learning

The use of e-learning tools (Web 2.0, Internet and Intranet) is associated with several advantages and disadvantages. The advantages are accessibility, interactivity and communication.

The accessibility of a course is improved for students with special needs, distance learning and part-time students, students who are absent, and for those who wish to revisit the lesson to consolidate prior learning. Such students can access the course remotely. Furthermore, this accessibility has a positive impact on the learning of those students who learn best by being able to watch a video, or interacting in a virtual environment instead of participating in the traditional classroom. They are able to repeat the lesson at their own pace away from the 'distraction' of the lesson. The diversity offered by e-learning methods allows multiple learning preferences to be addressed and provided under one technological umbrella, regardless of the range of abilities within the audience.

Students with disabilities or special needs may find that the customization afforded by e-learning allows knowledge objects to be tailored into a variety of formats to meet their individual requirements. For example, students with auditory impairment will benefit from script or subtitles on video elements where such facilities may not be possible in the normal classroom environment. Further, general access to school-based education may not be possible for some students outside specific hours, for example, disabled students may need the assistance of a carer who works during the day. E-learning will be especially assistive for profoundly deaf students through the use of subtitles, playback, and audio controls.

The functions offered through e-learning are available at a time to suit the learner and allow individuals to progress at their own pace. Students can work around their other commitments while still gaining access to e-learning on line. This is beneficial to students who have difficulties balancing the competing demands of home and school, such as child carers. It also helps those who feel intimidated by attending school, and these can be slowly introduced into the school population via the VLE.

Interactivity is an important element of e-learning. Learning occurs when students are engaged, and there is evidence that students benefit from actively engaging with their course using e-learning tools. Specifically, the advantages relate to feedback, practice and customization, and all these are features of a well-designed e-learning environment but not necessarily features of a tradition classroom environment (Sizer, 2001).

The instant feedback from an e-learning system has a dual function. First, the feedback allows students to receive accurate and timely progress reports with which they are able to monitor their own performance. This is an essential component in motivating students who need constant and appropriate feedback on their performance to date before they move on to the next stage of their learning. Second, such feedback is instantly available to the teacher, who is able to monitor progress and adopt the appropriate intervention strategy to ensure that the student remains on target. The quicker such intervention occurs, the greater the impact the intervention will have on student performance. Such intervention can occur promptly and this is particularly important where correction is vital before the student can move on to the next phase of the lesson.

Students who learn through practice are able to benefit by 'doing'. Within an e-learning environment, students can practise and re-practise in a non-formal environment, submitting the final version when they are ready. For example, Gmetrix software allows numerous attempts at practice questions from a bank of questions before official testing begins.

If students are able to self-direct their learning pathways, they are more likely to be engaged. E-learning offers flexible pathways that conventional classroom practice cannot. Online learning can start, stop and resume at a time convenient to the individual, and the pace of the learning can be customized to suit individual needs as opposed to the individual being dictated to by traditional school timetables or didactic teaching or highly structured courseware. Learners may not do as well when they are obliged to study different subjects in blocks of 50 or 60 minutes, five or six times per day. Varying the length of lessons and when lessons are conducted may provide greater educational benefits and e-learning can deliver education within such a flexible framework.

Through self-customization of their individual online work areas, students are able to tailor their learning environment in a manner that they feel is most conducive to their learning. Giving students ownership of their work areas creates a motivational aspect that is missing from the traditional lesson where students are told how to record their work and how to report on their progress. Student creativity through customization engages students in the learning process. The better the ability of an e-learning platform to create such an environment, then the greater the chances of learning occurring.

Communication facilities help students to feel part of a learning community and extend what they can experience. The areas in which VLEs are most effective are assessment, bulletin boards, ad hoc communications or instructions and 'stop press' items. It is these features which encourage student participation beyond the novelty of the first few weeks of a course. In particular, the communication element of a VLE: creates a forum for evaluating work created by others; enables staff to support distance learners; enables all participants to contribute to the overall learning process; and facilitates group work. Using the Internet, language students can talk to native speakers across the globe; virtual field trips can be undertaken to deserts, jungles, and mountainous regions by students who live in cities; students can participate in courses taught in other schools; and students can interact with their peers around the world. In addition, ICT enables the use of threads which have the advantage of keeping a catalogued record of inputs and this is especially important in terms of communicating instructions, updates, course alerts and communications specific to particular students. Videos of lessons can be saved online and students who are absent for various reasons, for example, illness, exclusion, participating in the school's inclusion unit, or holidays, can access these lessons at any time without being present physically in the classroom. In addition, students who wish to revisit the lesson for revision purposes are able to do so and this again serves as a means to consolidate prior learning.

Disadvantages of e-learning

While several advantages exist to support the use of e-learning tools as a means of engaging students in the learning process and from this engagement improving their learning opportunities, there are nonetheless several constraints to the effective deployment of e-learning tools. These disadvantages relate to the need for basic ICT skills; the ICT resources needed to access and use e-learning tools, including Internet access; the inability to work independently; and isolation.

Prior to participating in an e-learning environment, potential e-Learners must possess entry-level ICT skills. Students will require a working knowledge of various computer applications so that they are able to fully utilize e-learning resources. Regardless of how well designed, implemented and tested an e-tool is, unless the student has the necessary knowledge and skills to use the resource, the resource will not be used effectively.

In addition, compatibility issues with software need to be addressed so that the e-tool is able to function as intended. This may require the download and installation of various software updates as required, and this may have to be done by the user. The need to be able to do this before being able to learn using an e-learning platform may result in student disengagement.

Furthermore, access to a computer which is connected to the Internet is required and this Internet connection will have to be sufficiently fast to ensure that navigating the e-learning resource is smooth and fast; any disjointed transmission will result in the user becoming frustrated and then disengaging.

E-learning students need to take responsibility for their own time management and independently plan their own learning. However, as students are at least partly independent from the traditional classroom, these skills and studying without formal teaching may prove too difficult for some, and as a result they may be distracted and disengage.

A further disadvantage of e-learning is isolation. Students may feel isolated and unsupported while learning. If the student feels isolated, they may be less motivated and disengage from the learning process. They may suffer from anxiety as they are unable to seek the relevant help they require in order to give them an initial boost or the extra impetus necessary to move to the next stage.

Activity

Write a list of the features of a VLE. You may find it helpful to look at a VLE you are familiar with as you do this.

For each feature, state:

- How you could use the feature to help with your students' learning.
- How you could use the feature to improve your teaching.
- The advantages and disadvantages of the feature.

Classroom observation technologies

Developments in audio and video recording devices, with the ability to zoom in, record and playback, make it possible to record lessons in the classroom. The purpose of this is: to monitor individual student behaviour; to identify learning patterns specific to a group defined by, for example, gender, race or age; to provide a record of the lesson for students who are absent or those who might wish to revisit the lesson later, and to record the teacher's performance, perhaps in order to share good practice, for self-development, or to be used for the annual performance management review. This technology has the potential to improve both teaching and learning.

Once agreement and trust are established, audio and video recording has the potential to be a very useful resource for the entire school community. This technology serves as a tool for self-development, thus contributing effectively to improving teaching and learning. Learning objectives and lesson outcomes can be evaluated in action to ascertain if they were realistic and achievable. Individual student behaviour can be observed and if necessary remedial strategies can be planned away from the classroom. Teacher and support assistant movement around the classroom can be studied to ensure that all students receive some personal attention during the lesson. Finally, areas of strength can be shared with faculty members as a means of sharing best practice. Recorded lessons can easily be shared more widely among a cluster of schools and used for teacher training. A bank of such resources can be used: to strengthen the training of new entrants to the profession, in CPD for experienced teachers; and by the SLT and middle leaders as a means to standardize the grading of lesson observations for the purpose of performance management review and Ofsted preparation. The shared use of such data via online collaboration systems, for example, Mirasys and Wimba, may prove useful for teaching schools, and those schools that wish to share teachers and other staff among a confederation or family of schools. Recording lessons may improve the quality of CPD and training at a reduced cost.

However, there is the potential to alienate teachers who fear 'Big Brother' is monitoring them. Students may play up to the camera, thus rendering the monitoring purpose of the technology ineffective; recorded images may not capture the essence of the classroom, and may be misinterpreted away from the actual events in the classroom; teachers may be distracted from the actual job in hand, teaching to the camera rather than the class. For audio or video recording to be successful, teachers must feel secure that all recordings are kept for and replayed for agreed professional purposes. Furthermore, observers need to be trained so that they appreciate and understand that observing a lesson in such a way will be quite different to actually being in the classroom.

Software monitoring tools enable teachers via a central console to improve the efficiency of teaching and learning and behaviour management by observing students' screen displays while they work independently. Students' attention to the task is more focused as they are aware that their use of the computer may be monitored and recorded. This is often enough to keep students on task (Safer and Fleischman, 2005). Monitoring is further enhanced when teachers have access to the monitoring software using a portable device, such as a tablet PC or netbook as the teacher is able to monitor students' work while moving around the classroom. The same software may also enable teachers to control students' screen displays so that demonstrations to the whole class can be more easily seen by each student.

Activity

Consider whether a classroom teacher would welcome the introduction of video recording of lessons in place of lesson observations.

Case study: Outwood Grange Academy

Outwood Grange Academy provides education for 2200 students aged 11–18. The Academy is a designated specialist school for technology, the arts and leadership development, and was one of the first schools to be granted Teaching School Status. Furthermore, the Academy provides support to several other schools within its Family of Schools.

The Academy follows the educational strategies of the 'Deeps'. The Deeps structure is based on nine gateways organized into four Deeps: (1) Deep Leadership (Workforce Reform and Design and Organization); (2) Deep Learning (Learning to Learn, Assessment for Learning and Student Voice); (3) Deep Support (Information, Advice and Guidance and Coaching and Mentoring); and (4) Deep Experience (New Technologies and Curriculum Design) (Hargreaves, 2008).

All classrooms within the academy are equipped with a PC for the teacher which is connected to an IWB and is enabled for multimedia and Internet access. At several locations throughout the site there are multimedia PCs with Internet access for groups of staff and students, and in addition, there are numerous laptops, netbooks, iPads, slates and classrooms equipped with the ability to monitor teacher and student activity using Classwatch software. Teachers have access to a bank of electronic resources in terms of knowledge objects, statistical analysis and educational software tools all designed to enable them to better meet the individual needs of students. Students expect to receive reports on their performance at regular stages throughout the year highlighting where they are in relation to personalized targets. Rigorous interrogation of the data using the management information system (MIS) allows Outwood to measure actual performance against targets, and produce customized reports for end users, that is, students, parents, teachers, and the SLT. Outwood has created an information-on-demand system which allows for the early identification of concerns and from which appropriate intervention strategies can be implemented.

The Academy welcomes the introduction of new technologies to deliver its educational programme; however, any factor which has the potential to alter the relationship between teaching and learning is scrutinized very carefully to ascertain whether or not the proposed new technology is suitable and appropriate for the delivery of high quality education, taking into consideration various student learning approaches. This scrutiny is important because, for example, schools must be very careful to ensure that boring lessons which lead to student disengagement are not replicated by lessons which use 'boring PowerPoints' (Sizer, 2001). These too will lead to disengagement; however, they also have the additional costs of missed opportunity, depleted budgets, missed learning opportunities and possible student resistance to future innovation.

Outwood is investigating the potential of Cloud computing as an alternative to the established VLE. Cloud computing is Internet-based computing in which large groups of remote servers are networked so as to allow the sharing of applications, centralized data storage, and online access to computer services or resources. The rationale behind exploring this is to remove boundaries to learning. Students live complex lives where the technology and its uses at home are usually not the same as in schools (Bryant, 2010). Through using Cloud technology, students using the Internet will be able to access knowledge and learning objects more easily regardless of its location, and teachers will be able to share and collaborate on resource production. Teachers are unable to design and implement unique lessons for all the classes they teach (Wolf, 2011) as such a workload is not feasible given the need to balance the demands of work and their personal lives. Through the Family of Schools collaborating on such projects, teachers may be able to share these resources and cater for a greater variety of preferred learning styles. Even so, this new technology may not prove to be the way forward.

Outwood has also recently invested in several sets of WordWall by Visual Education, which utilize the new WordPad2 interactive student devices. These devices are marketed as being revolutionary in the sphere of student learning with commentators claiming almost miraculous outcomes. While such claims may be accurate for an individual group, it would be reckless for another teacher from a different school whose students have different learning styles and educational objectives to assume that by purchasing the device, they will automatically enjoy the same educational rewards. Outwood has researched this technology and initial impressions are favourable. Even so, instead of immediately adopting the e-tool throughout the academy, the adoption process has been slower in order to ensure that there is scope in individual schemes of work (the written curriculum) for such a technology to be beneficial to student learning, and that sufficient measures are adopted to ensure that teachers are trained in the use of the e-tool before it is rolled out academy-wide. This is achieved through various internal pilot schemes which ensure that the teachers concerned have the relevant skills to use the full potential of the new learning tool in advance of its use in the classroom (taught curriculum). Too often, schools rush to deploy new technologies without adequate planning and just hope for the best. These new technologies rarely live up to expectations, resulting in missed opportunities and financial loss. Being proactive with all aspects of investigation, design and implementation of e-tools and e-learning may not absolutely guarantee the successful deployment of a new technological tool, however, it will lessen the consequences of deploying the wrong e-tools and hence minimize misalignment in learning. This pro-active approach adopted by Outwood for deploying ICT technologies ensures that opportunities are seized, not wasted.

Whichever options are chosen, the misalignment of education and technology must be avoided at all costs. Outwood is very keen to avoid unnecessary expenditure on items which do not contribute to improved teaching and learning. Purchasing an e-tool today, then realizing that its operational costs are more than expected and that the expected outcomes are leading to misalignment, may easily be corrected by rendering the e-tool redundant. However, the costs may be significant, particularly for a large organization operating under tight fiscal restraint. Hence, Outwood is keen to assume nothing until the e-tool has been successfully matched with its own learning requirements, not those of a vaguely similar establishment described in a web-based advertisement.

Outwood is proactive in using features of existing tools to support its provision of e-learning. For example, an underlying assumption is that students will need to openly share ideas, working in cooperation and collaborating on projects. During the summer of 2010, Outwood changed its primary software from MS Office 2003 to MS Office 2010 with SharePoint server. This has allowed students, staff and administration to work collaboratively on class assignments, departmental projects and Family of Schools' initiatives without the constant battle of document synchronization, emailing attachments or posting to solid state storage devices. The understanding and use of these technologies are enabling Outwood to create learning tasks which are big enough to have out-of-the-classroom relevance within a real-world environment. Such authenticity is empowering students at Outwood with real-world tools to solve real-world problems.

Furthermore, the collaborative nature of the tools and the method of implementation adopted using the Deeps are leading to the creation of a co-construct model of learning. That is, teachers select material from prearranged schemes of work which must be displayed via the e-tools in order to meet the rubric of the syllabus; next, students are allowed to edit this using what knowledge objects and skills they deem necessary. This process moves learning away from the classroom and didactic lessons, ensuring that student ownership and empowerment via e-learning are present throughout Outwood.

By sharing resources across the Family of Schools, a greater wealth of knowledge, skills and visions is available to all stakeholders. Harvesting this potential and creating academy-wide alignment could produce significant returns. Students lead high tech lives outside school and decidedly low tech lives inside school. This new 'divide' is making the activities inside school appear to have less real-world relevance to the student. Through the Deeps, Outwood is constantly attempting to reduce this divide. As technology progresses very rapidly, schools cannot hope to keep abreast of all technological developments, let alone adopt them; nonetheless, they must ensure that the tools they do adopt are right for their students, ensuring that opportunities are not missed. The potential for technology misalignment is ever present and planning for tomorrow is essential today.

The introduction of new technologies into any school is usually heralded as 'the way forward', with phrases such as '21st-century technology for a 21st-century education' being used. Given the investment in time, money, and opportunity costs that is required for such technology to be effectively deployed as a means of improving the learning process, attention must be given to how the written, taught and assessed curriculum can benefit from such technology. New technologies have the potential to change both the way we think about education and the processes of teaching and learning.

Activity

Consider:

- What developments in ICT have changed the way you teach?
- Does ICT provide effective ways to improve students' learning or is it a distraction?

Summary

- Any ICT tool that does not contribute to improving learners' understanding has no role in the learning process.
- Teachers tend to adopt new technology more slowly than students.
- Different learners have different styles of learning. Choosing one technology tool which will meet the learning needs of all groups may prove difficult.
- Student-centred learning approaches learning from the standpoint of the learner. Using a VLE brings independence from the teacher and the classroom.
- Blended learning integrates e-learning and face-to-face teaching.
- Social learning allows students to explore concepts more easily through discussion with others, receiving feedback and sharing the way forward.
- The greater the alignment of the written curriculum, the taught curriculum and the assessed curriculum, the greater the amount of learning that occurs.
- In order to successfully engage and educate students using ICTs, remember the four Ps of Web 2.0: Personalization, Participation, Peer-to-Peer, and Predictive Modelling.
- When using ICTs to support learning, the purpose should be explicitly understood. Making use of technology for the sake of it may lead to students disengaging and could make the introduction of other technologies more difficult in the future.
- A common misconception is that all learning which is carried out using a computer is e-learning.
- The advantages of e-learning are accessibility, interactivity and communication.
- The disadvantages of e-learning are: the need for basic ICT skills; the ICT resources needed to access and use e-learning tools; the inability to work independently; and isolation.
- Lessons in the classroom can be recorded. The purpose of this is: to monitor student behaviour; to improve learning; to provide a record of the lesson for students who are absent or those who might wish to revisit the lesson later; and to record the teacher's performance.

Further reading

Hargreaves, D. (2008) *A New Shape for Schooling?* Specialist Schools and Academies Trust. London: DfE.

JISC (2006) 'In their own words: exploring the learner's perspective on e-learning', available at: http://www.jisc.ac.uk/media/documents/programmes/elearningpedagogy/iowtext.doc (accessed 14 November 2007).

Chapter 9

ICT in school administration and management

John Higgins

Introduction

This chapter reviews the current use of ICT in schools for administration and management; outlines the advantages and disadvantages; offers advice on selecting appropriate software; and considers the responsibilities of schools in collecting, processing and using data and current legislation.

Many school administration and management tasks can be performed more efficiently and effectively using ICT. A management information system (MIS) provides the information needed to do this (O'Brien and Marakas, 2011).

Administration and management tasks in schools

Most administration and management tasks in schools can be supported or completely carried out using ICT software and hardware tools. Some of these tools are standalone and others are bundled; some are aligned to a specific role, while others are general in nature and are able to support numerous school-wide tasks. Some schools use 'off-the-shelf' software and solutions to meet their individual needs, while other schools prefer to develop their own ICT tools to ensure that the tool chosen is developed to meet their specific requirements.

All schools' data are similar and the ICT tools used should do the following:

- Accept input from different sources and in different data types.
- Run customized queries and reports in a style required by the user.
- Generate data which is portable so that it can be shared.
- Be fit for purpose.

Exchanging pupil data sets between schools saves a great deal of administration time and serves as an e-record which follows the pupil as they progress through their school career. Pupil information can be imported into an existing school MIS even before the pupil has arrived on site. Essential data, such as pupils' names, addresses, next of kin, medical records, educational provision, and emergency contact details accompany the pupil, removing the need to constantly re-input data at the end of each year or Key Stage. This data can be used in conjunction with other data to complete individual, form and year group, departmental and school profiles.

Computer-based pupil attendance records can be used to monitor attendance. Data is collected year on year and saved for analysis purposes. This data can be used to monitor:

- *School attendance*: the data is used to compare school attendance with local and national trends and against national targets, to inform a school's leadership team (SLT) of areas of concern, enabling them to choose an appropriate strategy aimed at improving attendance figures.
- *Individual class registration records*: these show who is absent and from this, analysis can establish to what extent the 'missing' of lessons is impacting on pupil performance, and corrective measures can be implemented and monitored.

Pupils' attendance can be recorded in every period throughout the day and parents immediately informed of absences. Systems that allow the immediate input of attendance data to the computer system can quickly produce a report showing which pupils are absent. Attendance data can be input using a variety of methods, including desktop computers, OMR, swipe cards, or portable computers with communications links. If attendance is recorded during each period, the location of a particular pupil can be output on demand and a pupil's whereabouts can be tracked. Letters or emails to parents can be generated informing them of their child's absences from school, and this information can be summarized for the relevant members of staff and the attendance office. Some schools now have their morning and afternoon registration data linked to a text messaging service which immediately texts the parents informing them that their child is absent from school. In most cases, the parents are aware; however, in some cases they are not, and the ICT systems contributes to safeguarding procedures.

The collection of data for every aspect of a pupil's school life very quickly builds into a profile of the pupil which can contribute to identifying areas of underperformance or other concern. This information can be shared with parents and can explain why the pupil is under-performing and, when used with other data available in schools, may help reduce absenteeism.

Activity

Find out:

- How is attendance recorded in your school?
- Which software is used to process attendance data?
- What are the potential uses of attendance data?
- What is the attendance data actually used for?
- Is the software being used to its full potential?

Records of Achievement and other curriculum-related records of pupils' attainment and progress can be used as an eportfolio of evidence. Such records can include the recording, analysis and reporting of pupils' progress against National Curriculum targets, Assessing Pupils Progress (APP) and other customized tracking sheets. Aggregating these tracking sheets as the pupil progresses through the school builds a comprehensive document which evolves with the pupil. Teachers' comments, attendance statistics, examination entries and results, extra-curricular activities attended and behaviour to mention but a few, can contribute to the process of building a detailed eportfolio which will serve to inform teachers about a particular pupil and thus guide them to an appropriate course of action to correct under-achievement or stretch and challenge.

Curriculum mapping software, for example, Atlas Rubicon (http://www.rubicon.com/AtlasCurriculumMapping.php), can be used in conjunction with the school curriculum to establish individual learning pathways for pupils. Such pathways can serve as the hub for all curriculum initiatives. These pathways are supported by reference to specific schemes of work mapped to relevant resources. Such a system produces clarity and ensures reinforcement is provided to support, for example, the school's literacy and numeracy policies.

The school timetable can be modelled using ICT. Timetabling software is able to match individual pupils' needs to the constraints facing the school. Option block setting will create option sets providing certain criteria have been met: class size, number of classes and any other prerequisites such as a double science lesson and physical constraints such as the school only having one gym. These options can be imported into the timetable program which will match pupils to classes, classes to teachers, and teachers to classrooms. A multitude of lessons and day lengths can be selected. From this, the school can change the parameters of the timetable to examine if moving from a 25-period week to a 40-period week is necessary or, what a two-week timetable would look like. Further, constraints on the timetable due to part-time workers and changes to recommended learning hours can be manipulated very easily. Performing these editing and modelling tasks manually would be impractical because of the time it would take, however, using ICT, various models can be explored and analysed for effectiveness at the touch of a button.

An absent teacher may negatively affect pupils' learning. Staff cover software ensures that a replacement teacher with appropriate knowledge and skills is deployed to minimize the disruption caused to pupils' learning when a teacher is absent. Such software is designed to streamline the daily business of arranging and publishing a cover timetable for absent staff or special events as effectively, quickly and as fairly as possible. The software automatically assigns staff to cover on the basis of many factors including: the length of time since a teacher was last directed to cover; the number of non-contact periods lost by the cover teacher compared with other colleagues; whether the teachers are in the same faculty (it is preferable if a science teacher covers science), and whether the cover teacher is of the appropriate gender for covering, for example, PE lessons.

The construction of individual staff action plans can be assisted and coordinated with whole-school development and resource planning. The information collected can be related to payroll, CRB checks, safer recruitment training, staff qualifications and skills, all being used for the provision of individual and whole-school development planning. Appraisal and staff development can be organized, records kept and analysed, these being coordinated with staff job descriptions, staff responsibilities, and INSET records. A centralized audit of lesson observation, drop-ins, and learning walks can be analysed to establish common areas of teaching which need addressing. For example, is there a specific need for whole-school or individual development in teaching plenaries? Data analysis allows a focus on the areas which need attention, and therefore resources are channelled into specific areas of need, which is especially important if continuing professional development (CPD) budgets are tight.

Finance and budgeting software is used to facilitate the monitoring and control of spending to ensure budgets are not exceeded, or if they are, such over-spend is anticipated. A well-established system will provide a sound basis for forecasting, planning and analysis, including 'what if' modelling which is vitally important in today's economic climate. Budgets can be allocated to cost centres, such as departments. The software can produce analysis, contrasting spending against budget, showing actual cash flow against profiles of projected outgoings for the school and for cost centres. The software should help maintain records of purchases and sales, printing the appropriate documentation, such as purchase orders and invoices. Modern finance software has built-in features to advise on current Financial Services Authority (FSA) guidelines, ensuring that all purchases fulfil current legal requirements. A variety of standard reports are available to ensure that the report is pitched to the needs of various users, including audit trails, and historical expense analysis.

Asset tracking software is used to catalogue school equipment (computers, rooms, theatres, sports halls and other major capital items in short supply), and also serves as a booking system. Users can book facilities and resources that are fit for purpose. For example, if a teacher needs access to computer facilities for 12 pupils, rather than book an entire computer suite of 30 computers, they can book part of the facility or a smaller room, leaving the remaining computers available to be booked by other users. Further, such software may contain specific details about the resources being booked. For example, rather than book a high end iMac suite with specialist Music software installed for a word processing lesson, the user will be guided towards a general purpose facility which will be fit for purpose while freeing up the more specialized facilities.

Library automation software can be used to organize and monitor the borrowing of books and other resources from the school library or other resource centres. Bar codes are used to identify the books being loaned and these are linked to an already established unique pupil administration number held centrally on the school's MIS. Reminders and other notifications can be issued to pupils via tutor groups electronically through the MIS.

Campus messaging systems including TV broadcasts and audio announcements may be used to advertise school activities, serve as reminders about extra-curricular events, and congratulate groups and individuals as well as raising awareness of various school issues. The capture, storage and playback of video and/or CCTV can be used to deter cheating in examinations, improve pupil movement around the campus, and serve as a source for video upload to the school's sporting pages. This can also improve a school's safeguarding and monitoring provision. Advances in video storage, increased data speeds and portable recording and playback devices ensure that video feeds can be watched in real time or stored for later viewing.

When schools turn to ICT to assist with administration and management tasks, they often overlook software that they may already own because its full potential is not understood and therefore not realized (Higgins and Moseley, 2001). It is tempting to buy new application software that appears to offer an immediate solution to pressing problems because the software was promoted as being a complete and instantaneous solution to that problem. However, it may well be that a school already owns software that could be equally useful if appropriately used by a suitably experienced member of staff. Many schools have found that some administration and management tasks can be done effectively using general purpose software, for example, word processing, graphics, database, and spreadsheet software. Many of these programmes are application generators and these are able to move away from generic functions and produce custom-built applications with the potential to match sophisticated specialist software.

Activity

Make a list of the administration tasks done using ICT in your school.

- Which tasks would have to be done even if ICT was not available?
- Which tasks would not be done if ICT was not available?
- Does using ICT help or hinder school administration?

The advantages and disadvantages of using ICT

Schools generate and process vast volumes of data and this data is used to drive decisions. The greater the accuracy and completeness of the data, the faster the data becomes information. Information reduces uncertainty and strengthens the decision. Even so, while ICT can help pupils to learn and teachers to teach more effectively it is not the case that ICT will make a difference simply by being used (Higgins and Moseley, 2001).

Advantages

- An ICT system helps teachers with all aspects of their work and teaching can better target individual pupils' needs. Whole-school ICT-based profiling systems are used to record and report on pupils' progress, facilitating intervention strategies and individual curriculum pathways as appropriate.
- An ICT system can automatically provide up-to-date, reliable and accurate reports to the various stakeholders, including parents and teachers. This is a requirement of any system for school administration and management. For example, school, departmental and special spending must be monitored, updated and reported regularly with an up-to-date summary of spending in relation to budget. Using ICT, these reports can be automated and produced more frequently. Further, these reports can be generated and emailed to the recipient automatically at a pre-set time.
- Information can be distributed as and when required while remaining complete and secure through the use of password, encryption and rights protection. Often, there is a loss of quality when photocopies are made and security and control issues arise through the distribution of copies. ICT systems can distribute information across networks while maintaining integrity and confidentiality. Where such confidentiality is broken, the audit trail will locate the 'culprit'. Through the use of validation rules, the system will ensure that all data is complete, in a standardized format and organized in a manner which makes processing the data efficient.
- Record keeping is more orderly and reliable. Manual paper-based records may be lost or misplaced due to poor filing or loans not being returned. With an ICT system, all records are kept in a manner which allows for duplicate copies to made, backed up, and archived for future use. Many systems also include an audit feature so that school administrators can see who is doing what and when.

- Reports generated by an ICT system can be more uniform, flexible and focused than those produced by manual systems. They can be produced more often and for a greater variety of purposes. With ICT systems, mistakes can be edited and changes to formatting can be implemented immediately and disseminated to all stakeholders from one master template. For example, a focused summary of GCSE results for placing in local papers could be generated from the data returned to the school by the examination boards. This summary analysis may be edited by the school, or rearranged to focus on some unusual feature of the data. Similarly, timetable programmes may allow schools to adjust the curriculum to cater for pupils' interests. Timetabling software can show each pupil's subject choices. This provides very useful information about the choices of a particular population of pupils and the curriculum can be adjusted to meet pupils' expectations. This flexibility allows individual pathways to be explored and where possible implemented. Manually adjusting these parameters is impractical due to time constraints.
- ICT systems can serve as a focus for the standardization of methods throughout the school, providing, for example, a unified framework for recording and reporting assessments. SIMMS and Serco Facility, probably the most widely used MISs in UK schools, provide such a framework, ensuring that all data that is required is collected and therefore any reporting from the system is complete.
- Tracking the progress of specific groups of pupils is easier using ICT systems. Data sets can be sorted faster and more accurately when using a computer, compared to manual methods. Through the MIS, data can be sorted and compared to identify trends, perform comparisons between groups of pupils and identify areas of over- and under-achievement.
- Using an ICT system, searching for information about pupils who meet a specific range of criteria is made possible at the click of a button as opposed to trawling through extensive paper-based records. For example, locating a specific pupil's individual record is completed in seconds; with a manual system, this would take much longer.
- ICT systems force the demand for bigger and better data sets. Entering data into a system can be tiresome and lengthy; however, once the data is entered, it can be reused any number of times without additional input. Some information can be entered automatically, for example, through OCR, OMR, sensors and swipe cards. To cater for this demand with a manual system would require additional staff, however, with an ICT system; the same or fewer staff are required.

Disadvantages

Using ICT does not of itself bring benefits. If ICT is misapplied or installed without sufficient analysis, then fewer benefits will be gained and money will be wasted (Lucey, 2005). Advantages offered by a new ICT system may not be fully realized until all disadvantages have been identified and removed. From the outset, a clear set of aims need to be established and these include:

- What do you require from the system?
- When do you require the system to be fully operational?
- Where is the system to be deployed?
- Who is going to oversee and use the system?

The outcomes of these decisions influence what can be done in both the short and long term, and give rise to a range of resultant problems:

- ICT systems, especially MIS, can be expensive to purchase and install. The purchasing of hardware and software can be a major capital expense, and great care needs to be taken to ensure that such items are compared and evaluated against alternatives, thus ensuring that the right one has been selected. An initial audit of curriculum and management needs will establish what is required from the software; the findings of the audit should then serve as the driving force for any decision as to which systems to buy. Failure to understand your needs from the outset will lead to missed opportunities and wasted expenditure.
- Purchasing the correct equipment is only part of the expense; other factors need to be considered, for example, the purchase of new furniture. Many new desktop models are now single units which may affect the size of the computer's footprint. If the school is introducing laptops, is there any need for the traditional rows of tables found in many ICT rooms? Will power sockets and Wi-Fi points need relocating and are there enough of these? Storage units to house such devices need to be considered, and again, the additional cost.
- Most schools use ICT to support decision-making, and the increasing dependence on data by staff is increasing the workload and pressure being placed on data managers and administrative assistants. MIS and ICT tools aim to reduce workload; however, workload may not be reduced, but simply changed. This needs to be taken into account especially at busy times of the school calendar.
- With the advent of Web-based technologies, portable devices and Cloud computing (see Chapter 8), a number of schools are sharing staff calendars. This serves to improve the scheduling of meetings within federations of schools and highlights activities throughout a diverse organization. However, this also highlights discrepancies in workloads, potentially causing resentment among staff and fear of excessive monitoring.
- The introduction of new ICT systems may lead to extra work for the user. At least initially, the user may have to continue to use the current legacy system as well as being trained on the new system. If the user is a reluctant recipient of the system, then such perceived additional work will not be welcome. Work may be duplicated in the early stages of system implementation to ensure that the new system is fit for purpose before the legacy system is completely removed. The alternative would be for a direct implementation of the new system, however, this brings with it uncertainty as to whether the new system will work as expected.
- Hardware and software may not function for a variety of reasons. Whatever the cause of the system malfunction, the people who are relying on the system now need to find an alternative. The provision of hot swap tools will solve the problem; however, these incur an additional cost. Further, the repair of the fault takes time and if the item is returned to the supplier under warranty, this process will need additional monitoring and will take even longer.
- With any system, data portability is essential. Although due care and consideration will have been taken to ensure that data is portable between the new and legacy system, often, little consideration is given to the portability of data between the new system and external recipients of that data. If the recipient does not support the new data format, then they are unable to open the file.

- Backing up critical and sensitive information to various storage devices reduces the risk of losing the data due to system failure; however, such a method increases the risk of data being seen by unauthorized users which invokes various legal and ethical considerations. Encrypting the data is a solution; however, this too becomes an additional factor that needs to be addressed.

- Purchasing the ideal piece of software is by no means easy; however, once you have the software, time and financial consideration need to be given to the future of the software in terms of licensing, upgrades and new version releases. If the cost of these becomes too high, consideration of an alternative may be necessary which in turn necessitates more potential disruption and anxiety for staff, and the additional costs of training and installation.

- Modules within an MIS are compatible; however, consideration needs to be given to compatibility between software from different vendors and across various platforms. School MIS systems tend to be different from school financial systems, and unless these two critical systems can communicate, the advantages of sharing data may be lost. Many providers are aware of this and offer modules to cover all areas of school management so that schools can benefit from sharing data. In this situation, compatibility across platforms may not be an issue; however, the purchaser needs to be careful that they are not being locked in to a bundle of software from a particular supplier due to the features of a few of the modules within the bundle.

- Assuming that all computers can share a common suite of software can be a costly and frustrating error. Some computers within a school may be four or more years older than the latest and may not be capable of running the latest software and so have to be replaced at additional cost. In addition, schools need to ensure that all licences are appropriate for the software version and the number of installations.

- ICT systems influence where people work. Desktop computers dictate where people can work due to their size and power requirements. Laptop computers provide more flexibility; however, for such provision to be most effective, planning and a change of organizational ethos may need to be considered.

- The input of information to the MIS software may be time-consuming and, consequently, expensive, thus outweighing some of the advantages in using a computer-based system. Many systems demand that information must be entered via the keyboard, but this is likely to be relatively slow compared with data entry using swipe cards, OMR or other methods of Direct Data Entry. Furthermore, swipe card systems may be unreliable, and OMR forms may not be accurately completed, causing additional problems. Adopting various verification methods may help solve the problem of data accuracy; however, these also need to be carefully organized and may be time-consuming.

Factors to consider when choosing software

There is also a section on software selection and licensing in Chapter 4.

Software compatibility

When purchasing software, it is crucial to ensure from the outset that the type of software chosen is compatible with your current software and hardware. If you buy new software that is not compatible, then it may not be easily usable. For example, Apple software will probably not work on a PC, and if it does, you may find that some of the software features either do not function as expected or are not supported by future upgrades. Specifically, Casio FX calculator IWB emulators work across all platforms and are easy to install, providing they originate from a local CD device that is, they will not function across a network due to security and copyright issues. This may be a minor problem unless you do not have CD drives installed in all the computers used in Mathematics. Even so, factors which hinder the full utilization of software across all platforms should be avoided if possible.

End users will gauge the effectiveness of any ICT purchase by how the ICT tool is able to support the school. As demands and expectations on schools' data change in the light of curriculum changes, Ofsted frameworks, legislative requirements and census feedback from the DfE, schools will be expected to produce their own customized reports. Flexible alignment between the software facilities and the user's ability to use the application must occur; otherwise, the ICT tool could very quickly become unusable.

The ability to move data between applications that do not have the same default file types should be available. Further, given the continued development of VLEs and Cloud computing, software needs to handle data objects that are Sharable Content Object Reference Model-compatible (SCORM) to support Web-based learning and collaboration. This is increasing in importance as schools move into shared learning partnerships.

Data compatibility with all components of a school's information system is essential, whether these are standalone applications or in a MIS, in order to ensure that any output is based on complete, accurate and up-to-date input. For example, timetabling software will generate an analysis of the curriculum for each pupil that can be exported into other software, for example, a spreadsheet or word processor, in order to generate pupils' records of achievement. These records of achievement may reflect curriculum learning objectives, and as a result, the teacher now has a customized tracking sheet for all pupils in all classes plotted against internal and external targets. From this, examination entries can be extricated easily and uploaded to the examination board. Customizing output ensures that generic distribution of information is avoided and is replaced by purposeful end user-driven output.

Installation and training

Some questions to consider are:

- Who is going to install the software on PCs and the network, and are they technically proficient? Do they have the capacity and capability to perform the installation, testing and troubleshooting? Do they have sufficient access rights to change network policies and administration settings?
- Who is going to provide training for users? Are they competent in the delivery of such training? Will the training be 'in-house' or external, and is there an additional cost?
- If the software is a specialist application, for example, Sage accounting software (see Appendix 2), will training be provided for users as they become more advanced in the use of the application?
- Is user support via remote desktop connection or 'dialling-in' between the vendors and the user available, and what are the cost implications?
- Other sources of help and support: is there a telephone help line? Is there effective online help with built-in tutorials; manuals as hardcopy or downloads; FAQs; and user support groups?

User interface

The interface between the user and the application should be fit for purpose and not unnecessarily complicated. Although various interfaces exist such as menu-driven interfaces and natural language interfaces, by far the most popular is the Graphical User Interface (GUI). This uses graphical icons to represent functions, for example, an icon could be a drawing of a printer and when this icon is clicked, the application will print the active document. MS Windows and Apple operating systems make use of this type of interface which makes all functions easily accessible for even novices.

Data protection

The Data Protection Act (1998 and 2003) gives rights to individuals and greater responsibilities to those who hold personal data. Demonstration that the Act is being adhered to shows that your school operates with due diligence and responsibility. Breaches of the DPA can lead to claims for compensation, prosecution and bad publicity for your school. Schools hold information on pupils and in doing so must follow the requirements of the DPA. This means that data held about pupils must only be used for the specific purposes that are allowed by the Act. The rules regarding personal data also apply to employees, whether they are teaching or non-teaching staff.

The DPA uses several definitions which need to be understood in order to fully appreciate the implications of this legislation:

- *Personal data* means data which relates to a living individual who can be identified.
- *Processing*, in relation to information or data, means obtaining, recording or holding the information or data or carrying out any operation or set of operations on the information or data.
- *Data subject* means an individual who is the subject of the personal data collected.
- *Data controller* means a person who determines the purposes for which and the manner in which any personal data is, or is to be, processed.
- *Data processor*, in relation to personal data, means any person (other than an employee of the data controller) who processes the data on behalf of the data controller.

Schools are 'data controllers' under the DPA in that they process 'personal data' in which people can be identified individually. When data is obtained from data subjects, the data controller must ensure, so far as is practicable, that the data subjects (including pupils or their parents or carers) have, or are provided with, or have readily available to them, the following information, referred to as the 'fair processing information':

- details of the data that they hold;
- a statement of the purposes for which they hold the data;
- details of any third parties to whom the information may be passed.

The DPA applies to all personal data that is processed. It applies to paper files as well as electronic data, so that the principles apply to written records and notes that are kept, for example, in teachers' mark books. The DPA covers the collection, storing, editing, retrieving, disclosure, archiving and destruction of data and there are eight principles that must be adhered to as well as a number of conditions that apply.

The eight principles specify that personal data must be:

1   Processed fairly and lawfully.
2   Obtained for specified and lawful purposes.
3   Adequate, relevant and not excessive.
4   Accurate and up-to-date.
5   Not kept any longer than necessary.
6   Processed in accordance with the data subject's rights.
7   Securely kept.
8   Not transferred to any other country without adequate protection in situ.

Two key words in these principles are 'fairly' and 'lawfully'. What do they mean for schools in practice? The DPA sets out a 'fair processing' code. This requires data controllers to inform subjects about the purposes for which their personal data will be processed. This information should be provided at the time the personal data is obtained from the data subject, and should be comprehensive and transparent. 'Lawfulness' can be broken down into two areas:

•   The annual notification to the Information Commissioner needs to be comprehensive, setting out all the categories of personal data obtained, from whom it is obtained and to whom it is disclosed.
•   Obtaining the data subject's consent to data processing. Consent will only be valid if the fair processing information has been provided. Ideally, consent recorded in writing is the most appropriate.

Appropriate technical and organizational measures must be taken to guard against unauthorized or unlawful processing of personal data and against accidental loss or destruction of or damage to personal data. In particular, care needs to be taken when the data controller uses a data processor to process data on its behalf. If, for example, a school outsources its ICT maintenance and support function, the supplier will be a data processor for the purposes of the DPA. The additional obligations placed on data controllers using data processors are that:

•   The data controller must put in place a written contract stipulating that the data processor should take appropriate security measures in relation to the personal data it is processing.
•   The data controller must take reasonable steps to ensure compliance by the data processor with its security obligations, depending on the nature and volume of the personal data being processed on behalf of the data controller. Reasonable steps may range from requesting regular written updates from the data processor as to the security measures it is implementing, to full audits by the data controller involving visits to the data processor's premises.

Each school that processes data must notify the Information Commissioner annually. A school, like every other data user, must conform to the requirements of the DPA. In particular, this requires the school to formally notify the Office of the Information Commissioner of the following information:

- the purposes for which the school holds personal data;
- what data it holds;
- the source of the data;
- to whom the data is disclosed;
- to which countries the data may be transferred.

Activity

Investigate how your school would deal with a request to see all personal data stored electronically and on paper by:

- a teacher or other employee of a school;
- a parent;
- a pupil.

Passing on information

Schools hold information on all the stakeholders within their organization. This information is often shared at various times throughout the year with external agencies who offer support, advice and guidance to schools, for example, government agencies such as the DFE, examination boards and contractors who provide other support services. Schools need to ensure that they are confident that the recipients of such information adhere to the same data safeguarding measures as themselves.

Holding data

Schools retain files containing personal data on computer systems. However, there is some debate about how long such data should be retained after pupils have left school or employees have moved on. The fifth principle of the DPA states that personal data processed for any purpose or purposes shall not be kept for longer than is necessary for that purpose or purposes. As a general rule of thumb, a school should check on the stated purposes for which it is holding data, which could suggest an appropriate length of time, for example, finance data might be held for six years; and pupil and staff data might be held for seven years. This means that after seven years a school would not be able to provide copies of examination results or references.

Safe disposal

An aspect of data security that may be overlooked relates to the disposal of computing equipment. Schools have legal responsibilities to safeguard the personal data which may be saved on hard disks, for example, email and passwords. Deleting files or formatting a hard disk may not be sufficient since widely available software programs can recover some or all of this information. Schools are advised to check that the organization to which any equipment is given will provide a warranty that they securely erase all disks. It is advisable to consult your local technical support for advice. If the disks contain particularly sensitive information, then the industry recommendation is that they should be physically destroyed.

Summary

- Most administration and management tasks in schools can be carried out using ICT:
  - Exchanging pupil data sets between schools saves time spent on administration.
  - A pupil's data set becomes an e-record which follows them through school. This can be used to identify under-performance or other concerns.
  - The school timetable can be modelled using ICT. Timetabling software is able to match individual pupil's needs to the constraints facing the school.
  - Staff cover software ensures that a replacement teacher with appropriate knowledge and skills is deployed when a teacher is absent.
  - Staff development can be coordinated with whole-school planning.
  - Spending can be monitored to ensure budgets are not exceeded.
  - Asset tracking software can be used to catalogue school equipment.
  - Library automation software can be used to organize the loan of books and other resources from the school library.
  - Campus messaging systems can be used to advertise school activities, etc.
  - Some administration and management tasks can be done effectively using general purpose software, for example, word processing, graphics, database, and spreadsheet software.

- Advantages of ICT systems:
  - An ICT system can help teachers with all aspects of their work and identify an individual pupil's needs.
  - An ICT system can provide automatically up-to-date, reliable and accurate reports.
  - Information can be distributed when required while records remain complete and secure.
  - Record-keeping is more orderly and reliable.
  - Reporting can be more uniform, flexible and focused and reports can be produced more often and for a greater variety of purposes.
  - Tracking pupils' progress is easier using ICT systems.
  - Searching for information about pupils is faster and easier.

- Disadvantages of ICT systems:
  - ICT systems, especially MIS, can be expensive to purchase and install.
  - Other factors need to be considered, for example, the purchase of new furniture.
  - ICT may be expected to reduce workload, however, it may change patterns of work, not reduce workload.
  - Staff may fear excessive monitoring.
  - The introduction of new ICT systems may lead to extra work at least initially.
  - Hardware and software may not function for a variety of reasons.

    o Backing up information reduces the risk of losing the data; however, it increases the risk of the data being seen by unauthorized users.

    o After you have purchased software, you need upgrade it.

    o All computers may not be able to run a common suite of software.

    o Schools need to ensure that all software has appropriate licences.

    o ICT influences where people can work.

    o Data input using a keyboard may be more time-consuming and expensive than direct data entry (DDE), such as using swipe cards. However, DDE may be unreliable.

- Factors to consider when choosing software:

    o There is also a section on software selection and licensing in Chapter 4.

    o Software compatibility.

    o Installation and training.

- The Data Protection Act (DPA):

    o The DPA gives rights to individuals, and responsibilities to those who hold personal data.

    o Demonstration that the Act is being adhered to shows that your school operates with due diligence and responsibility.

    o Schools should make sure pupils and parents know what data they hold; and why they hold it.

    o The DPA applies to all personal data in paper files as well as electronic data, for example, teachers' mark books.

    o Personal data must be: obtained for specified and lawful purposes; adequate, relevant and not excessive; accurate and up-to-date; not kept longer than necessary; kept securely; and not transferred to any country without equivalent protections.

    o Schools should notify the Information Commissioner annually setting out what personal data it holds, the source of the data and to whom it is disclosed.

    o Schools should obtain consent to hold personal data, if possible, in writing.

    o Measures must be taken to guard against unauthorized or unlawful processing of personal data and against accidental loss or destruction of or damage to personal data.

    o When computer equipment is disposed of, schools must safeguard personal data which may have been saved on hard disks.

    o Personal data processed for any purpose shall not be kept for longer than is necessary.

Further reading

Imison, T. and Taylor, P. H. (2001) *Managing ICT in the Secondary School*, Oxford: Heinemann.

Jen-Hwa Hu, P., Clark, T. H. K. and Ma, W. W. (2003) 'Examining technology acceptance by school teachers', *Journal of Information and Management*, 41(2): 227–41.

Selwood, I. and Pilkington, R. (2005) 'Teacher workload: using ICT to release time to teach', *Educational Review*, 57(2): 163–74.

Chapter 10

ICT Policy

Introduction

Every school should have a whole-school policy for ICT and a plan for its implementation as ICT is both a cross-curricular skill and a subject in its own right. This should be a working document well grounded in what is happening throughout the school. It should include a realistic implementation plan and provide a clear vision for the future, providing targets for the overall development of ICT within the school in the current school year and in the long term.

There should be evidence of thorough and effective planning of the ICT curriculum, and a costed development plan for the provision of the necessary ICT resources.

Developing a whole-school ICT Policy: aims, audit, action

Writing an ICT Policy is not an exact, mechanistic process. Unique features of each school will find their expression in the ICT Policy. The following is not a prescription for writing an ICT Policy but some suggestions that will hopefully be helpful to those who attempt this task.

The first stage in developing an ICT Policy is to describe the long-term aims of the policy. Next, an audit of what is currently being done in the school should be carried out. When it is clear where the school is going and where it is starting from, an action plan can be developed that will help the school move forward.

The statement of the aims, the audit and the action plan are each likely to cover:

- the management structure for ICT;
- the ICT curriculum and its organization;
- the assessment, recording and reporting of pupils' work in ICT; and arrangements for moderation;
- provision of ICT resources; including hardware and software, and arrangements for security, disaster recovery, and the implementation of the Data Protection Acts;
- safeguarding and equal opportunities;
- health and safety;
- staffing and staff continuous professional development (CPD);
- funding.

It is unwise to plan in detail the development of ICT resources more than one year ahead. The underlying technology and associated costs change very rapidly and can have an immediate impact on what schools are able to do and how they can do it. The development of an ICT Policy is an on-going activity. The current policy can only be a snapshot of the school's intentions at the time it was written. Consequently, it is essential that the ICT Policy is reviewed and updated every year.

Aims

The aims are developed within the ICT Policy as the long-term goals that the school seeks to achieve. For practical purposes, the 'long term' can be considered to be a period of about five years. The aims should be realistic and achievable within the given time span. This is not the place for speculation akin to science fiction but an opportunity to state what the school wishes to work towards. It is necessary to think seriously and carefully about the aims of the school. However, as they are long-term goals, they should not be regarded as inflexible. They are a statement of intent that informs planning in the short term. The ICT Policy might begin with a statement of the overall aims, that is, a 'mission' statement. This is a general statement of intent. More detailed aims will follow, perhaps organized under the sub-headings used in this chapter or concise aggregates of these where this is more meaningful (see the example ICT Policy on p. 155).

It is important that the aims should clearly represent the ambitions of the school with regard to the development of ICT in the long term. If the ICT Policy is to engage the efforts of the whole school, the aims should reflect the views of the whole school. It is therefore important that the views of those who are closely involved with ICT in the school are balanced by the views of others who have different perspectives. While the ICT Coordinator may have well-informed opinions about the direction that the development of ICT in the school should take, it is probable that he or she will have (and probably should have) a highly partial viewpoint. If the ICT Coordinator is asked to write the aims, it is essential that these are thoroughly evaluated by more impartial members of staff. The statement of aims determines how ICT will be developed in the school. It is ultimately used to direct funding and other resources to particular departments, teachers and resources. It is prudent to ensure that the statement of aims represents as broad a perspective as is possible.

Management structure

Often, when a policy statement is required, the Headteacher will ask the person in charge of the relevant subject department, or the person who has the responsibility for the coordination of the cross-curricular theme, skill or dimension, to write it.

Let us suppose that the Headteacher asks the HoD Mathematics to produce a written policy document showing how the Mathematics curriculum is to be implemented throughout the school and to outline forward plans for the department. The HoD Mathematics will know what will be taught, when it will be taught and who will teach it. Arrangements for assessment will relate to how teaching within the Mathematics department is organized. The HoD Mathematics can expect that all those timetabled to teach Mathematics can do so! Writing a policy document within a well-known and well-defined subject area, such as Mathematics, is not easy but who is able to write the policy and what issues it will address are relatively clear. This is not always so when an ICT Policy is written.

When developing ICT Policy, the need to organize some aspects of ICT across the curriculum may be a complicating factor. Pupils' experiences of ICT may happen in many, perhaps all, subjects and out of school. Management structures will be needed to support a whole-school approach. It is likely that the planning of the curriculum; assessment, recording and reporting; access to ICT resources; and CPD will all be coordinated throughout the whole school. Consequently, developing a whole-school ICT Policy may be a somewhat more complex task than writing a policy that predominantly addresses issues within the relatively well-defined focus of a traditional subject department. Moreover, it may not be entirely realistic to expect that all the teachers who might be asked to teach, use and assess ICT will already have sufficient skills to do so. As a result, the development of ICT Policy could involve the whole school. The HoD ICT should not be left to write the school's ICT Policy although s/he is likely to make a substantial contribution to it.

A management structure will be needed that is sufficiently effective and authoritative to organize the development, implementation, monitoring and evaluation of the ICT Policy throughout the school. While this will inevitably redefine itself as the ICT Policy is developed and put into practice, it is useful to have, at least, the foundations of a suitable management structure in place at the beginning. The discussion assumes that there is the following personnel in place:

- An ICT Coordinator who reports directy to senior management. The ICT Coordinator should be responsible for organizing pupils' ICT experiences throughout the curriculum into a coherent, integrated framework. The ICT Coordinator should have the skills to work with other teachers. In some schools the ICT Coordinator is referred to as the ICT Director.
- An HoD ICT who is responsible for the ICT department and discrete ICT.
- An ICT Manager who is responsible to the ICT Coordinator. The ICT Manager will have the technical skills required for the management of the school's ICT resources and will have time allocated to do this task. The ICT Manager is the line manager for ICT technicians.
- A Coordinating Group for ICT chaired by the ICT Coordinator. This committee considers the school's ICT Policy and implementation plan, and reviews practice. Membership of the Coordinating Group includes the HoD ICT and representatives from different subject departments, preferably HoDs. The subject department representatives will prevent important decisions affecting the whole-school curriculum being made by a few ICT specialists acting alone. These subject representatives will have the responsibility for ensuring that decisions regarding the ICT curriculum and resources reflect the needs of the whole school. Heads of subject departments are responsible for ensuring that their departmental schemes of work support the school's ICT Policy. In some schools, this committee is divided into two: a small executive committee consisting of a senior manager, the ICT coordinator and the HoDs of departments that make considerable use of ICT in teaching; and an open committee which all teachers and other staff can attend. This arrangement ensures quick decision-making and a wide catchment for new ideas and uses of technology.
- A requirement that every teacher is responsible for teaching ICT and using ICT to support learning.

Management structures should be explicit and should include arrangements for the monitoring the effectiveness of management itself. This might include regular reviews of performance in relation to agreed targets with prior agreement over the action to be taken if there is under- or over-performance. Accurate, independent minutes of meetings will also help indicate whether management is functioning effectively.

The curriculum and its organization

When writing the aims, a decision will have to be made regarding the approach to organizing the ICT curriculum that is desirable in the long term. The hybrid ICT approach places the teaching and assessment of discrete ICT in specialist classes, and encourages pupils to make use of ICT throughout the curriculum wherever this is appropriate. Discrete ICT gives pupils guaranteed access to an entitlement curriculum. However, it may not provide rich contexts in which pupils can explore the variety of uses of ICT. The cross-curricular approach delivers ICT through other subjects but many schools have found it difficult to implement effectively. The issues affecting the ICT curriculum and its organization are reviewed in Chapter 2; however, it has been found that a hybrid approach is most effective.

Assessment, recording and reporting

When it has been decided how the curriculum will be organized, a means of assessing, recording and reporting pupils' attainment and progress should be planned. Whichever system is seen as desirable, it must result in at least an individual summary of what each pupil can do and the progress each is making so that this can be reported to parents. There will also need to be some well-understood and clear mechanism for moderation of the assessments made by different teachers. Some possible arrangements are reviewed in Chapter 3.

ICT resources

Hardware

The ideal mix of hardware, and how it will be distributed throughout the school, should be described. As there is unlikely to be sufficient hardware to meet all requirements, schools should employ the hardware available in the way that best supports their approach to organizing the ICT curriculum.

The hybrid ICT approach leads to a distribution of hardware that is a compromise between centralizing all the ICT hardware in a few ICT rooms and distributing the hardware throughout the school. The specialist ICT facility is developed so that ICT can be taught to large classes. Possibly three or four ICT rooms will be needed and these could be located in different parts of the school. Small clusters of computers are also maintained in various locations throughout the school, where access is easy. For example, a cluster of computers located in the school library will be readily accessible and can be supervised easily. In some instances, clusters are located in specific classrooms where they will be heavily used, for example, a few computers may be permanently located in science for data logging experiments; and trolleys with laptops and/or tablets provided elsewhere. This approach can provide adequate facilities for specialist ICT studies, and ease of access for all pupils in all subjects.

If the cross-curricular ICT approach is adopted, hardware should be distributed to easily accessible locations throughout the school. One or more computers could be located in each classroom. While this makes ICT hardware available to each class, there are considerable disadvantages associated with this particular strategy. A more realistic alternative is to distribute the hardware in clusters throughout the school, and provide trolleys with laptops and/or tablets. This may be done in a way similar to the distribution arising from the hybrid ICT approach. However, in this case, it is likely that the specialist ICT facility will be greatly reduced or entirely absent.

If ICT is taught only as a discrete subject, all ICT hardware can be concentrated in ICT rooms with little or no hardware distributed around the school. Unfortunately, the hardware may then not be easily accessible to classes in subjects other than ICT.

The decision to standardize on one type of hardware, introduce a limited choice or make available the widest possible range of types of hardware is also important. With the same computers in use throughout the school, the cross-curricular ICT, discrete ICT and hybrid ICT approaches to organizing the curriculum can be associated with the particular ways of distributing ICT hardware described above. The introduction of even a limited choice of hardware affects this association. For example, if a school has chosen the hybrid ICT approach with the distribution of ICT hardware described above, it is anticipated that pupils will be taught how to use ICT in their specialist classes and will use ICT throughout the curriculum. However, if pupils are taught ICT on one type of hardware, and are then expected to use ICT on a different type of hardware, it is unlikely that they will be able to do so without additional instruction from the subject teacher. This defeats the intention of the hybrid ICT approach that pupils will learn ICT skills in specialist classes, and then use them throughout the curriculum without further specialist teaching about the hardware.

Similarly, if the cross-curricular ICT approach is adopted, pupils may not, in practice, have easy access to suitable hardware. They may not be able to use the hardware that is available because of all the different types deployed throughout the school. These problems are exacerbated if the school has decided to make available the widest range of ICT hardware possible. Even so, there are good reasons to ensure that pupils do experience a range of different types of computers: it is unlikely they will always have available to them the type of computer they are familiar with at school; and the underlying technology changes so rapidly that even the same type of computer may eventually be used in radically different ways.

When ICT is taught as a discrete subject, pupils' access to hardware can be more closely regulated. Standardized hardware could be used throughout pupils' planned ICT curriculum or more variety introduced in a planned way as and when this is seen as being desirable.

Software

How the school believes that continuity, progression and differentiation are best achieved in pupils' experiences of ICT software should be written into the aims of the ICT Policy.

Software should be easy to use and understand, for pupils working at different levels of ability. Using the software should make it more likely that pupils will make progress in both ICT and the subject in which they are using ICT. It should not make it more difficult. For example, if a spreadsheet is being used in Business Studies to generate graphs that show where the break-even point occurs, it should be easier to use the spreadsheet than draw the graphs by hand. Pupils who have difficulty understanding the concept of the break-even point should be able to use the spreadsheet to explore this concept, easily generating the graphs that will help them understand it.

Pupils should have available to them a range of software, that supports their learning as their knowledge and understanding of ICT develops. A single piece of software with different levels of access of increasing difficulty is ideal. Alternatively, different pieces of the same type of software of increasing complexity may be made available as pupils progress. Similarly, there may be a decision that certain features of software will be used in Year 7, with additional features in Year 8, and so on. In each case, there is an assumption of planned access and that this is shared with pupils, so that pupils learn to use progressively more complex software.

The decision to standardize on one type of software, introduce a limited choice or make available the widest possible range is also important. With standardized software in use on the same type of hardware, the three approaches to the curriculum characterized can be associated with the particular ways of distributing ICT hardware described. The use of even a few different examples of the same type of software can affect pupils' ability to make use of ICT easily any time and anywhere. For example, if a school has chosen the hybrid ICT approach with the associated distribution of ICT hardware described above, it is anticipated that pupils will be taught how to use software, such as a word processor, in their specialist ICT classes and will use it throughout the curriculum. However, if pupils are taught how to use one word processor in their ICT class and are then expected to use a different word processor in another subject, it is unlikely that they will be able to do so without some additional instruction or support from the subject teacher. This defeats the intention of the hybrid ICT approach that pupils will learn how to use ICT software in specialist classes and then use it throughout the curriculum without additional specialist teaching.

Similarly, if the cross-curricular ICT approach is adopted, pupils may not effectively have easy access to suitable software because they are unable to use that which is available to them. These problems are exacerbated if the school has decided to make available the widest range of ICT software possible. However, there are good reasons to ensure that pupils do experience a range of different types of software: it is unlikely that they will always have available to them the type of software they have been used to in school; and even the same software may change considerably between different versions.

With the discrete ICT approach, pupils' access to software can be more closely regulated. Standardized software could be used throughout pupils' planned ICT curriculum or more variety introduced as and when this is seen as being desirable.

The means of distribution of software throughout the school should also be decided. Distribution can be done either using a client server network or on local hard disks or a combination of these. Distributing software over a network tends to slow down the network significantly and it is important that network applications run as fast as possible, for example, when using web browsers for Internet access. Consequently, it is usual for an image to be created for a networked PC and, typically, this image is installed on the local hard disks of all the PCs in an ICT room. The same image could be used throughout the school with different images at specialist locations. For example, specialist software for music applications may only be required only on those computers used by the Music department.

Setting up, installing, testing and maintaining an image can be very time-consuming so that it is preferable to have only a small number of images in use throughout the school. A record should be kept of what software is included in each image and where that image is installed, and back-ups of the images should be stored securely. If this is done, it should be relatively easy to overcome software malfunction by re-installing the image. Taking this approach reduces the work involved considerably and can make security much easier to maintain.

Security

An effective means of ensuring the security of ICT resources may be described in the aims. ICT resources are expensive, and often have a high re-sale value. Schools that do not carefully secure their ICT resources are likely to have them damaged or stolen. It may be that the general security precautions implemented in the school are adequate. However, additional measures may need to be taken (see Chapter 4).

Unfortunately, security measures will have an impact on pupils' access to ICT resources. For example, pupils may be prevented from using ICT resources because supervision is not available at the time access is required. Security is important in ensuring computer equipment is not damaged or stolen. However, it should be remembered that the school's ICT resources are provided to help pupils learn. A balance must be found that allows reasonable access to ICT resources when pupils need to use them, and that keeps them secure.

Disaster recovery

An ICT Policy may also include within its remit procedures for disaster recovery. All hardware and software may malfunction at some time. Schools would be advised to have in place appropriate procedures for replacement and recovery. These might include:

- Back-ups of all software and data files on a regular basis (see Chapter 4).
- Preventative maintenance of all hardware.
- Arrangements to repair or replace broken hardware within agreed time limits.
- Arrangements to run vital software elsewhere. For example, if as a result of a fire, the school is destroyed, or otherwise inaccessible, some software may still be needed. Such software should be identified and arrangements to run it at another location should be made.

Data protection

A comprehensive ICT Policy may also include reference to the measures the school has taken to conform to the requirements of the Data Protection Acts (2003 and earlier). These Acts stipulate that all organizations keeping any personal information on living and identifiable people should register them with the Data Protection Registrar and this applies whether the information is stored electronically, on paper or otherwise. The legislation covers both school pupils and employees and regulates what can be done with personal information. Schools should consider the implications of the Data Protection Acts very carefully when using computers to manage information about pupils, employees and others. Data protection legislation is reviewed in Chapter 9.

Safeguarding and Equal Opportunities

Relevant aspects of the school's Safeguarding and Equal Opportunities Policies may be re-stated, re-interpreted, and elaborated in the ICT Policy with reference to ICT. This topic is dealt with more extensively in Chapter 5.

Pupils' access to ICT resources affects their access to the curriculum. If pupils do not have the same level of access to ICT resources, they cannot have the same opportunities to develop their knowledge, skills and understanding of ICT. This is not only a matter of making ICT resources available to all. It is also necessary to monitor and supervise pupils' actual access to and use of ICT resources to ensure that the arrangements made are effective in ensuring equal access.

An important part of safeguarding and equal opportunites in practice is the publication of acceptable use policies (AUPs). These are likely to be expressed differently for staff and pupils and cover a range of issues including esafety. Essentially, they are guidelines to what is acceptable behaviour when using the school's ICT resources. The AUP for pupils should be displayed prominently throughout the school wherever ICT resources are in use by pupils, see Figure 10.1.

Staffing and CPD

Clearly, the ideal is that the all teaching staff in a school should be fully competent in a wide range of ICT skills and knowledgeable about the full potential of ICT. However, this is probably too ambitious. Stated aims should be more realistic estimates of what levels of skill are required to deliver the chosen approach to the ICT curriculum.

If the discrete ICT approach is chosen, only a small number of staff must have ICT skills and knowledge but they should have the full range of skills and in-depth knowledge. With the hybrid ICT approach, in addition to these ICT specialists, more of the staff will need to know how to use the ICT resources in ways relevant to their subjects. With the cross-curricular approach, a much larger number of staff will need to be capable of using ICT, teaching ICT and assessing pupils' ICT capability. However, these teachers may only need expertise relevant to their particular subjects. For example, an English teacher may only need to know only how to use a word processor and desk top publishing software, how to support pupils' use of this software in the classroom, and how to assess pupils' competency in these.

CPD will be needed to raise all teachers' ICT skills to the required standard. This can be made available through a variety of mechanisms. ICT skills are often self-taught. Many teachers invest their own time in learning ICT skills for themselves. Whilst individual teachers can make considerable progress in developing their own ICT skills, small groups of teachers can often support each other more effectively. Skills learnt by individuals attending short day or evening courses can be cascaded to the group. Residential weekends can sometimes be helpful in sustaining impetus. The strategy for providing CPD in ICT should be agreed and clearly stated in the ICT Policy.

Funding

Realistic estimates of the total cost of each element of the ICT Policy will help in evaluating the affordability of the proposed curriculum model. Total costings will provide a measure of the magnitude of the investment that needs to be made by the school. Funding should be planned expenditure that can be relied on each year.

Activity

Discuss what provision for ICT you would like in your school.
  Record your discussion under these headings:

- The management structure for ICT.
- The ICT curriculum and its organization.
- The assessment, recording and reporting of pupils' work in ICT; and arrangements for moderation.
- Provision of ICT resources; including hardware and software, and arrangements for security, disaster recovery, and the implementation of the Data Protection Acts.
- Safeguarding and equal opportunities.
- Health and safety.
- Staffing and staff continuous professional development (CPD).
- Funding.

Audit

An audit is a statement of what is being done. It is essentially a descriptive process. In order to plan how to reach the long–term goals the school has set for itself when determining its aims, the starting points must be known. An audit describes exactly what is being done so that the school can plan what it will do in order to achieve its long-term aims.

It may be useful to present the audit in at least two different ways. There should be a detailed audit which is thorough and comprehensive. Such an audit will be required to enable administrative control to be exercised so that, for example, insurance claims are accurate. There may also need to be a summary audit, as the detailed audit, although necessary, is not often immediately meaningful to teachers and others involved in managing the curriculum.

For example, in a detailed audit, a computer may consist of a mouse, a keyboard, a system unit and a monitor. Each of these would be described in detail. For example, a system unit, model Lenovo H330 Desktop PC, containing an Intel Core i5-2320 processor; 4 Gbytes of RAM memory; a 500 Gbyte hard disk; 6 USB ports; connections for HDMI, VGA and Gigabit Ethernet; a memory card reader; and a DVD drive. The serial number and location would also be recorded. There may be separate sections in the detailed audit for system units, keyboards, monitors and other component parts. However, a detailed audit of this nature does not always present a clear view of what is available for use in the classroom. Teachers may find it more useful to know, for example, that a PC is available for use in Room 11. The summary audit should express the contents of the detailed audit in a form useful to teachers, curriculum planners, governors and others to whom a detailed audit would be confusing and, possibly, meaningless.

What the school needs to know

Below is a list of some of the questions schools may wish to ask when considering aspects of ICT Policy. It is not suggested that it is necessary or desirable to always include the answers to all of these questions. However, the answers should be known. They will often appear in more detailed appendices to the ICT Policy. The policy itself will be a meaningful summary which may be less comprehensible if too much detail is included.

Management structure

- What is the current management structure for organizing the staff involved in delivering the ICT curriculum?
- Which roles and responsibilities have these staff in relation to ICT?
- What are the strengths and weaknesses of the existing management structure?
- How is the effectiveness of management procedures monitored?
- How often are the results of monitoring reported and to whom?
- What are the strengths and weaknesses of these procedures?

The curriculum and its organization

- Do different groups of pupils have a different curriculum for ICT?
- If so, which groups of pupils have which curriculum?

For each different group of pupils in each year:

- How is the delivery of the ICT curriculum currently organized?
- Which timetable structures are used to deliver ICT?
- In what subjects is ICT taught?
- What ICT is currently taught in these subjects?
- In which subjects is ICT used?
- What use is currently made of ICT in these subjects?
- What are the strengths and weaknesses of the existing curriculum?
- How is curriculum provision monitored to ensure that the expected curriculum is delivered to each pupil?
- Which external syllabuses or specifications are used, especially for assessment at the end of Years 11 and 13?
- Which groups of pupils have access to which external syllabuses or specifications?
- How is the effectiveness of these arrangements monitored?

- How often are the results of monitoring reported and to whom?
- What are the strengths and weaknesses of these procedures?

Assessment, recording and reporting

For each different group of pupils in each year:

- How is ICT assessed?
- Are logs, profiles, eportfolios, coursework, controlled assessment or written examinations used in assessment?
- Are these on the VLE, on the network or on paper?
- For what purpose does assessment take place?
- Is it formative or summative?
- In which subjects is ICT assessed by which teachers?
- Are the requirements for I/GCSE and other external assessments met?
- What are the strengths and weaknesses of the existing arrangements for assessment?
- How is the effectiveness of assessment procedures monitored?

For each different group of pupils in each year:

- What assessment evidence and what records are collected?
- When are these collected?
- What administrative routines are used to collect the assessment evidence?
- What summaries of the results of assessment are prepared?
- When are these prepared?
- Is a statement bank used for feedback?
- How is this edited?
- What assessment evidence and what records must be retained and for how long?
- What arrangements are made for the storage of the assessment evidence and the associated records?
- Which teachers have what roles and responsibilities in collecting the evidence, summarizing it and ensuring the safe and secure storage of it?
- What are the strengths and weaknesses of the existing arrangements for collecting the evidence?
- How is the effectiveness of procedures for collecting the evidence monitored?

For each different group of pupils in each year:

- How is pupils' progress and attainment reported?
- When is it reported?
- What are the statutory requirements?
- Are these requirements met?
- Which teachers have what roles and responsibilities in reporting progress and attainment?
- What are the strengths and weaknesses of the existing arrangements for reporting progress and attainment?
- How is the effectiveness of these arrangements monitored?

For each different group of pupils in each year:

- What assessment evidence is moderated?
- Are there exemplars of pupils' graded work available that can be used to ensure standards are maintained from year to year?
- How is moderation of assessment organized?
- What moderation is done for internal assessments?
- What moderation is done for external assessments?
- When is moderation done?
- What record of the moderation process is retained and for how long?
- Where are these records stored?
- Are the moderation requirements for GCSE and other external assessments met?
- Which teachers have which roles and responsibilities in the moderation process?
- What are the strengths and weaknesses of the existing arrangements for moderation?
- How is the effectiveness of moderation procedures monitored?

Hardware

- Is there a hardware inventory?
- How regularly is the hardware inventory updated?
- Does the hardware inventory cover all the separate pieces of computer equipment in the school?
- For each piece of equipment, is there recorded on the hardware inventory, at least, the serial number, description, cost of purchase, location used and the name of the person responsible for it?
- What other information is kept on the hardware inventory about each piece of equipment?
- Is there a summary hardware inventory that gives the same information in terms that are readily understandable by teachers and curriculum planners?
- Is there a detailed plan of the school's network showing exactly where the network cable is accessible and the range of wireless connections?
- Who is responsible for keeping the hardware inventory and network plan up-to-date?
- What are the strengths and weaknesses of the existing arrangements for keeping a detailed, complete and up-to-date hardware inventory and network plan?
- How is the effectiveness of these arrangements monitored?
- How often are the results of monitoring reported and to whom?
- What are the strengths and weaknesses of these procedures?

Software

- Is there an inventory of software?
- How regularly is the software inventory updated?
- Does the software inventory cover all the programs and data files owned by the school?
- What information is kept on the software inventory about each program or data file?
- For each piece of software, is there recorded, at least, the serial number, description, cost of purchase, licence conditions and location?

- Is there a summary software inventory that gives the same information in terms that are readily understandable by teachers and curriculum planners?
- Who is responsible for keeping the software inventory up-to-date?
- What are the strengths and weaknesses of the existing arrangements for keeping a detailed, complete and up-to-date software inventory?
- Which checks are made to ensure that unlicensed software is not used?
- How is the effectiveness of these procedures monitored?
- How often are the results of monitoring reported and to whom?
- What are the strengths and weaknesses of these procedures?

Security

- What physical security precautions are taken to guard against unauthorized access and theft?
- For example, what locks, grills, laminates, alarms, anchors, and disk safes are used?
- Where are physical security precautions used?
- Are computers kept in secure locations?
- Who is responsible for checking that physical security precautions are satisfactory?
- What precautions are taken to restrict access to software to those authorized to use it?
- What system of passwords and user identity numbers and permissions is used?
- Who is given passwords and user identity numbers, and how are permissions varied for groups of users?
- How often are passwords and user identity numbers changed?
- Who is responsible for setting up new users and deleting old users and setting permissions?
- Can unauthorized users access network cables or otherwise gain access to the network?
- What measures are taken to protect the network cable from physical misuse, and the wireless network from unauthorized access?
- What steps are taken to protect the computer system from viruses and other malware?
- Who has overall responsibility for all aspects of security?
- How often do they report and to whom?
- How is the effectiveness of these arrangements monitored?
- How often are the results of monitoring reported and to whom?
- What are the strengths and weaknesses of these procedures?

Disaster recovery

- What back-ups of software are made?
- How often are back-ups of software made?
- What system of organizing regular back-ups is used?
- Where are back-ups stored?
- Are there at least three back-ups stored on site, locally off-site and remotely off-site?
- Who is responsible for taking back-ups and organizing the system of back-ups used?
- What preventative maintenance is carried out?
- How regularly is preventative maintenance carried out?
- What arrangements are made for repair or replacement of broken hardware?

- What arrangements have been made for software maintenance on a day-to-day basis and in the longer term?
- What arrangements have been made to run mission critical software if the school's computer systems are unavailable?
- Who has responsibility for ensuring that suitable arrangements are made for disaster recovery?
- How often are the results of monitoring reported and to whom?
- What are the strengths and weaknesses of these procedures?
- How is the effectiveness of these procedures monitored?

Data protection

- What systems containing personal data are registered with the Data Protection Registrar?
- What arrangements are made to collect personal data?
- What is the purpose for which the personal data is collected?
- Is the purpose for which the personal data collected clearly stated?
- Is the personal data collected relevant to the purpose it is used for?
- To whom is personal data disclosed and under what circumstances?
- How long is personal data kept?
- What arrangements are made for parents, pupils and others to look at personal data about them stored on electronic and paper files at the school?
- What charge is made?
- How are parents, pupils and others informed of these arrangements?
- What arrangements are made to ensure personal data remains accurate?
- What arrangements are made to have inaccurate data changed?
- Who is responsible for ensuring that the school meets the provisions of the Data Protection Acts?
- How often are the results of monitoring reported and to whom?
- What are the strengths and weaknesses of these procedures?
- How is the effectiveness of these procedures monitored?

Safeguarding and equal opportunities

- What monitoring is done of access to ICT resources?
- What is recorded during monitoring?
- Who does the monitoring?
- How often?
- Where and how often are the results of monitoring reported?
- What rules and constraints are used to ensure equal and safe access to ICT resources?
- When is access to ICT resources supervised and when is unsupervised access allowed?
- Who is responsible for and who supervises access to ICT resources?
- Are staff and pupils aware of what is meant by cyberbullying and what to do if they experience this?
- Can staff and pupils sceptically evaluate information?
- What information is allowed to be accessed or blocked on school networks?
- Are filters in use? What rules do these follow and can they be bypassed?

- Who should staff and pupils report to if they accidentally access pornography, or receive phishing emails?
- What precautions are taken to protect computers from viruses and pharming?
- Who should users contact if they encounter what they believe to be symptoms of a virus?
- What should users do and who should they inform if they encounter other users making illegal use of computers, for example, downloading music which is under copyright?
- When is it checked that computers are physically safe to use?
- What checks are made?
- Do checks include the full range of recommendations (see Chapter 5)?
- Are Equal Opportunities strategies in ICT congruent with those stated in the school's Equal Opportunities policy or other policies?
- Who is responsible for monitoring that equal opportunities issues are identified and appropriate action is taken?
- What data is collected to enable effective monitoring and at what time intervals?
- What gender, ethnic origin and age are staff who teach and use ICT on a regular basis? Who monitors this and where and when do they report?
- How often are the results of monitoring reported and to whom?
- Is there an acceptable use policy (AUP) for pupils?
- Is this displayed next to all computers pupils use?
- Is there an AUP for staff?
- How are staff made aware of the implications of an AUP?
- What are the strengths and weaknesses of these procedures?
- How is the effectiveness of these procedures monitored?

Staffing and CPD

- Who teaches ICT, helps pupils make use of ICT and assesses ICT?
- What ICT skills do they currently have?
- What ICT skills do they need?
- What arrangements are made for ICT CPD?
- Who provides the ICT CPD?
- Who is responsible for ensuring that an adequate programme of CPD is available?
- How often are the results of monitoring reported and to whom?
- What are the strengths and weaknesses of CPD provision?
- How is the effectiveness of this provision monitored?

Funding

- What are the current costs and sources of funding for each element of the ICT Policy?
- Which procedures are used to ensure spending remains within budget?
- Who is responsible for spending the budget?
- Which procedures are used to monitor the effective use of funds?
- Which criteria of effectiveness are used?

- Who is responsible for monitoring the effective use of funds?
- How often are the results of monitoring reported and to whom?
- What are the strengths and weaknesses of these procedures?
- How is the effectiveness of these procedures monitored?

How the school can find out what it needs to know

There are two basic strategies:

- The SLT or persons nominated by the SLT can find out what the current situation is by asking administrators, teachers, pupils, parents, caretakers, and ancillary staff. The opinions of all those involved can be sought through meetings, interviews, and questionnaires. Meetings and interviews are recorded or notes taken so that points raised can be thoroughly investigated at a later date. Questionnaires are carefully analysed and there should be opportunities for informal comments to be made. Those involved in collecting the evidence should meet together to discuss the results of their investigations. A detailed audit report and a summary are be produced.
- An individual involved with and well informed regarding the current situation can be asked to write a detailed audit report and summary.

The advantage of the first option is that a thorough, detailed and extensive audit report is likely to be produced. Unfortunately, the process of producing the audit report will be very time-consuming. The second option will lead to the production of an audit report in a much shorter time but it is more likely that there will be omissions or bias in the report. In each case, the audit report and summary should be discussed by the ICT Coordinating Group and revised accordingly. The whole staff should then have the opportunity to comment before the final version is agreed.

Activity

Describe the provision for ICT in your school. Record your findings under these headings:

- The management structure for ICT.
- The ICT curriculum and its organization.
- The assessment, recording and reporting of pupils' work in ICT; and arrangements for moderation.
- Provision of ICT resources, including hardware and software, and arrangements for security, disaster recovery, and the implementation of the Data Protection Acts.
- Safeguarding and equal opportunities.
- Health and safety.
- Staffing and staff continuous professional development (CPD).
- Funding.

Action

The aims stated within the ICT Policy are an indication of the long- term goals of the school; the audit is a comprehensive, detailed statement of the current circumstances within the school; an action plan is a programme for immediate implementation. The action plan consists of a number of action statements. An action statement should say what will be done in the next school year, who will do it, and what constitutes success. As such, these action statements should be recognized as being immediately achievable by those who will be involved in their implementation.

The action statements will direct the school from the audit towards the aims. That is, the action statements will indicate what the school should do in the short term to achieve the aims of the ICT Policy in the long term, starting with current circumstances in the school. However, what can be done will be constrained by the resources available to do it. It is useful to write all the proposed action statements and estimate the cost of implementing them before considering the constraints that limited funding will inevitably impose. If all the desired progress towards the aims cannot be achieved within available funding, a costed list of action statements will assist in prioritizing what can be done.

Some action statements will be attainable within existing resources, or with limited additional funding. For example, changing the management structure may only require some adjustment of existing responsibilities and the allocation of a limited amount of time for meetings. In contrast, some action statements will not be attainable without considerable additional expenditure. For example, developing and extending the ICT curriculum to include groups of pupils who currently do not have an adequate experience of ICT. This may require the purchase of large quantities of additional ICT hardware and software, or the employment of extra teachers with specialist ICT skills, knowledge and understanding, for example, in programming.

It may be worth considering whether action statements can be implemented by extending the functionality of existing resources. This can often be done for relatively little cost. For example, additional equipment or component parts could be purchased that extend the functionality of the school's hardware, i.e., more memory could be purchased for the computers, allowing a wider range of educational software to be run. Similarly, an intensive, well-structured programme of CPD could improve the ICT skills of existing staff, avoiding the need to employ more or different staff.

The action statements that can be funded from next year's budget indicate what will be done towards the realization of the aims of the ICT Policy. These are the action statements that should be included in the school's ICT Policy.

Activity

Discuss what could be done to improve the provision for ICT in your school.
Record your discussion under these headings:

- The management structure for ICT.
- The ICT curriculum and its organization.
- The assessment, recording and reporting of pupils' work in ICT, and arrangements for moderation.

- Provision of ICT resources, including hardware and software, and arrangements for security, disaster recovery, and the implementation of the Data Protection Acts.
- Safeguarding and equal opportunities.
- Health and safety.
- Staffing and staff continuous professional development (CPD).
- Funding.

Presentation of the ICT Policy

ICT policies may be presented in a variety of ways. The proposed approach to arriving at a whole-school ICT Policy described in this chapter may be reflected in the final form of the ICT Policy. This way of presenting the ICT Policy clearly separates the long-term aims, the audit of ICT resources and the actions to be taken in the next school year. Separate sections can be useful in keeping their content in focus and up to date. The aims provide a relatively static indication of the overall goals that should be taken into account when planning. A separate audit section provides a framework for the administrative work that will need to be done from day to day. The action section indicates what should be done in the next school year, providing clear, short-term objectives for day-to-day working. This separation of the aims, audit and action sections may assist clarity in planning, and provide useful working documentation which can be a focus for the day-to-day organization, administration, and implementation tasks that must be done.

However, presentation of the ICT Policy with separate sections for each of the aims, the audit and the actions to be taken, can obscure inter-connections between them. For example, when reading the aims section, it may not be clear what is currently being done to achieve them or what the starting point was. In this case, it may be difficult to evaluate progress without reference to the audit and action sections. Similarly, a separate audit section gives an up-to-date snapshot of the resources currently available but does not indicate why these are made available or what is being done to remedy deficiencies. The action section may provide a concise summary of what is being done but will not provide a useful rationale for doing it or show how the actions now being taken contribute to long-term developments. For these reasons, schools may prefer to present the aims, the audit and the actions to be taken in a more integrated format when compiling the version of the ICT Policy that will be distributed to governors, parents, staff and inspectors. If the ICT Policy is presented with the associated elements of the aims, audit and action sections summarised and grouped together, it may be more comprehensible. For example, see the example ICT Policy below. It is not uncommon for schools to present their ICT Policies in this way to create a more informal, readable document. Greater detail, and the separation of the aims, audit and action sections of the ICT Policy are useful for day-to-day planning and management. However, the ICT Policy may be more comprehensible and meaningful to governors, parents, staff and inspectors if these separate sections are then presented in an integrated, summarized form. More detailed information can be included as appendices.

Some sections of the ICT Policy may be best expressed as posters. For example, the AUP for pupils could be a copy of the poster that is displayed where pupils use computers and that informs them of what they can and cannot do when using school computers.

An example of a school ICT Policy

The purpose of an ICT Policy is to provide an overview of what is happening in the school, and and its purpose and direction. The example ICT Policy below is a summary policy. It does not incorporate all the detailed planning that underpins it, though some of this could be incorporated as appendices. Some possible appendices are shown. The ICT Policy should be comprehensible to governors and useful to teachers. Consequently, only significant developments are described.

Manor School ICT Policy for the school year beginning Sept. 20XX

Mission statement

The school intends to provide all pupils with opportunities to acquire knowledge, skills and understanding of ICT in breadth and in depth, so that they can use ICT to support their learning throughout the curriculum, and are well prepared for work, or further study when they leave Manor School.

Management structure

The school wishes to establish an ICT Coordinating Committee that will be chaired by the Deputy Head (curriculum), and will include the ICT Coordinator, the HoD ICT and all ICT teachers, the ICT Manager and technicians, and one representative from each subject department. This committee will have oversight of the whole ICT curriculum, and overall responsibility for planning and implementation of ICT Policy, collectively and as named individuals.

At present, there is an ICT Coordinator who is responsible for all aspects of the use of ICT throughout the school. The ICT Coordinator chairs the ICT group which is regularly attended by teachers of Design Technology, Mathematics and Music but no other subject departments. The ICT Group meets once or twice a term. Minutes are not taken. This group has very little influence on curriculum coordination and development planning. No other ICT teachers attend other than the ICT Coordinator; the ICT Manager does not attend and no ICT technicians attend.

By the end of September, all subject departments will nominate a representative to attend the ICT Coordinating Committee. This committee will meet for the first time during October, and thereafter at least once each term. The Deputy Head (curriculum) will organize and chair meetings. Minutes will be taken. During the Summer Term and by the end of it, the ICT Coordinating Committee will review and update the ICT Policy. The Deputy Head (curriculum) will report progress to the Headteacher and governors as required but at least annually.

The curriculum and its organization

The school aims to deliver a core programme of study in discrete ICT lessons during a single one-hour period per week for all pupils in KS3 and two hours per week in KS4. All pupils will be entered for a vocational course equivalent to a GCSE, such as, Cambridge National Certificate. Optional courses leading to IGCSE ICT and GCSE Computing will be available for those who choose further study in KS4 and this will involve a further three hours of timetabled discrete ICT each week and one hour each week after school. Pupils' experiences of ICT throughout the curriculum will be coordinated with their studies in discrete ICT lessons to ensure progression and continuity.

Pupils' experiences of ICT are not yet fully coordinated across the whole curriculum. Pupils in Key Stage 3 are timetabled for ICT for approximately one period per week for one term per year as part of a Technology carousel that also involves Design Technology and Music. As a result, pupils' experiences of ICT are restricted and are often too narrow and superficial. All pupils are entered for the Cambridge National Certificate at the end of Year 11 but no pupils are entered for I/GCSE or other external assessment in ICT or Computing.

From the start of the next school year, it is expected that pupils in Key Stages 3 and 4 will be timetabled for at least one period of discrete ICT per week, and will complete the Cambridge National Certificate by the end of Year 10. In Year 11, a few pupils will be able to choose to study for IGCSE ICT and GCSE Computing; other pupils will concentrate on subjects where they will be more successful in external examinations.

A plan for the coordination of discrete ICT and the use of ICT throughout the curriculum is needed. To begin with, a curriculum audit will be completed by Christmas. The ICT Coordinator will ensure that the plan is considered by the whole staff, approved by the ICT Coordinating Committee and complete by Easter. This will be distributed to Heads of Department in the week following the Easter holidays for inclusion in their curriculum plans for the following school year. The Deputy Head (curriculum) will ensure that any necessary adjustments to the organization of the timetable are made. It should be possible to implement the plan within the level of ICT staffing and resources anticipated at the start of the next school year.

Assessment, recording and reporting

The school will report pupils' progress and attainment in ICT to parents once each year in accordance with the whole school policy on assessment, recording and reporting, and in such a manner that statutory requirements are met. Teachers will assess and record pupils' progress and attainment in discrete ICT classes. Pupils' progress and attainment in subjects other than ICT will be assessed and and a summary grade recorded by their teachers who will inform each pupil's ICT teacher. This will be integrated with assessments made in discrete ICT. A centralized record of pupils' progress and attainment will be assembled by the ICT coordinator. The ICT coordinator will moderate all assessments, and establish consistent standards throughout the school based on a portfolio of examples of pupils' work at different levels of attainment.

At present, the above system is in place except that the integration of the assessments made in discrete ICT with those made in other subjects is poor, and there is no satisfactory system of internal moderation. As Heads of Departments present their new curriculum plans for the next school year, the Deputy Head (curriculum) will ensure that these include appropriate proposals for assessment, recording and reporting. Centralized recording and reporting will need extending in the next school year to incorporate these assessments and those done by the new ICT specialist teachers. The ICT coordinator will ensure this is done, and that pupils' reports include a summary of their progress and attainment in ICT. Proposals for instituting a practical system of internal moderation will be included in the next ICT Policy.

Hardware and software

The school intends to provide four ICT rooms with 30 computers in each and five clusters of five computers located in the library, the Business Studies area, the Design Technology base room, the Humanities block and the Music studio. There will be a staff workroom with six PCs. All computers will be networked, and access to a wireless network will be available throughout the school. A full range of software will be available to include: word processing, graphics, spreadsheet, database, games construction, and audio and video editing. Where additional software specific to particular subjects is required, this will be chosen by the teachers concerned in consultation with the ICT Coordinator. As far as is possible and desirable, a standardized menu will be used, giving all pupils and teachers access to the same software in the same way in all locations. A VLE will be used to distribute subject-specific electronic resources, for example, worksheets, data, audio and video.

The school presently has three ICT rooms containing 30 networked PCs. There is a cluster of five networked PCs in the library and five PCs in the Business Studies area and five PCs in the Humanities block. The staff work room has six PCs. User interfaces may be different and pupils may encounter a range of software that does the same tasks but is operated in different ways. The wireless network is not accessible from some classrooms.

Some 30 PCs will be purchased to be installed in a new ICT room accessible from the library. The five PCs currently in the library will be moved to the Design Technology base room. A further five PCs will be purchased for the Music studio. The ICT Coordinator will produce a map of the school showing where there is access to the wireless network and additional routers will be installed where they are likely to be most effective.

The HoD ICT will be responsible for the choice of software. Software will be open source and industry standard where possible and this will be made available throughout the school. Where necessary, additional licences will be purchased for the software currently in use. A whole-school VLE will be set up to for all subject areas and provide subject-specific resource materials and teacher-researched Internet links for student use with password-protected areas set up where necessary. The VLE will be set up, maintained and developed by the ICT Manager. Heads of Department are asked to periodically review content on their subject's area of the VLE and individual teachers should report difficulties to the ICT Manager.

Planning, development, and implementation will be the responsibility of the ICT Coordinator who will make a written progress report to the Deputy Head (curriculum) at the end of each term. These developments should be completed by the start of the next school year.

Security, disaster recovery and Data Protection

The school aims to protect hardware, software and data by:

- Placing grilles over the windows of ICT rooms where these are on the ground floor.
- Extending the school's burglar alarm system into ICT rooms and surrounding corridors.
- Attaching all computers to walls or desks using steel cables.
- Locking all rooms containing ICT hardware when this is not in use.
- Restricting access to networked software by giving teachers and pupils their own individual user identification numbers and passwords.
- Allowing users to change their passwords when they wish.
- Setting permissions for groups of users.
- Performing an automatic virus check each time a user logs on to the network.
- Installing network cabling so that it is inaccessible.
- Requiring a password for access to the school's wireless network.
- Backing up all fileservers each day to a local server and each week to a remote server.
- Correcting hardware and software faults as they arise, and carrying out preventative maintenance once each year during the summer holidays.
- Establishing mutual support arrangements with a local business or another school so that in the event of widespread and serious damage to ICT systems, mission critical software can still be run.
- Meeting the statutory requirements of the Data Protection Acts.

At present, the above arrangements have been implemented but not always comprehensively. For example, some but not all computer equipment is secured to walls or desks. Back-ups of the fileserver are taken once per week overnight to a remote file server. Arrangements for meeting the requirements of the Data Protection Acts are ad hoc and inconsistently implemented. There is no arrangement for running mission critical software elsewhere.

The ICT Coordinator will identify hardware which is not secured to walls or desks, and produce a list for immediate action. The cost of extending back-ups will be explored. Arrangements for meeting the requirements of the Data Protection Acts will be clearly stipulated and their effectiveness assessed. Mission critical software will be identified and arrangements considered that will allow this to be run at another location. Procedures should be reviewed by Christmas and put into place by the end of the school year. The ICT Coordinator will report to the Deputy Head (curriculum).

Safeguarding and Equal Opportunities

In ICT, in addition to implementing whole-school policies for Safeguarding and Equal Opportunities, it will be ensured that pupils' access to ICT resources is supervised and monitored. There is no unsupervised access during timetabled classes and no access at other times. It is intended that a computer club will be run at lunchtimes and after school each day in the library beginning at the start of the next school year. These will be organized by the HoD ICT and will be supervised by a rota of teachers who will register pupils' attendance. These registers will be used to monitor access. If some groups are found to be under-represented, the reasons for this will be investigated by the ICT Coordinating Committee, and appropriate corrective action determined case by case.

The Acceptable Use Policy for pupils is produced as a poster and reads as shown in Figure 10.1.

Acceptable use of ICT

You may use ICT in school to help you with your work provided you stick to these rules:

- You are responsible for your own behaviour on the Internet and when using ICT.
- Do not tell anyone else your user ID or password.
- Make sure you only access suitable websites.
- Report unsuitable websites immediately to your teacher.
- Be careful in the language you use, particularly in email and other communications.
- Only contact online people you know or those the teacher has approved.
- Do not send chain letters.
- Only visit chat rooms when given permission to do so.
- Report cyberbullying to your teacher.
- Do not get involved in cyberbullying using social networking sites, texting or other methods.
- Do not download illegal files or attempt to install downloaded software.
- Do not attempt to bypass school security or hack into the school network.
- Do not post personal information online. For example, full names, telephone numbers and addresses (including email addresses) should not be posted.
- Do not arrange to meet someone you have only met online unless this is part of an approved school project.

If you do not follow these rules, you will be warned and may be banned from using the school network and the Internet.

Figure 10.1 Rules for acceptable use of ICT in school

Staff Acceptable Use Policy

All staff who use the school ICT network are required to read the staff AUP and sign it (Figure 10.2).

Staffing and CPD

The school intends to ensure that all teachers have the skills, knowledge and understanding to enable them to use ICT where necessary in their all their professional activities, and to support pupils who use ICT to learn.

The school has two specialist ICT teachers, the HoD ICT and one main-scale teacher. Some 90 per cent of the entire teaching staff can use a word processor with around half of these having a good in-depth knowledge. Around 70 per cent of teachers currently have the skills to use subject-related software, and of these 20 per cent can use a wider range of ICT software which is not related to their subject.

Acceptable Use Policy for Staff

Use of the Internet

- Use of the Internet at school should be to enhance teaching and learning or for administrative purposes.
- Limited personal use is acceptable before and after school, at lunchtime and during breaks.
- Accessing inappropriate or indecent materials will result in disciplinary action and the police may be informed.
- Be cautious when posting personal information online including on social networking sites and blogs.
- Do not post material that damages the reputation of the school or would cause parents and others concern about your suitability to work with children.
- Do not be 'friends' with, or communicate with, pupils on social networking or similar websites, for example, Facebook.

Use of email

- The school will provide you with an email address.
- Use this email address for school business.
- You must use your school email address to communicate with pupils. You must not use your personal email address.

Use of the school ICT network

- Each member of staff has a unique user identification.
- Immediately change your password from the password you are given by the ICT Manager.
- Change your password at least once each term.
- Passwords should not be obvious; and should include alpha and numeric characters; and a mix of upper and lower case.
- Never tell anyone your password or write it down.
- When you use ICT rooms with pupils, make sure that the pupils' AUP is on display and that pupils' behaviour is acceptable.
- When accessing school registration and administration software, do not leave the computer unattended and make sure pupils cannot see what is displayed on the screen.
- Do not use removable media on the school network if you have used it on other computers. Viruses and other malicious software can be transmitted to the school network from memory sticks that have been infected elsewhere.
- Personal ICT devices, for example, smart phones, should not be connected to the school ICT network without prior approval from the ICT Manager.
- Departmental purchases of new ICT hardware should be approved by the ICT Manager.
- Software installed on the school network should be approved by the ICT Manager.
- Software must be licensed.
- If you suspect that illegal or inappropriate content has been accessed on a computer, it should be immediately turned off and secured. Do not attempt to check whether content is illegal by accessing it. Contact a member of Senior Management immediately.
- You must have the permission of the ICT Manager to take school ICT equipment home.

Use of the school laptop

- The school will provide you with a laptop which may be used in school and elsewhere.
- If the laptop goes missing or is stolen, inform the ICT Manager as soon as possible. If there is a related insurance claim, you are responsible for the excess of £150 and should discuss this with the school's Finance Manager. The school's insurance does not cover the laptop if it is left in an unattended car unless it is locked out of sight in the boot.
- You are responsible for backing up data or programs you have stored on your laptop or on removable media.
- The laptop is supplied with software installed which includes MS Windows, Microsoft Office and the Adobe Creative suite.

- Anti-virus software is installed on the laptop and this updates automatically.
- You must ensure that additional software installed by you is licensed and appropriate for use in an educational setting. Requests for additional software to be purchased by the school should be made to your Head of Department.
- Should any faults occur, advise the school's ICT Manager as soon as possible. The school cannot guarantee to provide a substitute laptop while it is being repaired.
- Costs incurred by staff accessing the Internet from home are the responsibility of the teacher, and not chargeable to the school.
- School telephone lines must not be used for Internet access.
- Government and school policies regarding appropriate use, data protection, computer misuse and health and safety must be respected and promoted by all users of the laptop, at school and at home.

If you have any questions or concerns regarding the above, please contact the Deputy Head (curriculum).

You are required to sign that you have read this AUP and agree to it. If you have borrowed a school laptop, you must sign for it at the start of each term. Please see the Deputy Head (curriculum) to do this.

Figure 10.2 Staff acceptable use policy

The school intends to employ one additional specialist ICT teacher from the start of the next school year and to redeploy an existing member of staff to teach ICT. As the focus of development in the next school year is the ICT curriculum, CPD for staff will prioritize those activities that support this. This will be based around a support group comprising the HoD ICT and the three specialist ICT teachers and other teachers who plan to use ICT in their subjects. CPD for those not immediately concerned with teaching ICT will be planned for the following school year.

Funding

Estimated expenditure for this school year is shown in Table 10.1.

Table 10.1 Estimated expenditure on ICT

Item	Cost
An additional ICT room adjacent to the library with 30 PCs and five PCs for the Music studio Example of PC that could be purchased: Lenovo H330 Desktop PC @ £449 each Intel Core i3 processor; Windows® 7; 4GB memory; 500GB hard drive; 20″ monitor, mouse and keyboard	£15,715
Software: Open Office, Adobe Creative Suite, etc. – estimated cost	£6,000
Rewiring, lighting, etc. where required – estimated cost	£5,000
Furniture: chairs, blinds, etc. where required – estimated cost	£3,500
Additional routers and installation – estimated cost	£1,000
Additional security measures	£1,500
Total	£32,715

These purchases will be organized by the ICT Coordinator. Orders must be approved by the Deputy Head (curriculum) and Deputy Head (finance) before they are issued.

Appendices

1   Summary and detailed curriculum audit (when available).
2   Summary and detailed hardware inventory.
3   Summary and detailed software inventory.
4   Security audit.
5   Arrangements for disaster recovery.
6   Job description for the ICT coordinator.
7   Job descriptions for the new ICT teachers.

Activity

Look at a range of example of school ICT policies. You could search Google using the keywords 'ICT Policy secondary school'.

Compare and contrast different policies with the example given above.

Summary

This chapter recommends developing a whole school ICT Policy by determining the aims of the school, conducting a thorough and detailed audit, then deciding what action will be taken within the next school year.

If possible, an effective management structure should be put in place before the development process begins. For example, a school might establish an ICT Coordinating Group with the responsibility for coordinating ICT throughout the school. This could be chaired by a member of the SLT. The ICT Coordinator, the HoD ICT, specialist ICT teachers, a representative from each subject department, the ICT Manager and ICT technicians could be invited to attend. The subject representatives will have responsibility for the implementation of the school's ICT Policy within their departments.

The ICT Policy may be presented with separate sections for the aims, the audit and the action. This can help focus the planning and review process, and assist with day-to-day organization and administration. However, an ICT Policy may be more meaningful if it is then presented in an integrated manner, with the related sections of the aims, the audit and the action adjacent to each other (see the Manor School ICT Policy on p. 155).

Further reading

Buckinghamshire ICT Curriculum Support Team (n.d.) *On-Line Handbook for School ICT Coordinators*, available at: http://www.bucksict.org.uk/ICT%20Coordinators%20Handbook/ (accessed 7 June 2012).

Syllabuses and specifications for external assessment

There are a very wide variety of external assessments available from a wide range of Awarding Organizations (AOs) throughout England, Wales and Northern Ireland. AOs are also referred to as examination boards and awarding bodies.

Ofqal lists those organizations and qualifications that are registered and regulated on the Register of Regulated Qualifications (Ofqal, 2011c). At the time of writing, there are over 180 AOs, some of which offer only one or two specialist qualifications and others which offer a wide range of general qualifications. It had been suggested that these could be merged into one awarding body but this suggestion was rejected by Ofqal (Gardner, 2011). There is also a very wide range of different qualifications available and the DfE maintains a list of qualifications that will be funded for teaching in state schools (DfE, 2011a).

The AOs most likely to be used in English secondary schools are shown in Table A.1 and these can be contacted through their websites.

The level of qualifications suitable for 11- to 19-year-olds is described in the National Qualifications Framework (NQF). A summary of levels 1–3 is given in Table A.2 and it is described in detail on: www.direct.gov.uk.

The level of a qualification is a guide to the difficulty of the content and entries tend to be age-related. In general, most candidates will be entered for GCSE qualifications at age 16 and A-level qualifications at 18. Even so, students can be assessed at any age at any level. For example, some schools enter pupils for Functional Skills qualifications at the end of Key Stage 3.

Qualifications are often referred to as being 'vocational' or 'academic'. Vocational qualifications tend to be more employment-related than academic qualifications. At level 2, Cambridge Nationals and BTECs would be considered to be vocational qualifications, whereas GCSE or IGCSE would be thought of as academic. This is likely to affect whether assessment is mainly coursework, controlled assessment or examinations.

AOs provide a range of support materials for teachers for the qualifications they provide. What is available varies between AOs and you should look at the AO's website and check provision with the ICT subject officer at the AO. It is particularly important to check out in detail the subject content and the way in which the qualification is assessed. This information will be found in the specification.

Some support materials are freely available to anyone accessing an AO's website. For example, the AQA GCSE ICT specification and a scheme of work can be freely downloaded from the website, and you can contact 'Ask AQA' online if you have any queries. There are also freely available specimen assessments for each component of the assessment, for example, specimen question papers and specimen data files.

Table A.1 Awarding organizations' websites

Awarding organization	Website	Based in
AQA	www.aqa.org.uk	Manchester
Edexcel (includes: BTEC)	www.edexcel.com	London
OCR (includes: CIE)	www.ocr.org.uk	Cambridge
WJEC	www.wjec.co.uk	Cardiff
CEA	www.rewardinglearning.org.uk	Belfast

Table A.2 The National Qualifications framework levels 1–3

NQF level	Examples of qualifications
Entry	Functional Skills (FS) at entry level
1	FS at level 1
	GCSE grades D–G
2	FS at level 2
	GCSE grades A*–C
3	A-levels

In contrast, access to other materials is sometimes restricted. For example, at the time of writing, AQA restrict access to their Secure Key Materials which includes:

- previous question papers and mark schemes;
- controlled assessment tasks;
- examples of candidates' work with commentaries by Principal Examiners;
- reports on the examinations.

In order to access the Secure Key Materials, you have to register and will need to provide the centre number of your school. These restrictions can make it difficult for those who do not work in a recognized centre to obtain information about the qualifications.

Because of the number and range of qualifications available, examples of the content and assessment methodology have been selected from those available at level 2.

GCSE ICT

Pupils may take courses based on the specifications that Ofqal approve for GCSE ICT. A GCSE ICT specification must meet the requirements of the national subject criteria for GCSE ICT (Ofqal, 2009a). Copies of specifications can be downloaded from the AO's website.

A comparison of the GCSE ICT specifications available from Edexcel and AQA is in Table A.3. The AQA GCSE ICT full course is compared with the Edexcel GCSE ICT single award as these are both single GCSE courses. AQA also offer a GCSE short course which is half a single award, and Edexcel also offer a double award.

The most obvious difference between the specifications is that the AQA has three units that are assessed, of which two are marked by teachers, while Edexcel has only two units, one of which is marked by teachers. The time AQA allows for controlled assessment is

Table A.3 A comparison of the AQA and Edexcel GCSE ICT specifications

AQA GCSE ICT – full course	Edexcel GCSE ICT – single award
3 assessed units: Unit 1 – systems and applications Unit 2 – applying ICT Unit 3 – practical problem solving	4 assessed units: Unit 1 – living in a digital world Unit 2 – using digital tools
The type and timing of the assessment: Unit 1 – written paper – 90 minutes Unit 2 – controlled assessment – 25 hours Unit 3 – controlled assessment – 25 hours The units can be taken in any order. Candidates can re-sit units.	The type and timing of the assessment: Unit 1 – written paper – 90 minutes Unit 2 – controlled assessment – 40 hours The units can be taken in any order. Candidates can re-sit units.
The weighting of the assessment: Unit 1 – 40% Unit 2 – 30% Unit 3 – 30%	The weighting of the assessment: Unit 1 – single 40% Unit 2 – single 60%
What is assessed: Unit 1 Section A: 10 short answer questions Section B: three extended answer questions Section C: one essay from a choice of two questions Unit 2 – solve one or more tasks in context provided by the AO Unit 3 – solve one practical problems out of six provided by the AO	What is assessed: Unit 1 – five compulsory questions. Each question includes multiple choice, short answer and extended writing. Unit 2 – one task made up of four activities.
Teacher involvement in marking: Unit 1 – AO marked Unit 2 – teacher marked; AO moderated Unit 3 – teacher marked; AO moderated	Teacher involvement in marking: Unit 1 – AO marked Unit 2 – teacher marked; AO moderated
Results reported as grades from A*–G. Grade A* is the highest grade available.	Results reported as grades from A*–G. Grade A* is the highest grade available.

also very different from the time Edexcel allows. Both specifications cover the national subject criteria for GCSE ICT and it can be expected that the majority of the subject content will be common across the specifications. However, the way each organizes this content is very different.

Arrangements for organizing GCSE assessment are under continuous review. An outcome of the Wolf Report (2011) is that all GCSEs taken after summer 2013 will be linear with examinations at the end of the course. There is also likely to be more external assessment with much less internal assessment carried out in schools. IGCSEs are already linear and externally assessed – see below. In addition, spelling, punctuation and grammar will be assessed after summer 2013.

IGCSE

IGCSE courses are available internationally and are popular in English independent schools (BBC, 2009). Specifications for IGCSE ICT are available from Edexcel and CIE and these are compared in Table A.4.

Table A.4 A comparison of the Edexcel and CIE IGCSE ICT specifications

Edexcel IGCSE ICT	CIE IGCSE ICT
Assessed through: Paper 1 – A Written paper Paper 2 – A Practical paper	Assessed through: Paper 1 – A Written paper Paper 2 – A Practical paper Paper 3 – A Practical paper
The timing of the assessment: Written paper – 90 minutes Practical paper – 3 hours	The timing of the assessment: Written paper 1–2 hours Practical paper 2–2.5 hours Practical paper 3–2.5 hours
The weighting of the assessment: Written paper – 50% Practical paper – 50%	The weighting of the assessment: Written paper 1 – 40% Practical paper 2 – 30% Practical paper 3 – 30%
What is assessed: Written paper – compulsory multiple-choice and short-answer questions. No choice of questions. Practical paper – a computer-based examination, taken under controlled conditions, which consists of structured activities.	What is assessed: Written paper 1 Practical papers 2 and 3 – a computer-based examinations, taken under controlled conditions, which consists of a number of practical tasks.
Teacher involvement in marking: Written paper – AO marked Practical paper – AO marked	Teacher involvement in marking: Written paper 1 – AO marked Practical paper 2 – AO marked Practical paper 3 – AO marked

Subject content
Written paper:
  ICT Systems
  Impact of ICT
  Use ICT Systems
  Find and Select Information
  Develop, Present and Communicate
Practical paper
  Use ICT Systems
  Find and Select Information
  Develop, Present and Communicate
  Information
	Subject content set out in eight interrelated sections:
	Types and components of computer systems
	Input and output devices
	Storage devices and media
	Computer networks
	Data types
	The effects of using ICT
	The ways in which ICT is used
	Systems analysis and design

Results reported as grades from A*–G. Grade A* is the highest grade available.	Results reported as grades from A*–G. Grade A* is the highest grade available.

Restrictions that stopped state schools from offering IGCSE qualifications have been lifted (DfE, 2010). Edexcel and CIE IGCSE courses are assessed through examination only and this is thought to be more rigorous and manageable than the controlled assessment used in GCSE. 'Controlled assessments are cumbersome and time-consuming and restrict the ability of schools like Manchester Grammar School to provide inspirational teaching for the most able pupils' (Ray, cited in BBC, 2009).

IGCSE is much more manageable in schools than GCSE and assessment is more comprehensive, thorough and rigorous. The organization of the assessment is more straightforward than for GCSE and does not require teachers to mark and moderate it as it is assessed through papers set and marked by the AO. Assessment is at the end of the course rather than modular.

GCSE Computing

Some pupils in some schools have the option of studying GCSE Computing or a similarly named course: OCR – GCSE Computing; and Edexcel and AQAc GCSE Computer Science. Specifications are significantly more technical than I/GCSE ICT and designed for 'mechanics' rather than 'car drivers'. At the time of writing, these specifications and supporting resources are under development.

Functional Skills (FS)

Functional Skills (FS) are the elements of English, Mathematics and ICT that provide learners with the skills and abilities they need in their everyday lives and at work. FS qualifications are available in each of English, Mathematics and ICT separately. The subject content of the FS ICT qualifications offered by AOs is closely based on the national FS criteria for ICT (Ofqal, 2009b). Specifications for FS ICT are available from several AOs and those from Edexcel and AQA are compared in Table A.5.

The above FS in ICT assessments from Edexcel and AQA are very similar in outline, but there are differences:

- Edexcel require candidates to have access to the Internet in section A but not in section B so that candidates' access to the Internet must be turned off while they are

Table A.5 A comparison of the FS ICT specifications from Edexcel and AQA

Edexcel FS in ICT (at Level 2)	AQA FS in ICT (at Level 2)
Separate assessment at levels 1 and 2; and entry levels 1, 2 and 3.	
Assessed through a computer-based test which is 2 hours in length.	
There are four opportunities to take the test each year and it can be taken within a 5-day period.	
Format of the test:	Format of the test:
Candidates complete a task using ICT.	Candidates are provided with a Candidate Booklet which guides them through a series of activities they must complete using familiar software.
Data files are provided beforehand.	
In Section A of the test, candidates need access to the Internet.	
In Section B, Internet access is not allowed. Candidates print their work.	One activity involves the use of simulated Internet access, email and office applications.
	Data files are provided beforehand.
	Candidates print their work.
The test is set and marked by the AO.	The test is set and marked by the AO.
Subject content: exact conformity to the FS in ICT subject criteria.	Subject content: exact conformity to the FS in ICT subject criteria.
Pass or Fail at the level entered.	Pass or Fail at the level entered.

sitting the examination. AQA do not allow Internet access at any time during the examination.

- Edexcel's candidates will be familiar with the software they are using as it will be the same software they use each day. AQA uses a Flash simulation of a PC desktop with email, a web browser, a spreadsheet, and folders, and this has to be installed on school computer systems beforehand so that candidates can use it during the test. Some common software features are not fully implemented and the speed at which pupils can work may be affected.

When considering which FS in ICT specification to provide in school, teachers should work through a complete test so that they can judge the likely response of their pupils.

Cambridge Nationals, BTEC and DiDA

Cambridge Nationals replaced OCR Nationals which were the most popular ICT vocational qualification taught in secondary schools. Students learn transferable skills that are practical and relevant, and are needed in future study and the workplace.

Cambridge Nationals are available at NQF levels 1, 2 and 3. They assess the application of ICT skills through their practical use. At levels 1 and 2 pupils can be entered for the Award, Certificate or Diploma (see Table A.6).

The Cambridge National qualifications in ICT are unitized and at level 2, units are graded Pass, Merit and Distinction. There are currently 11 units grouped into four strands: Business Information Systems; Creative; Technical; and Learner-initiated project. At least 20 per cent of each unit is externally assessed with the remainder internally assessed and moderated by teachers. The Business Information Systems strand has two units and one of these must be chosen for the Certificate and the Diploma.

Unit 1 is assessed through a one-hour written paper that is marked by the AO but other units have centre-assessed tasks which are marked by teachers and moderated by the AO. Quality of written communication is assessed in all units. Model centre assessed tasks can be downloaded free from the OCR website. Candidates can re-sit units.

BTEC Firsts are also vocationally related qualifications and these are available through Edexcel. They are available in a similar range of subjects to OCR Nationals. ICT is reinterpreted as Information and Creative Technology.

Table A.6 Cambridge Nationals award, certificate and diploma

Cambridge Nationals at levels 1 and 2	Units to be taken	Guided learning hours	Equivalence in school league tables
Award	Units 1 and 2	60	No equivalent
Certificate	1 and 2 plus two optional units	120	1 GCSE
Diploma	1 and 2 plus six optional units	240	Has the content of 2 GCSEs but no qualification from 2014 can count as more than 1 GCSE

Table A.7 BTEC First award, certificate and extended certificate

BTEC First at level 2	Number of units required	GCSE equivalence
Award	Unit 1 or Unit 2; and Unit 3 and a choice of optional units to make up a total of 120 guided learning hours	1
Certificate	Unit 1 and Unit 2 and Unit 3 and a choice of optional units to make up a total of 240 guided learning hours	Has the content of 2 GCSEs but from 2014 no qualification can count as more than 1 GCSE
Extended Certificate	Unit 1 and Unit 2 and Unit 3 and a choice of optional units to make up a total of 360 guided learning hours	Has the content of 3 GCSEs but from 2014 no qualification can count as more than 1 GCSE

BTEC First helps learners prepare for employment. It is available at level 2 with clear progression routes to the next stage of education, for example, to BTEC National at level 3, or into employment. This section focuses on level 2 and at this level pupils can be entered for the Award, Certificate or Extended Certificate (see Table A.7).

All BTEC Firsts are graded as Pass, Merit and Distinction.

The mandatory units are entitled:

Unit 1:   The Online World
Unit 2:   Technology Systems
Unit 3:   A Digital Portfolio

There is a range of interesting optional units available, for example:

Unit 4:   Creating Digital Animation
Unit 7:   Creating Digital Video
Unit 13: Website Development

Units 1 and 2 are assessed through a one-hour online test; Unit 3 and other units are internally assessed.

DiDA (the Diploma in Digital Applications) qualifications are also available from Edexcel. DiDA is available at level 1 and level 2 but only level 2 is reviewed here (see Table A.8).

There is one mandatory unit: Unit 1: Using ICT. There are four optional units and these are:

Unit 2: Multimedia
Unit 3: Graphics
Unit 4: ICT in the enterprise
Unit 5: Games authoring

Candidates complete a project for each unit and showcase their achievements in an eportfolio. The eportfolio is internally assessed by teachers and moderated by Edexcel. There are no formal written examinations. The grades awarded are pass, credit, merit and distinction.

Table A.8 Edexcel AiDA, CiDA and DiDA

DiDA at level 2	Number of units required	Equivalence	Guided learning hours
Award – AiDA	Unit 1	1 GCSE	30
Certificate – CiDA	Unit 1 + 1 optional unit	Has the content of 2 GCSEs but from 2014 no qualification can count as more than 1 GCSE	60
Extended Certificate – CiDA+	Unit 1 + 2 optional units	Has the content of 3 GCSEs but from 2014 no qualification can count as more than 1 GCSE	90
Diploma DiDA	Unit 1 + 3 optional units	Has the content of 4 GCSEs but from 2014 no qualification can count as more than 1 GCSE	120

Level 3

A very wide range of level 3 qualifications are available from AQA, Edexcel and OCR and other AOs. Some indication of these is given in Table A.9 and further information is available on the relevant website.

Table A.9 Level 3 qualifications from AQA, Edexcel and OCR

Qualification	AQA	Edexcel	OCR
A-level Applied ICT	✓	✓	✓
A-level ICT	✓		✓
A-level Computing	✓		✓
BTEC National		✓	
BTEC Apprenticeships		✓	
14–19 Diploma		✓	✓

Software for school administration and management

John Higgins

This appendix reviews some of the software schools use for: finance, management information systems (MIS), resource management, school ICT self-review, school organization, and virtual learning environments (VLEs).

Category

Finance

Company

Corero Progresso Finance PLUS

Contact details

Serco Learning
Winchester House
Stephenson's Way
Wyvern Business Park
Derby
DE21 6BF

Website

www.sercolearning.com

Description

Corero is a school financial management package which is part of the SERCO family of applications. Corero includes real-time access that enables users to review up-to-date departmental income, pay and non-pay costs, budgets and commitments. Users can raise requisitions, authorize requests and acknowledge receipt of goods and services using the web. Users can import budgets directly from spreadsheet packages, and budgets and actual expenditure can be exported into these spreadsheets using common file formats. There are extensive search facilities and a comprehensive suite of reports available to users. A full audit trail is available.

Category

Finance

Company

WCBS

Contact details

Somerset House
Magdalene Street
Glastonbury
Somerset
BA6 9EJ

Website

http://wcbs.co.uk

Description

WCBS's financial package is called PASS and is modular-based. The modular software delivers a single view of a school's finances. Each PASS Finance module integrates fully with Microsoft Office products. The Fees Management (Billing) module streamlines the billing and cash collection processes. The Grant Management module removes the administrative burden of processing parental income-based grant or bursary applications. This module is aimed at reducing workload and helping schools to maintain charitable status. The Nominal Ledger and Bank Reconciliation module combines analysis options with extensive management reporting. The Fixed Assets module allows for the maintenance of an integrated fixed asset register as part of the school accounting system. The Purchase Ledger module keeps track of all incoming invoices. The Commitment Accounting (Order Processing) module establishes a disciplined purchase order management process to aid auditing. The Payroll module has been designed to specifically meet the needs of independent schools. If your school manages commercial initiatives, the Sales Ledger module extends analysis and reporting to these business transactions. The School Shop module allows you to manage the school shop. The HR module is designed specifically to meet the requirements of HR departments within independent schools.

Category

Finance

Company

Sage

Contact details

Sage (UK) Limited
North Park
Newcastle upon Tyne
NE13 9AA

Website

www.sage.co.uk

Description

SagePayroll software is used to pay employees and for submitting PAYE data to HMRC online. It is recognized by HMRC and is suitable for businesses with over 10 employees. This software takes into account current legislation and is specifically used to automatically calculate statutory payments and deductions, such as: tax, National Insurance, sick pay and maternity pay. The software records all the information required by law, storing all employee information, details of all starters and leavers, together with historical data for up to seven years and this can be submitted to HMRC electronically as required. The school can track HMRC submissions by status and sender. Sending data direct from the software means you won't have to spend time manually filling in and submitting forms. The school is able to receive electronically PAYE updates from HMRC, such as changes to employee tax codes, and apply them directly to employees' records. The school is able to make payments direct from the software, paying employees and HMRC online. Other features allow for the forecasting the impact of pay rises, bonuses and overtime. Further, Sage 50 Payroll allows you to store other employee information, including: personal information, appraisal records, job and salary history, absence and holidays, and other related documents.

Category

Management Information Systems (MIS)

Company

SIMS

Contact details

5 Mercian Close
Cirencester
Gloucestershire
GL7 1LT

Website

www.capita-sims.co.uk

Description

SIMS manages student registration and truancy systems, student performance, personalized learning, exam organization, timetable construction, cover management and a range of other school activities. It maintains real-time information to support schools in conducting regular and comprehensive self-evaluations, helping them target resources, support personal development and monitor behaviour patterns. Through the use of integrated desktop tools, teachers are able to access information, analyse and input pupil data. Further, SIMS provides web access through the SIMS Learning Gateway, which allows teachers and parents to access the data in SIMS from home.

Category

Management Information Systems (MIS)

Company

Serco Learning

Contact details

Winchester House
Stephenson's Way
Wyvern Business Park
Derby
DE21 6BF

Website

www.sercolearning.com

Description

ERCO's MIS offers a range of tools to support a school's MIS. Data is entered once but then has many uses so there is no need for duplicate data entry. Student information, including: date of birth, photo, contact details, next of kin, siblings, medical details, and SEN, are easily accessible. Reporting is based on analysis of real-time data including behaviour, assessment and absence information. Customized student reports, such as end of term or end of year, can also be generated. The ePortal provides direct, real-time access to information relevant to each stakeholder within the school, via the web. Each user within the school is issued with a unique and secure ID and password to access the MIS. Student behaviour can be logged so that details of positive and negative behaviour can be recorded. These include merits, bullying, and disruptive behaviour, with a comments box to include any relevant details. Behaviour can be escalated to a relevant staff member and detention can be issued and recorded. An electronic document storage facility is available to store all letters, reports, and other important documents. Each item relating to a specific student can be attached to their record. Attendance Records, including lesson-by-lesson registers, can be taken quickly and analysed to identify patterns or trends.

Category

Management Information Systems (MIS)

Company

WCBS

Contact details

Somerset House
Magdalene Street
Glastonbury
Somerset
BA6 9EJ

Website

http://wcbs.co.uk

Description

3Sys is the MIS from WCBS which provides users with a flexible management information system through the use of user-defined fields. 3Sys includes a database search facility and full Microsoft Office suite integration.

Category

Management Information Systems (MIS)

Company

Viglen Ltd

Contact details

7 Handley Page Way
Old Parkbury Lane
Colney Street
St Albans
Hertfordshire
AL2 2DQ

Website

www.viglen.co.uk

Description

The Viglen Learning Platform (VLP) is a Virtual Learning Environment (VLE) designed for education. The VLP has many features. There are built-in communication tools that can be set up so that all or some of them are available to users of the system. The system provides an arena where members work together, both synchronously and asynchronously. Some of the available tools for communication and cooperation are: an internal messaging system, email, chat, SMS notifications, discussion forums, process-oriented writing tools, notice-boards, and newsgroups. There are tools for administration, reporting and evaluation. The system automatically generates reports that quickly and efficiently provide a comprehensive overview of the progress of a group or individuals within the learning cycle. The Production and Management of Learning Resources tool allows for the production, organization, maintenance and reuse of learning resources. This tool handles all types of digital content, both self-produced as well as those imported from other sources. Course content can be organized in a variety of different ways, by topic, chronologically or by function. For more advanced users, the system can be provided with the e:plus content management module.

Category

Management Information Systems (MIS)

Company

Core Education and Consulting (Talmos)

Contact details

> Solutions
> Brough Business Centre
> Skillings Lane
> Brough
> HU15 1EN

Website

www.coreeducation.co.uk

Description

Teachers are able to collaborate and share resources across departments, the school and more widely. Talmos Connect offers teachers the ability to manage and deliver lessons and homework directly from their timetable. Teachers can attach lesson plans to their timetable and can deliver their lessons directly from their timetable and make resources available for students to view. Teachers can access their personal work space and networked resources from home; and there are lesson planning tools that allow the teacher to set, receive and mark homework. The quick assignment tool allows the teacher to place resources directly onto the timetable for instant homework setting or provision of specific resources to aid learning. With the use of SIMS Web Parts teachers have access to SIMS. Students can access their assignments and personal work areas from home, and are able to access resources such as the library system, revision and assessment systems, and classroom content. Surveys, forums, wikis and blogs within the MIS encourage discussion and debate in a safe and secure environment. The Homework Tracker enables teachers and students to view the progress of work, submissions, marking and teacher commentary. The Student Council can create an area to collaborate and display information using notice-boards, forums, RSS feeds and podcasts. I-space, the personal portfolio area, is used to create, organize and display students' work. Social networking is encouraged through RSS feeds, forums, surveys and questionnaires. Parents can see their child's attendance, assessment and behaviour information as well as lesson plans plus homework status and other details. Talmos includes integration with other schools' ICT systems such as Microsoft Exchange, web mail and other VLEs such as Moodle.

Category

Resource Management: Print Management

Company

PaperCut

Contact details

Netop
55 Old Broad Street
London
EC2M 1RX

Website

www.papercut.com

Description

PaperCut is print management software which is designed to save paper and money by promoting the responsible use of a school's printing facilities. The software runs on Windows, Mac, Linux and Novell and in mixed environments. Logs record who, what, when and where printing is done. You can set quotas that assign limits to users' printing, and manage printers, for example, monitoring toner levels remotely. Printing is possible from wireless user-owned devices and over the Internet. Printing can be charged to users' accounts and can be shared by multiple users. Printouts can be watermarked. Clustering and load balancing increase efficiency and distribute wear and tear.

Category

Resource Management: Library Management

Company

Micro Librarian Systems

Contact details

Arden House
Shepley Lane, Hawk Green
Marple,
Stockport
Cheshire
SK6 7JW

Website

www.microlib.co.uk

Description

Eclipse is a dynamic online library portal designed for secondary school and college libraries. The program has an intuitive user interface with a reporting package. For example, the Head teacher can access reports specifically designed for inspections; and track progress in reading by gender, ethnicity and other groupings. The acquisitions module is used to create purchase orders and manage a budget. Editing facilities allow maintenance of the resources catalogue. The asset register can be used for all school's loaned resources including text books and portable devices. Eclipse can be integrated with the school's VLE and this integration allows automatic updates of student data from the MIS system. Teachers can integrate information literacy skills into lesson plans and support such lesson plans more effectively through improved awareness of available resources. The Student interface allows multiple search options to help develop student information literacy skills. Students can write book reviews and read reviews from other students. The floor plan shows students the location of resources within the library and enables them to reserve resources and manage their own account. Students watch video clips of authors talking about their books.

Category

Resource Management: Classroom Management Software (CMS)

Company

Netop (Vision Pro)

Contact details

55 Old Broad Street
London
EC2M 1RX

Website

www.netop.com/classroom-management-software

Description

Vision Pro is a classroom management application that allows teachers to observe and control students' desktops. Teachers can view an expandable thumbnail image of each student's screen on their computer, so they can monitor their students' activities from their desk. In addition, teachers can share their own screen with students and display what one student is doing on other students' computers. Vision Pro allows for the control of students' Internet use, allowing the teacher to select which websites they want the class to view and which websites to restrict. The teacher can open a file, application or website, in one operation, for an individual or the whole class, and can operate their students' computers without having to leave their desk. Students cannot exit the applications the teacher has launched, open other files, access the desktop or restart their computers. The teacher can render all students' screens blank in a single click, locking students' keyboards and mice. The teacher can shut down, wake up, start, restart or turn off all the computers in the class or just the ones selected. There are over 20 annotation tools to give the teacher's on-screen presentations more impact. The teacher's screen display can mirror the seating plan in the classroom. The teacher can label students' screenshots and rearrange them on-screen. Teachers can send and receive instant messages to/from a student, a group or the whole class.

Category

Resource Management: Screen Capture

Company

Snagit

Contact details

Douglas Stewart
EDU Limited
57 Fleet Road
Fleet
Hampshire
GU51 3PJ

Website

www.techsmith.com/snagit-features.html

Description

Snagit is used to capture any item seen on a computer screen in order to provide feedback to or communicate with students. The teacher can create screen videos for demos or quick reviews, sharing these items instantly to, for example, YouTube or Facebook. The user can grab their entire desktop, a region, a window, or a scrolling window with a single hotkey or click. Custom graphics can be made by taking multiple screen captures and putting them together to create a new graphic. The teacher can draw attention to a specific part of their image, by spotlighting one specific area and magnifying it. Snagit blurs and darkens everything else so that the students' attention is focused. Snagit will tell you what you've spelled wrong and help create consistently error-free callouts. All screen captures are automatically saved.

Category

Resource Management: Video/CCTV and Audio Management

Company

Milestone Systems UK and Ireland

Contact details

The College Business Centre
Uttoxeter New Road
Derby
DE22 3WZ

Website

www.milestonesys.com

Description

Milestone's IP-based surveillance solution has central control of all connected cameras, devices, and user accounts. There is: access to live cameras and recorded video; task-oriented tabs; and an adaptable user interface that can be tailored to your working environment. You can customize the software to fit your needs by integrating analytics, business systems and third-party applications.

Category

Resource Management: Classroom Video Management

Company

Classroom

Contact details and website

www.classwatch.co.uk

Description

Classwatch systems provide high resolution digital video and audio recording of classrooms and other teaching spaces. Classwatch can be used by teachers to improve teaching and share best practice. Recordings can be used for CPD and the development of teaching skills, and for feedback to pupils, staff and OFSTED. Recordings are fully secure.

Category

School ICT Self-Review

Company

ICT Mark

Contact details

NAACE
PO Box 6511
Nottingham
NG11 8TN

Website

www.naace.co.uk

Description

The ICT Mark is an accreditation scheme available within the UK which recognizes schools achieving national standards in the effective use of technology. Schools holding the ICT Mark have demonstrated that they are committed to using technology to improve their overall effectiveness and efficiency in using ICT to support teaching and learning. Ofsted and DfE continue to recognize the fundamental role of ICT in learning, teaching and management and the ICT Mark recognizes good practice. There are six elements to NAACE's Self-Review Framework (SRF): Leadership and Management; Planning; Learning; Assessment of ICT Capability; Professional Development; and ICT Resources. The framework enables schools to assess their level of development against national standards. Self-assessment using the ICT Mark criteria is a due-diligence exercise for the provision of ICT within schools, ensuring that investment in, and use of ICT equipment to support teaching and learning, administration and planning are fit for purpose.

Category

School organization: Timetable

Company

October ReSolutions Ltd (TimeTabler)

Contact details

3 Crown Green
Lymm
Cheshire
WA13 9JG
United Kingdom

Website

www.timetabler.com

Description

TimeTabler is designed to provide a workable school timetable, matching student subject choices. option blocks, teachers and rooms. TimeTabler allows: the scheduling of part-time teachers; setting, e.g. in Mathematics; staggered lunch-breaks; variable days; split-site schools; consortium days, and shared teaching post 16.

Category

School organization: Staff Cover

Company

October ReSolutions Ltd (Staff Cover)

Contact details

As above

Website

www.timetabler.com

Description

StaffCover links directly to the TimeTabler program. It allows you to see who is absent (and whether for all or part of the day); the names of any special events needing cover (e.g. a French exam); the names of any supply teachers available (and, if you wish, whose timetable they should cover); and which staff who, although present, are doing special tasks in their non-contact periods and so are not available to do cover. StaffCover then automatically assigns cover staff on the basis of several factors. The weightings of all the factors used to calculate the cover have standard default values but you can modify them if you wish. These factors include: the length of time since a teacher was last used for cover; the number of non-contact periods lost compared with other colleagues; whether the teacher to be covered is in the same faculty as the covering teacher (e.g. a Science teacher to cover Science); whether they are of the same gender for covering PE or Games; and whether the cover teacher prefers to cover classes with older or younger children. StaffCover automatically assigns staff to cover; however, the user is free to edit the recommendations. Once the cover is approved, the program will print out a cover timetable for the staff notice-board and individual slips to be given to each affected teacher, or emails can be sent automatically. The program keeps a record of all cover in order to provide full statistics at any time. At any time, you can re-calculate the entire cover, and tomorrow's cover can be prepared in advance. Split-site schools can be run as two sites or one, and statistics can be combined or kept separate.

Category

School organization: Options

Company

October ReSolutions Ltd (Options)

Contact details

As above

Website

www.timetabler.com

Description

Options is a program for analysing and organizing the subject choices that students make in the optional part of their curriculum. Options is designed to streamline the annual process of arranging students' subject choices into option blocks suitable for timetabling. The program aims to achieve the highest satisfaction rate for the students, and to let them study the subjects they have chosen.

Category

Virtual Learning Environments (VLE)

Company

Research Machines (RM)

Contact details

New Mill House
183 Milton Park
Abingdon
Oxon OX14 4SE
United Kingdom

Website

www.learningplatform.rm.com

Description

The RM Learning Platform consists of a range of features and tools that include: a virtual learning environment (VLE) to manage resources and courses; a dynamic Web-based portal environment to communicate and collaborate with all stakeholders; an integration tool with the MIS to create accounts and share key data with teachers, parents and learners; and comprehensive assessment tools to record and monitor learners' targets and progress.

Category

Virtual Learning Environments (VLE)

Company

Moodle

Contact details and website

http://moodle.org

Description

Moodle is open source software. It is a tool for creating online dynamic websites. Moodle must be installed on a web server, either on site or via a web hosting company. The focus of Moodle is to provide educators with tools to manage and promote learning. Moodle has features that allow it to scale to very large deployments, to accommodate many thousands of students, yet it can also be scaled down for primary school or education hobbyist use. Moodle can facilitate full online courses as well as augment face-to-face courses (blended learning). Many users utilize the activity modules (such as forums, databases and wikis) to build richly collaborative communities of learning around their subject matter (following the social constructionist tradition), while others prefer to use Moodle as a way to deliver content to students (such as standard SCORM packages) and assess learning using assignments or quizzes.

Category

Virtual Learning Environments (VLE)

Company

itslearning

Contact details

The McLaren Building
46 The Priory Queensway
Birmingham
B4 7LR

Website

www.itslearning.com

Description

itslearning offers personalized learning for students. itslearning Mobile, offers a 3rd generation mobile platform designed for mobile phones and PDAs. The system provides access to Web 2.0 components, including Google maps, Flicker, Delicious and YouTube, and there is dynamic integration with the MIS. Students can create a personal learning blog. The eportfolio allows the creation of a collection of private and assessment portfolios for reflective learning. Students can select from a range of skins to choose their own look and feel within their eportfolio. Students can create multimedia content, text authoring and embed web 2.0 content. Audio and video conferences allow for online discussions with sound and video. Using the collaborative writing feature, users can submit working drafts for comments from teachers and classmates. Projects can be created around courses, topics, and other users invited to join and participate. There are secure messaging, email and contacts features. The calendar can be used to manage personal and school-related activities. A planner tool for teachers or school administrators is provided for making plans for single lessons and longer periods. Learners can be set individual goals and learning objectives for a specific time period and recent performance monitored. Teachers can create online tests with a wide range of interactive question types and feedback tools. Assignments provide open tasks and essays for individuals or groups with a mandatory deadline. Online exams can be taken in a secure environment. Attendance is tracked for easy reporting purposes. There is a customizable interface for different levels and ages of students. Accessibility features support users with dyslexia and the visually impaired. The interface uses a variety of languages including: UK English, US English, Spanish, French, German, and Italian. Parents and guardians can follow their child's progress. Users can connect to external courses and content, including other VLEs around the world. SCORM compliance allows courses to be imported and exported. A Bulletin Board permits new and messages to be added to your course. Lessons can be created with various multimedia elements and free and commercial content is available from a range of vendors. There is a search engine and you can archive old courses.

Category

Virtual Learning Environments (VLE)

Company

Frog Trade Ltd

Contact details

Dean Clough
Halifax
West Yorkshire
HX3 5AX

Website

http://frogtrade.com

Description

FROG allows users to build most things that can be found on the Internet (e-learning, social networks, video sites and various multimedia elements). FROG is a secure safe environment within the school from which students can work, collaborate and communicate. Teachers can create their own lessons and resources without having advanced technical understanding.

Category

Virtual Learning Environments (VLE)

Company

Netop

Contact details

55 Old Broad Street
London
EC2M 1RX

Website

www.netop.com

Description

The NetOp Learning Centre is an integrated Learning Management System (LMS) and a Content Management System (CMS) which facilitates the deployment of knowledge upgrades to managers, employees, students, customers and other partners. Specifically, the NetOp Learning Centre enables an organization to: establish a common portal for all online course activities; manage courses and users; develop content including courses, exams, quizzes, and questionnaires; create forums for user groups and individual discussions; combine traditional learning methods with online courses, creating a blended learning environment; and generate statistical reports on user behaviour. The NetOp Learning Centre is constructed to be used as an online course tool and as a presentation tool in classroom education and training sessions. It is accessible from any PC with Internet connection.

Glossary

Every area of interest has its own technical language or jargon. This is especially true of both ICT and Education. Technical language is helpful to experienced professionals and other knowledgeable practitioners as it helps them communicate shared understandings more precisely. However, for those training to work in these specialisations, or taking an interest in them for the first time, this jargon can be confusing. This glossary should be helpful to those needing some clarification of the technical language used by those with expertise in teaching and managing ICT in secondary schools.

Algorithm   A set of rules to solve a problem.

Amend   To change.

American Standard Code for Information Interchange (ASCII)   The ASCII coding system is used to uniquely represent characters and other information as bit patterns or binary codes. When files are in ASCII form, they are readily transferred between different pieces of software.

Analogue   The representation of data as a range of variable voltages. Only specialist computers represent data in analogue form. Most computers represent data in digital form.

Analogue to Digital Converter   A hardware device to convert analogue voltage to binary digital numbers which can be processed by a computer.

Ancestral system   The ancestral system for multi-layered file backup consists of layers of backups (copies) of a file or a disk, taken in chronological order. In its simplest form, it consists of the son (the latest copy), the father (the previous copy) and the grandfather (the copy before the previous copy). These copies are usually kept in increasingly secure locations.

Applications software   Software designed to do a specific job. For example, software for word processing and timetabling.

Attainment Target (AT)   An attainment target is a subdivision of a NC subject into recognisable sections that are assessed separately.

Backing storage   A means of storing programs and data outside the computer's RAM memory. Hard disks and memory sticks are backing storage. Backing storage is non volatile which means that it retains its contents when the power is switched off.

Backup   A backup of a file is another copy of it. The ancestral system is often used to organise multi-layered backups.

Bar code   A code represented by a series of vertical black and white lines, often used to store an identity number. For example, pupils could be issued with an identification card with a bar code on it that is used to store their identification number. This identification card could be read by a bar code reader when pupils register their attendance.

Bar code reader   A hardware device used to read a bar code. This could be a light pen, a laser scanner or a swipe card reader.

Binary   The base 2 number system. Binary numbers are represented using bits. The only digits used are 0 and 1. This number system is easy to represent using the digital electronics found in computer systems.

BInary Digit (BIT)   A BInary Digit or BIT takes the value 1 or 0. Patterns of bits make up coding systems that are used to represent information. ASCII is such a coding system.

Browser   A piece of software used to browse the information available on the Web servers. For example, Microsoft Internet Explorer, Mozilla Firefox and Google Chrome.

Buffer   Extra memory that acts as an intermediate store between a sending device and a receiving device. For example, a printer buffer is extra memory, usually built into the printer itself, which is used to hold information waiting to be printed.

Byte   A byte is a set of bits used to represent one character. There are normally eight bits to the byte.

CD   CDs can store text, sound, pictures, music and video and can be used as backing storage. The information on them can be accessed quickly and they store around 700 MB.

Cell   The intersection of a row and a column in a spreadsheet.

Central Processing Unit (CPU)   The main part of the computer, where all the processing takes place. It consists of the Control Unit (CU), the Arithmetic and Logic Unit (ALU) and the memory (RAM and ROM). The processor box or system unit of a modern desktop computer usually contains the CPU, a hard disk and at least one DVD drive.

Character   One of the symbols that can be represented by a computer. Characters include A to Z, 0 to 9, and punctuation marks.

Character code   A code used to represent characters, e.g. ASCII.

Character set   All the characters that can be represented using the character code used by a computer.

Check digit   An extra digit attached to a number. It is calculated from the original digits in the number, using a predetermined formula. It can be re-calculated to check that none of the digits in the number have been altered. The right most digit in an ISBN number is a check digit.

Clip Art   Clip Art is graphic images or pictures that have been prepared for importing into a word processor, DTP and other software. A wide range of Clip Art is available with illustrations for a range of different situations. You can choose a suitable piece of Clip Art to illustrate their document. Most clip art is copyright free but you should check this before using it.

Computer Aided Design (CAD)   CAD is the use of graphics software to help produce effective 2D and 3D designs. The graphics software used for CAD contains detail features not found in less powerful graphics software.

Computer Aided Manufacture (CAM)   Using a computer to control the manufacture of a product.

Computer Assisted Learning (CAL)   Using software to learn about another subject. For example, in Mathematics, using software to practise multiplication tables, or, in Geography, using a simulation program that explores the environmental and other problems that arise when controlling an oil slick in the sea.

Concept keyboard A specialised keyboard with no pre-set keys. It can be programmed to work with overlays with pictures or simplified keys. Can help support disabled users.

Control character Control characters are used to control the operation of peripherals, in particular, printers. They are part of a computer's character set, and have an ASCII code. Although they are always present in wordprocessing documents, they are not usually visible on the monitor screen or printout.

Control system An ICT system used to monitor and control environmental conditions. For example, a control system to monitor the temperature and humidity in a greenhouse, making adjustments so that these stay within acceptable limits.

Corrupt data Corrupt data is data that has been altered so that it is no longer meaningful. Data can be corrupted by accidental failure of the software or hardware being used. It may also be corrupted by malicious actions by hackers or by viruses.

CPD (Continuing Professional Development) Training that helps teachers maintain their professional skills, knowledge and understanding. See INSET.

Crash When a computer 'crashes', it stops working. Crashes can be associated with hardware failure, for example, a hard disk crash; or software failure, for example, a programming error.

Create Set up for the first time.

Cursor Often a rectangular block one character in size, or a vertical line, that appears on a monitor screen, often at the point at which the next character entered through the keyboard will be displayed. The cursor often flashes on and off to attract attention.

Cursor control keys The 'arrow' keys on a keyboard used to control the movement of the cursor around the screen.

Cyberspace The mental visualisation or conceptualisation of the Internet.

Data Data is input to a computer in its most basic form. It can take the form of numbers, characters, control codes, and voltages from sensors.

Database A means of storing and accessing information. The information is structured by sub-dividing it into tables, records and fields. The stored information can be searched and sorted and reports can be produced.

Data capture Data capture is the collection of data for input to a computer. Data capture can be online, e.g. Point of Sale terminals at supermarket checkouts, or off-line, e.g. questionnaires.

Data logging The use of sensors to measure environmental conditions. The sensors are connected to a computer which records the measurements made.

Data preparation Data preparation is the conversion of written or printed information into a form that can be processed by the computer. It usually involves using a keyboard to enter data written on a source document so that it can be saved on backing storage.

Data processing Computers input, process and output data. In commerce this activity is often called 'data processing'.

Delete Remove. For example, a file is deleted from a disk when it is removed from it.

Demonstration disk A demonstration disk contains a demonstration version of software. Demonstration discs are often sent to intending purchasers so that they can evaluate the software for themselves. The software on a demonstration disk may be complete but often there is some essential feature, such as printing, omitted. This is to encourage potential purchasers to buy a full copy of the software.

Denary   The base 10 number system. This is the number system people use. The digits available are 0 to 9.

Department for Education (DfE)   This Government department oversees the provision of education throughout England and Wales.

Desk Top Publishing (DTP)   DTP combines graphics and wordprocessing in a format typical of a newspaper or magazine with text in columns, varying character sizes, photographs and other illustrations.

Digital   The representation of data as codes made up of 1's and 0's. These can be stored in the computer as 5 volts and 0 volts, respectively, using two state, digital electronics.

Direct Data Entry (DDE)   DDE is data entry directly to the program that is processing the data. For example, using bar code readers or swipe card readers to input pupils' identification numbers, stored in bar codes, to a piece of software that is currently in use.

Documentation   Documentation for a piece of software includes a description of how to install the software on a computer, what it does and how it is used.

Dot matrix printer   A printer which has a print head consisting of a matrix of steel pins. Character shapes are made up from a pattern of dots. Dot matrix printers are relatively slow at printing but are cheap to buy and run. They can print text in draft or Near Letter Quality. A wide range of fonts and graphics can be printed.

DVD (Digital Versatile Disks)   DVDs store text, sound, pictures, music and video and can be used as backing storage. The information on them can be accessed quickly and they store around 4.7 GB.

Edit   Amend, delete or insert.

Electronic Data Interchange (EDI)   The exchange of information in electronic form over a network. For example, examination entries can be sent from schools to the GCSE examination boards using EDI over the national telephone network, and the examination results can be returned to schools in a similar manner.

Electronic Funds Transfer (EFT)   A paperless method of transferring money between bank accounts using a communications network.

Electronic mail (email)   A paperless method of communication across networks. Schools can send email via an Internet service provider, such as Everything Everywhere. Transmission can be almost instantaneous.

Error message   A computer will occasionally detect an error when running software and display an error message. It should be possible to find out what the error is and what action to take from the error message itself, from the reference manual or from help built into the program.

Execute   To execute software is to run or use it.

Expert system   Software that allows users to recognise particular situations, providing help and advice on the appropriate action to be taken.

Fibre optics   The use of very thin fibre glass strands to transmit information encoded as pulses of light. The underground cabling used to distribute cable television is a fibre optic cable. Fibre optic cable can transmit very high volumes of information. Television signals, computer data and video conferencing are all possible using fibre optic networks.

Field   A field is an item of information within a record. A column in a table is all the instances of the same field.

File   A file contain programs, data, pictures, etc.and can be stored on backing storage.

Filename   The name of a file stored on backing storage. This is unique within a folder.

Fileserver   A computer attached to a network whose main function is to enable network stations to access shared files stored on one or more hard discs that are connected to the network.

Flowchart   A graphical representation of the flow of data through a computer, or an algorithm.

Font   A set of consistently shaped characters, for example, the Times New Roman font.

Format   The format is the structure of the information, for example:

1   Formatting a hard disk prepares its structure for use with a particular computer system. An unformatted hard disk cannot be used.
2   The layout of a wordprocessing document.
3   The characteristic layout of a file, record or field.

Front end processor   A small computer used to control communications between a larger mainframe computer and the terminals and other peripherals connected to it.

Gigabyte   Gigabytes are a measure of the storage capacity of a computer's memory or backing storage. 1 Gigabyte is 1024 Megabytes.

Global village   It has become just as easy to use ICT to communicate with someone at the other side of the world as with someone in the next room. Consequently, in cyberspace everyone lives 'next door'. This is the global village.

Graphics   Pictures, images or symbols which can be processed by a computer. They can be displayed on the screen, saved on disk, and imported into DTP and other software.

Graphics pad   A graphics pad is a peripheral which allows the user to transfer line drawings to the computer by drawing on a sheet of paper that is resting on it.

Graphics software   Software that allows the user to paint or draw on the screen, using a range of design tools, colours and patterns.

Graphic User Interface (GUI)   A user interface that avoids the need to remember complex, text based operating system commands by providing a visual interface that uses windows, icons, menus and pointers. These can represent commands, processes or objects such as hard discs. To make a selection from a menu or to activate an icon, the user points at it and clicks a button on the mouse. Also known as a WIMP interface.

Graph plotter   An output peripheral that produces detailed pictures and diagrams on paper using one or more pens.

Hacker   An unauthorised user of a computer system who has broken into the system, possibly by discovering a valid user identification number and its associated password, or by bypassing them. Hacking is an illegal activity. Pupils should be strongly discouraged from hacking.

Hard copy   Printout.

Hard disk   Hard disks are high capacity magnetic backing storage. Internal hard disks are built into the computer and can have a capacity of 1 TB or more; external hard disks are usually portable and connect to a computer using a USB cable.

Hardware   The physical components of a computer system.

Head of Department (HoD)   The person in charge of coordinating a subject department in a secondary school. For example, the HoD Mathematics.

Help   Instructions showing how to use a piece of software that are accessible using the software when it is running. Also known as online help.

Help line   A telephone information service sometimes provided by hardware retailers, software vendors and others. Users who are having difficulty can ring the appropriate help line for immediate assistance in overcoming their particular problem. Many help lines are free to owners of a particular product; others are free during the guarantee period; some make a charge for their services.

Hexadecimal   The base 16 number system. Allowable digits are 0 to 9 and A to F. This is often used with computer systems to abbreviate binary codes, making them more memorable. For example, the binary code, 1101 0011, is hexadecimal D3.

High level language   A programming language that is relatively close to the English language, making it more comprehensible. For example, Python and C++.

Icon   A picture that represents a command, function, process, device or tool.

Information   Information is data that is meaningful to us. For example, the data 19122010 is a meaningless number until it is known that it is a UK date, the 19th December 2010. This is information.

Information and Communication Technology (ICT)   The use of computer based technology to store, process and communicate information.

Information System (IS)   An information system is the organisation of human and other resources, including ICT, into a coherent system for the purposeful processing of information. For example, a school might use a Management Information System to store information about the timetable and pupils' records.

Initial Teacher Education (ITE)   ITE and ITT courses include the Post Graduate Certificate in Education (PGCE) and the Bachelor in Education (BEd) degree. They are the courses that prepare students to teach in primary and secondary schools, and lead to the award of Qualified Teacher Status (QTS).

Initial Teacher Training (ITT)   See Initial Teacher Education.

Ink jet printer   A printer that uses ink jet technology. A jet of ink is squirted onto the paper to form characters. There is no contact between the paper and the print head.

Input   Data supplied to a computer system.

INSET (IN-SErvice Training)   Training that is undertaken whilst a teacher is employed by a school. INSET is often structured so that it can be completed part time or outside of regular teaching hours.

Interactive processing   Interactive processing takes place when the user and the computer are in active two-way communication.

Interface   The interconnection between two different systems or devices. See Graphic User Interface.

Internet   The Internet is a network of networks. These networks are interlinked to enable communications between their users on a global scale.

Interrogate   See Search.

IPD (Initial Professional Development)   Initial professional training for student teachers. See CPD and INSET.

Joystick   A lever used to move a pointer or other image around a monitor screen. Joysticks are often used with computer games and may be built into a games console.

Key field   Every record in a database should have a unique key field or primary key which identifies the record.

Key guard   A metal or plastic cover that is fitted to a keyboard to prevent keys being depressed unless there is a specific intention to do so. They can give access to some keys but not others.

Key-to-disk   A method of data preparation where data is entered at a keyboard and saved on disk.

Kilobyte (K)   Kilobytes are a measure of the storage capacity of a computer's memory or backing storage. A kilobyte is 1024 or 2^{10} bytes.

Laptop   A portable computer that is small enough and light enough to be carried around. They have an LCD screen which folds up for use. They can be powered by batteries or mains electricity allowing their use in a variety of locations.

Laser printer   Laser printers are expensive to buy and run but produce very high quality printing. A wide variety of fonts and graphics can be printed. Laser printers are fast in comparison with dot matrix, ink jet and daisy wheel printers.

Laser scanner   A hardware device that scans patterns of light reflected off it by a laser beam. These are input to a computer.

Liquid Crystal Display (LCD)   The technology used to provide screen displays on calculators, laptops, tables, smart phones, etc..

Load (or Open)   To retrieve from backing storage.

Local Area Network (LAN)   LANs are computer networks located in one room or in a single building.

Logo   From the Greek word 'logos' meaning 'word'. A high level language designed to guide a small turtle around the screen. Logo is an artificial intelligence language.

Machine code   Program instructions in binary code that can be executed by a computer.

Magnetic Ink Character Recognition (MICR)   A method of input where characters printed in magnetic ink are read directly into a computer. This method of input is used to process cheques.

Mail merge   The merging of a data file and a standard letter template, to produce personalised mail. Mail merge is a common function of word processing software.

Mainframe computer   A large, fast computer, probably having a variety of peripherals, including a high capacity backing store and terminals, and telecommunications links.

Management Information System (MIS)   A comprehensive, integrated information system for management and administration. Many MIS for schools also incorporate software that has links with aspects of management of the curriculum.

Mark sensing   An input method where pencil marks on paper are detected. Their position on the paper determines their meaning. The National Lottery uses mark sensing to input customers' number choices (see also Optical Mark Recognition).

Master file   A data file which is used to store most of the data for a particular application. It is updated from a transaction file.

Megabyte (K)   Megabytes are a measure of the storage capacity of a computer's memory or backing storage. A megabyte is 1024 kilobytes or 2^{20} bytes.

Memory   The part of the CPU that is used to store programs while they are running and data while it is being processed. Memory is RAM (Random Access Memory).

Memory stick   Memory sticks store up to around 32GB. They are small, light and portable and are widely used. They are usually plugged into the USB port on a computer.

Menu   A list of tasks which can be carried out by a computer progam. The user selects a task from the menu.

Merge   To combine one or more files into a single file.

Microprocessor   A single microchip containing all the elements of the CPU. Some microprocessors have built in memory but most supplement this, using additional RAM memory.

Model   A representation of a real or an imagined system. Computer based models can be constructed using a spreadsheet. For example, financial models are used in managing schools.

Modem   A MOdulator/DEModulator. Used to convert digital data output by a computer to analogue signals that can be transmitted along a telephone line and vice versa.

Moderation   Moderation is the process of ensuring that assessment has been carried out to the same standards by different assessors. This may involve assessors checking each others' work and meeting to discuss discrepancies.

Monitor   A screen used to display the output from a computer.

Mouse   A hand held input peripheral having one or more buttons on top and a ball or optical sensor underneath. When the mouse is moved over a flat surface, a pointer on the screen moves in a corresponding direction.

Mouse pointer   The on-screen representation of the mouse. This can take several forms depending on the mode of operation. Its most common forms are an arrow head and an 'I'.

Multiaccess   When many users are connected to, and in simultaneous communication with a single computer by means of terminals, this is multiaccess computing.

Multimedia   The combination of text, sound, pictures, music and video.

Multitasking   When one user, on one computer, is apparently running more than one program at the same time, this is multitasking.

National Curriculum (NC)   The Programmes of Study that schools may provide for pupils from 5 to 18 years old. The NC specifies which subjects pupils study and provides a framework for their assessment.

Netbook   A smaller version of a Laptop computer. Usually A4 size. Optimised for Internet browsing and email.

Network   A network is a system of interconnected cables. For example, networks can be used to connect computers; the telephone network connects telephone users.

Network station   A terminal connected to a computer network.

Non volatile   ROM memory is non-volatile, that is, its contents are permanent. They are retained when the computer is switched off. Information stored on backing storage is also non-volatile.

Notebook   A smaller version of a Laptop computer. Usually A4 size.

Off-line   Not connected to a network or connected but not in communication with it.

Online   Connected to the network and using it to communicate.

Open (or Load)   To retrieve from backing storage.

Operating system   The operating system is a program that makes a computer's hardware more easily accessible and useable by applications software. An operating system is always present when a computer is used.

Optical Character Recognition (OCR)   An input method that can read printed characters. Special fonts are often used.

Optical Mark Recognition (OMR)   An input method that reads marks on a document. The position of the mark is interpreted as information. For example, it is used for recording answers in multiple choice examinations, and for selecting National Lottery numbers.

Passive Infra Red detector (PIR)   A device attached to a burglar alarm system that uses infra red radiation to detect the presence of intruders.

Password   A code that restricts access to a computer system. Usually associated with a User Identification Number.

Peripheral   A peripheral is a hardware device that is connected to a computer system but is not a part of the computer itself. For example, a printer is a peripheral.

Personal Digital Assistant (PDA)   A hand-held computer with calendar and address book, e.g. a smart phone.

Pixel   The smallest area of a screen that can be used in building up a picture, i.e. a dot on the screen.

Pointer   An arrow or similar symbol which appears on the monitor screen. The position of the pointer is controlled by a mouse.

Port   A connector used to link peripherals to a computer.

Portable   Portable computers can easily be moved from one location to another; portable programs can be easily run on a variety of different computers.

Primary key   See key field.

Printout   The output from a printer.

Procedure   A set of instructions that performs a specific task. A procedure is a part of a computer program but it is not a complete program.

Processor   See Microprocessor.

Program   A set of instructions used to control the operation of a computer.

Programmer   A computer programmer designs, codes, tests and documents programs for a computer.

Programmes of Study (PoS)   A Programme of Study is a list of the topics that should be studied. Specifically, it is the content of each subject of the NC at each key stage.

Programming language   A language that allows a computer user to control the computer. For example: Logo, Visual BASIC, Python and C++.

Pull-down menu   A feature of a Graphic User Interface where a hidden menu can be revealed, that is, pulled down, by pointing at it.

Query   See Search condition.

Random Access Memory (RAM)   RAM is read/write memory that is used to store programs while they are being executed and data while it is being processed. It is supplied as modules that plug into the computer's motherboard. RAM is volatile.

Range check   A check that a data value is within realistic limits. For example, the number of months in a year must lie in the range 1 to 12.

Read Only Memory (ROM)   Memory within the computer's memory that can only be read. ROM is non-volatile.

Real time processing   The processing of input data which takes place so fast that when more data is input the results of the processing are already available. Real time processing occurs in real time, i.e. as it happens.

Record   A record is a collection of related fields. A row in a table in a database.

Record of Achievement (RoA)   A comprehensive, summative document assembled by teachers, pupils and others, that illustrates a particular pupil's achievements in a wide range of activities. It may include academic examination results, work placement records, and swimming certificates.

Run   To run a piece of software is to use it. See also execute.

Save   To record on backing storage.

Scanner   A peripheral used to input photographs, line art and pictures into a computer. It can also be used to convert printed text into a form suitable for input to a word processor.

Scroll   The display on a monitor screen is said to 'scroll' when it moves off the screen at the top and onto the screen at the bottom, automatically, at the same time. More accurately, this is known as 'vertical scrolling'.

Search   Look for.

Search condition   A search condition is used to determine which records are selected when searching a database. Search conditions may be simple, for example, an instruction to find the information about all those pupils whose name begins with the letter 'B'. Simple search conditions can be combined using logical operators, such as AND, OR and NOT.

Senior Leadership Team (SLT)   The SLT usually consists of the Headteacher and the Deputy Headteachers. In some schools, some senior teachers may be included in the SLT.

Sensor   An input device used to sense physical conditions. For example, a heat sensor.

Smart card   Smart cards contain an embedded chip so that the data stored on them is more secure than the data stored on stripe cards. The are used for bank and credit cards and have replaced stripe cards for this application.

Smart phone   A phone with a large touch screen that can access 3G and 4G mobile phone and wireless networks. Can browse the Web and access email; can access contacts and calendars, and run SatNav.

Software   Computer programs.

Sort   To put into order.

Source document   A document or questionnaire used for data capture. It is the source of the data input to the computer.

Speech recognition   A method of input to a computer by speaking to it. Computers have limited ability to recognise speech. Consequently, commands are likely to be spoken in a strictly defined and restricted language. Normal spoken conversation is not faultlessly recognised.

Speech synthesis   Sounds generated by a computer which synthesise human speech. A wide variety of words can be spoken but synthesised speech often lacks fluidity.

Spooling   Spooling is a method of queuing output directed to a printer before printing it. For example, when a user prints from a network station, the printed output is stored as a file on the network fileserver. This file enters a queue of files waiting to use the printer. One consequence of this that documents do not begin to print when pupils try to print them; consequently they try again; this adds another copy to the queue; and leads to multiple copies of the same file being printed later.

Spreadsheet   Spreadsheets are used to calculate and display financial and other numerical information in columns. Graphs can be generated, numerical models constructed and 'what if?' scenarios explored.

Standalone   A computer that is not connected to any other computer is being used in standalone mode, i.e. it stands alone.

Statement bank A database of standard comments for inclusion in reports, records of achievement, and other documents. The selected statements can usually be modified, if necessary, before printing.

Stripe card A plastic card containing a magnetic stripe which stores a limited amount of data. See smart card.

Surfing Surfing the Internet is the act of browsing through information on web servers throughout the world.

Systems analysis and design The in-depth analysis of the software and hardware requirements of a computer based system and its detailed design.

Tablet A tablet is a portable computer that is small enough and light enough to be carried around. They have an LCD touch screen and can be used without a keyboard. They are usually powered by batteries allowing their use in a variety of locations. They communicate via wireless or mobile phone networks. Operation and functionality is similar to a large smart phone.

Teacher Assessment (TA) The teacher's assessment of a pupil's attainment.

Technical documentation Documentation written for technical specialists. For example, ICT technicians.

Terminal A hardware system used to communicate with a computer over a network. Dumb terminals consist of a keyboard and monitor combination with no processing power of their own. These are often connected to mainframe computers. Desk top PCs can be used as 'intelligent' terminals. These have their own on-board processing power, and can be connected when the requirement arises.

Terrabyte Terrabytes are a measure of the storage capacity of a computer's memory or backing storage. 1 Terrabyte is 1024 Gigabytes.

Tracker ball A hardware device with the same function as a mouse. A tracker ball has a ball and buttons accessible on its upper surface. Instead of moving the mouse to control the screen pointer, the ball is turned while the tracker ball unit remains stationary.

Transaction file A file used to store data captured since the last master file update. The transaction file is used to update the master file.

Turnaround document A printout which has data written on it and is then used as a source document.

Turtle A programmable robot with wheels. A turtle is used to learn how to control the movement of mobile robots on a flat surface. It is often controlled using LOGO or a similar programming language.

Update To bring a file or document up-to-date by amending, editing, inserting or deleting data.

USB (universal serial bus) A type of connection which is used to attach external devices to a computer, e.g. a memory stick or an external hard disk.

User documentation Documentation written for users. User documentation should be user friendly. It should help users install software on a computer and explain how to use it.

User friendly Easy for users to operate and understand.

User Identification number (User Id.) A unique User Identification number is given to every user so that the computer can recognise them. Each User Id. is usually associated with a password, thus helping to prevent unauthorised access to computer systems.

User interface   The way in which a computer system communicates with users. For example, a Graphic User Interface (GUI).

Utility   A program which is used to do a task that is useful only in relation to the organisation and use of a computer system, for example, a utility program can be used to format a disk.

Validation   A check that data is realistic. A range check is one type of validation check.

Verification   A check that what is written on a source document is accurately transferred to a computer readable medium.

Virtual reality   A model world constructed using ICT. The rules governing relationships in a virtual reality model may be very unreal.

Virus   A virus is a computer program that 'infects' a computer system, usually without the user's knowledge. Viruses can reside in the computer's memory or on a hard disk. They may be harmless but more often they cause damage. The 'Form' virus, for example, may destroy wordprocessing files. When a virus is detected, it should be destroyed before further use is made of the computer system on which the virus was found.

Visual Display Unit (VDU)   A keyboard and screen used as a dumb terminal. The computer's screen, or monitor, is often inaccurately referred to as a VDU.

VLE (Virtual Learning Environment)   A VLE allows teachers to provide learning resources and assignments via the Web. Students can log in to the VLE from anywhere they have access to the Internet. Assignments can be uploaded or completed online. Students can access grade profiles so they know what progress they are making.

Volatile memory   Volatile memory looses its contents when the computer is switched off. RAM memory is volatile.

Wide Area Network (WAN)   A network spread over a wide area, possibly international, making use of both permanent cable connections and temporary connections using the telephone network.

Window   A rectangular subdivision of the screen which enables the user to look at the output from a program. There may be more than one window open on the screen at the same time.

Windows, Icons, Menus and Pointers (WIMP)   See Graphic User Interface.

Word processing   The preparation of letters and other documents using a computer.

Wordwrap   A feature of a word processor. When typing beyond the right hand margin, the word automatically carries over to the next line. This is wordwrap.

World Wide Web (The Web)   The Web is a multimedia information service accessible over the Internet. Information is provided on web servers by many different organisations throughout the world.

WYSIWYG (What You See Is What You Get)   What is displayed on the screen is what will be printed on the printer. This phrase is particularly used in connection with word processors.

Bibliography

Anderson, T. (ed.) (2008) *The Theory and Practice of Online Learning*, Athabasca, CA: AU Press.

AQA (2010) 'GCSE ICT, Unit 2, The Assignment: Applying ICT, Specimen Teachers' Notes', available at: http://www.aqa.org.uk/resource-zone/ict/gcse-ict.php (accessed 2 September 2011).

Assessment Reform Group (1999) *Beyond the Black Box*, available at: http://assessment-reform-group. org/publications/ (accessed 4 January 2013).

Assessment Reform Group (2002) *AfL: 10 Principles*, available at: http://assessment-reform-group.org/ publications/ (accessed 4 January 2013).

Association for Achievement and Improvement through Assessment (n.d.) Report, available at: http:// www.aaia.org.uk (accessed 23 September 2011).

Barkley, S. (2009) 'Do you know the four Ps of Web 2.0?', available at: http://www.gnaka.com/ general/do-you-know-the-four-ps-of-web-20-by-shawn-barkley (accessed 7 June 2012).

BBC (2009) 'Q&A GCSE v IGCSE', available at: http://news.bbc.co.uk/1/hi/education/7924496.stm (accessed 9 September 2011).

BCS (2011) *The Business Case for Information Technology and Computing Education*, available at: http:// academy.bcs.org/upload/pdf/business_case_for_computing_education.pdf (accessed 1 April 2011).

Becta (2008) 'How do boys and girls differ in their use of ICT?', available at: http://dera.ioe.ac.uk/ 8318/1/gender_ict_briefing.pdf (accessed 7 March 2012).

Becta (2010) *Harnessing Technology Schools Survey: 2010*, available at: http://dera.ioe.ac.uk/1544/1/ becta_2010_htss_report.pdf (accessed 13 December 2011).

BESA (2010) *ICT Provision and Use in 2010 2011*, available at: http://www.besa.org.uk (accessed 13 December 2011).

BIS (2010) *New Industry New Jobs, Skills System Case Studies, BIS Report*, URN 10/930.

Black, P. and Wiliam, D. (1998) *Inside the Black Box*, London: ARG.

Bradley, C. (2009) *Ofsted Subject Inspections*, available at: http://moodlexchange.com/?p=338 (accessed 4 April 2012).

Bryant, C. (2010) 'A 21st century Art room: the remix of creativity and technology', *Journal of Art Education*, 63(2): 43–8.

Burns, J. (2012) 'ICT to be replaced by computer science programme', available at: http:// www.bbc.co.uk/news/education-16493929 (accessed 4 April 2012).

CAS (2011) *Computing at School*, available at: http://www.computingatschool.org.uk (accessed 1 April 2011).

Childnet International (n.d.) *Why Is e-Safety Important?*, available at: http://childnet.com/kia/traineete achers/why.aspx (accessed 17 March 2012).

Childnet International (2005) *Promoting Internet Safety through the 'Jenny's Story' Film*, available at: http:// www.childnet-int.org/downloads/js_executivesummary.pdf (accessed 7 March 2012).

CIHE (2010) *The Fuse, Igniting High Growth for Creative, Digital and Information Technology Industries in the UK*, cited in BCS (2011).

Coates, S. (2011) *Second Report of the Independent Review of Teachers' Standards*, London: TSO.

Crawford, R. A. (1997) *Managing Information Technology (IT) in Secondary Schools*, London: Routledge.

Crawford, R. A. (1998) *What is IT Capability? An Investigation into Notions of What Constitutes IT Capability*, available at: http://www.moorsideuk.co.uk/roger/ (accessed 18 July 2011).

Crawford, R. A. (2010) *Edexcel IGCSE ICT*, Harlow: Pearson.

Crawford, R. A. (2011) *ICT Capability in English Schools*, Saarbrucken: Lambert Academic Publishing.

Crawford, R. A. (2012) 'Understanding and using assessment and delivering feedback', in N. Denby (ed.) *Training to Teach*, London: Sage.

Crawford, R. A. and Jenkins, I. (2001) 'Management strategies for delivering Information and Communication Technology (ICT) in English secondary schools', *Journal of Themes in Education*, 2(4): 367–79.

Culley, L. (1986) *Gender Differences and Computing in Secondary Schools*, Loughborough: Loughborough University Press.

DCSF (2007) *Cyberbullying*, available at: http://www.digizen.org/downloads/CYBERBULLYING.pdf (accessed 15 March 2012).

DCSF (2008) *Assessing Pupils' Progress in ICT at Key Stage 3: Standards File – Pupil (A to F)*, Nottingham: DCSF Publications.

Denby, N. (ed.) (2012) *Training to Teach*, London: Sage.

DfE (2010) 'Government announces changes to qualifications and the curriculum', available at: http://www.education.gov.uk/16to19/qualificationsandlearning/a0061424/government-announces-changes-to-qualifications-and-the-curriculum (accessed 28 June 2012).

DfE (2011a) *Section 96 Qualifications*, available at: http://www.education.gov.uk/section96/index.shtml (accessed 9 October 2011).

DfE (2011b) 'Performance table reform and transparency will raise standards and end perverse incentives', available at: http://www.education.gov.uk/16to19/qualificationsandlearning/a00192510/performance-table-reform-and-transparency-will-raise-standards-and-end-perverse-incentives (accessed 21 October 2011).

DfE (2011c) *Training Our Next Generation of Outstanding Teachers*, London: DfE.

DfE (2011d) *The Framework for the NC: A Report by the Expert Panel for the NC Review*, London: DfE.

DfE (2012a) *Removing the Duty on Maintained Schools to Follow the ICT Programmes of Study, Attainment Targets and Statutory Assessment Arrangements*, available at: http://www.education.gov.uk/consultations/index.cfm?action=consultationDetails&consultationId=1802&external=no&menu=1 (accessed 4 April 2012).

DfE (2012b) *ICT Curriculum*, available at: http://www.education.gov.uk/schools/teachingandlearning/curriculum/a00199693/use-of-ict (accessed 4 April 2012).

DfE (2012c) *Teachers' Standards*, London: DfE.

DfEE (1995) *Code of Practice: On the Identification and Assessment of SEN*, London: DfEE.

Directgov (n.d.) *Preventing Your Child from Downloading and File Sharing*, available at: http://www.direct.gov.uk/en/Parents/Yourchildshealthandsafety/Internetsafety/DG_071136 (accessed 15 March 2012).

Emmerson, K., Paterson, F., Southworth, G. and West Burnham, J. (2006) *Making a Difference: A Study of Effective Middle Leadership in Schools Facing Challenging Circumstances*, National College of School Leadership, available at: http://www.nationalcollege.org.uk.

English, F. W. and Steffy, B. E. (2001) *Deep Curriculum Alignment*, New York: Scarecrow Press.

Gardner, R. (2011) 'Ofqual rejects call for one exam board', *The Independent*, 16 December.

Gove, M. (2012) 'Seizing success', transcript of speech to made to the Annual Leadership Conference at the NCSL, available at: http://www.education.gov.uk/nationalcollege/conference2012 (accessed 1 July 2012).

Hargreaves, D. (2008) *A New Shape for Schooling?*, Specialist Schools and Academies Trust, London: DfE.

Hay McBer (2000) *Research into Teacher Effectiveness: A Model of Teacher Effectiveness*, London: DfEE.

Higgins, S. and Moseley, D. (2001) 'Teachers' thinking about information and communications technology and learning: beliefs and outcomes', *Journal of Teacher Development*, 5(2): 191–210.

Honey, P. and Mumford, A. (1992) *The Manual of Learning Styles*, 3rd edn, Maidenhead: Peter Honey.

HSE (n.d.) 'PAT: portable appliance testing FAQs', available at: http://www.hse.gov.uk/electricity/faq-portable-appliance-testing.htm (accessed 7 March 2012).

HSE (2006) 'Working with VDUs', available at: http://www.hse.gov.uk/pubns/indg36.pdf (accessed 7 March 2012).

Imison, T. and Taylor, P. H. (2001) *Managing ICT in the Secondary School*, Oxford: Heinemann.

Independent Schools Council Teacher Induction Panel (ISCtip) (n.d.) *Teacher Induction*, available at: http://www.isc.co.uk/about-us-2/teacher_induction (accessed 21 March 2012).

Jen-Hwa Hu, P., Clark, T. H. K. and Ma, W. W. (2003) 'Examining technology acceptance by school teachers', *Journal of Information and Management*, 41(2): 227–41.

JISC (2006) 'In their own words: exploring the learner's perspective on e-learning', available at: http://www.jisc.ac.uk/media/documents/programmes/elearningpedagogy/iowtext.doc (accessed 14 November 2007).

Kennewell, S., Parkinson, J. and Tanner, H. (2000) *Developing the ICT Capable School*, London: RoutledgeFalmer.

Kennewell, S., Parkinson, J. and Tanner, H. (2003) *Learning to Teach ICT in the Secondary School*, London: RoutledgeFalmer.

Knowsley, J. (2012) 'Pushed to the brink', *TES*, 1 June, p. 26.

Leask, M. and Pachler, N. (2005) *Learning to Teach Using ICT in the Secondary School*, London: Routledge.

Livingstone, S. and Bober, M. (2005) *UK Children Go Online: Final Report*, ESRC e-Society programme, available at: http://www.citizensonline.org.uk (accessed 21 October 2011).

Lucey, T. (2005) *Management Information Systems*, London: Thomson.

Mansell, W. (2010) 'Taking the easy path? Why BTECs have doubled', *TES*, 27 August.

Milner, A. (1989) *Girls and the New Technologies*, MESU.

MIT (Massachusetts Institute of Technology) (n.d.) *MITOPENCOURSEWARE*, available at: http://ocw.mit.edu/about/ (accessed 7 March 2012).

Moore, C. D. (2005) 'How should the KS3 ICT National Curriculum be taught so that it delivers capability at KS4?' available at: http://www.teacherresearch.net/tr_ma_4480_cdmoore.pdf (accessed 18 July 2011).

National Strategy (2008) *The Framework for Secondary ICT: Overview and Learning Objectives*, London: TSO.

NComputing (2009) 'Case study: New College, Leicester', available at: http://www.ncomputing.com/docs/casestudies/education/en/casestudy_leicester_edu.pdf (accessed 6 January 2012).

NCSL (2003) *Heart of the Matter: A Practical Guide to What Middle Leaders Can Do to Improve Learning in Secondary Schools*, available at: http://www.nationalcollege.org.uk/docinfo?id=17209&filename=heart-of-the-matter.pdf (accessed 30 March 2012).

Next Gen Skills (2012) *A Consultation Response to the DfE: Removing the Duty on Maintained Schools to Follow the ICT PoS, ATS and Statutory Assessment Arrangements*, Next Gen Skills, available at: http://www.nextgenskills.com.

North Yorkshire (n.d.) *Child Protection Basic Awareness*, available at: http://www.safeguardingchildren.co.uk/basic-awareness.html (accessed 15 March 2012).

NUT (2012) *First Post*, on http://www.teachers.org.uk (accessed 16 February 2012).

O'Brien, K. and Marakas, G. M. (2011) *Management Information Systems*, Maidenhead: McGraw-Hill.

Ofqual (2009a) *GCSE Subject Criteria for Information and Communication Technology*, London: Ofqual.

Ofqual (2009b) *Functional Skills Criteria for ICT*, London: Ofqual.

Ofqual (2011a) *GCSE, GCE, Principal Learning and Project Code of Practice*, London: Ofqual.

Ofqual (2011b) *GCSE Subject Criteria for ICT*, London: Ofqual.

Ofqual (2011c) *The Register of Regulated Qualifications*, available at: http://register.ofqual.gov.uk/ (accessed 9 September 2011).

Ofsted (1995) *Information Technology: A Review of Inspection Findings, 1993/4*, London: HMSO.

Ofsted (2003) *Good Assessment Practice in ICT*, London: Ofsted.

Ofsted (2009a) *The Annual Report of Her Majesty's Chief Inspector of Education, Children's Services and Skills, 2008/09*, London: TSO.

Ofsted (2009b) *The Importance of ICT: ICT in Primary and Secondary Schools 2005/2008*, London: Ofsted.

Ofsted (2010) *The Evaluation Schedule for Schools*, London: Ofsted.

Ofsted (2011) *The Annual Report of Her Majesty's Chief Inspector, 2010/2011*, available at: http://www.ofsted.gov.uk/resources/annualreport1011 (accessed 8 June 2012).

Ofsted (2012) 'Young people are not being sufficiently challenged in ICT lessons', available at: http://www.ofsted.gov.uk/news/young-people-are-not-being-sufficiently-challenged-ict-lessons (accessed 2 July 2012).

Owen, G. (1992) 'Whole school management of IT', *School Management*, 12(1): 29–40.

Pelgrum, W.J. (2001) 'Obstacles to the integration of ICT in education: results from a worldwide educational assessment', *Journal of Computers and Education*, 37: 163–78.

QCA (2007a) *ICT: Programme of Study: Key Stage 3*, London: QCA.

QCA (2007b) *ICT: Programme of Study: Key Stage 4*, London: QCA.

Rodeiro, C.L.V. (2010) *Uptake of ICT and Computing Qualifications in Schools in England, 2007–9*, Cambridge: Cambridge Assessment, Research Division.

Safer, N. and Fleischman, S. (2005) 'Research matters: how student progress monitoring improves instruction', *Educational Leadership*, 62(4): 81–3.

Selwood, I. and Pilkington, R. (2005) 'Teacher workload: using ICT to release time to teach', *Educational Review*, 57(2): 163–74.

Shah, S. (2012) 'Back to the drawing board for ICT education', *Computing*, 26 January.

Sirius Corporation (2011) *Case Study: Bishop Fox's Community School*, available at: http://www.siriusit.co.uk/clients/education/bishop-foxs-community-school (accessed 13 December 2011).

Sizer, T. R. (2001) 'No two are quite alike: personalized learning', *Educational Leadership*, 57(1): 6–11.

Smithers, A. and Robinson, P. (2011) *The Good Teacher Training Guide*, Centre for Education and Employment Research, University of Buckingham, available at: http://www.buckingham.ac.uk/wp-content/uploads/2010/11/GTTG2011.pdf (accessed 29 December 2012).

Somekh, B. (1996) 'Value conflicts in the management of innovation: supporting IT innovation in ITT in the UK', *Journal of IT in Teacher Education*, 5(1–2): 115–37.

TES (2011a) 'This week's poll', *TES Magazine*, 5 August.

TES (2011b) 'Resource of the week', *TES*, 16 September.

The National Strategies (2009a) *Assessing Pupils' Progress Materials: ICT*, available at: http://webarchive.nationalarchives.gov.uk/20110202093118/http://nationalstrategies.standards.dcsf.gov.uk/node/157533 (accessed 2 September 2011).

The National Strategies (2009b) *Assessing Pupils' Progress in ICT*, Assessment Guidelines, available at: http://webarchive.nationalarchives.gov.uk/20110202093118/http://nationalstrategies.standards.dcsf.gov.uk/node/157533 (accessed 2 September 2011).

TTA (1996) *Teachers Make a Difference, Post Conference Report*, London: TTA.

Vasagar, J (2012) 'Michael Gove to scrap "boring" ICT lessons', *The Guardian*, 11 January, available at: http://www.guardian.co.uk/politics/2012/jan2011)./michael-gove-boring-it-lessons (accessed 4 April 2012).

Volman, M., van Eck, E., Heemskerk, I. and Kuiper, E. (2005) 'New technologies, new differences: gender and ethnic differences in pupils' use of ICT in primary and secondary education', *Journal of Computers and Education*, 45: 35–55.

Wolf, A. (2011) *Review of Vocational Education: The Wolf Report*, DfE, available at: https://www.education.gov.uk/publications/eOrderingDownload/The%20Wolf%20Report.pdf (accessed 7 October 2011).

Woolard, J. (ed.) (2009) *Computer Programming in Key Stage 3*, available at: http://www.computingatschool.org.uk/data/uploads/CPinKS3.pdf (accessed 4 April 2011).

YouTube (n.d.) *Joe's Story*, available at: http://www.youtube.com/watch?v=cJAYMaT5BJg (accessed 7 March 2012).

Index

Note: page numbers in **bold** refer to a figure or a table.